Bombing Civilians

Bombing Civilians

A Twentieth-Century History

EDITED BY YUKI TANAKA AND MARILYN B. YOUNG

THE NEW PRESS

NEW YORK
LONDON

Requests for permission to reproduce selections from this book should be mailed to:
Permissions Department, The New Press, 38 Greene Street, New York, NY 10013.

Published in the United States by The New Press, New York, 2009
Distributed by W. W. Norton & Company, Inc., New York

LIBRARY OF CONGRESS CATALOGING-IN-PUBLICATION DATA

Bombing civilians : a twentieth-century history / edited by Yuki Tanaka and Marilyn B. Young.
   p.   cm.
Includes bibliographical references and index.
ISBN 978-1-59558-363-5 (hbk.)
   1. Military history, Modern—20th century.   2. Civilian war casualties—History—20th century.
3. Bombing, Aerial—History—20th century.   4. World War, 1939–1945—Casualties.   5. World War,
1939–1945—Aerial operations, American.   I. Young, Marilyn Blatt.   II. Tanaka, Toshiyuki, 1949–
D431.B66 2008
358.4'14—dc22

2008027814

The New Press was established in 1990 as a not-for-profit alternative to the large,
commercial publishing houses currently dominating the book publishing industry.
The New Press operates in the public interest rather than for private gain,
and is committed to publishing, in innovative ways, works of educational, cultural,
and community value that are often deemed insufficiently profitable.

www.thenewpress.com

Composition by NK Graphics
This book was set in Granjon

Printed in the United States of America

2   4   6   8   10   9   7   5   3   1

In memory of Erick Markusen, the pioneer scholar of genocide studies who passed away before completing his contribution to this book

CONTENTS

INTRODUCTION

Yuki Tanaka

Suddenly
There was a brilliant white-hot flash.
Buildings crumbled,
Fire blazed,
Smoke swirled all around,
Wires dangled everywhere,
And a writhing mass of humanity fled for safety

This passage from a poem by Hiroshima victim Sadako Kurihara graphically depicts the horror experienced not only by A-bomb victims but by all who have suffered air raid attacks: fire, smoke, flight. Yet the attackers, hundreds of meters in the air above, have little sense of what is happening down below. For the bomber crews, the people on the ground are entirely abstract; they are targets. By contrast, the experience of their victims is of the most terrible concrete reality. The sharp juxtaposition of abstract and concrete is a phenomenon unique to aerial bombing.

The premium placed on aerial bombing in modern warfare owes much to the relative safety of the attackers and the complete vulnerability of the victims. The psychological remoteness of pilots and bombardiers from the reality of the horror on the ground is well described by Charles Lindbergh, who flew the first solo, nonstop flight across the Atlantic, in 1927. Lindbergh also flew combat missions in the Pacific theater as a consultant for the commander of the U.S. Army Air Forces, General Henry Arnold, during World War II:

You press a button and death flies down. One second, the bomb hanging harmlessly in your racks, completely under your control. The next it is hurtling down through the air and nothing in your power can revoke what you have done. . . . How can there be writhing, mangled bodies? How can this air around

you be filled with unseen projectiles? It is like listening to a radio account
of battle on the other side of the earth. It is too far away, too separated to hold
reality.

The origin of aerial bombing can be traced to the use of hot-air balloons
in warfare in the late eighteenth century. Initially, balloons were used simply to determine the size and position of enemy forces, but militarists soon
realized their potential for dropping grenades and other harmful objects
on enemy troops. The use of airplanes in the early twentieth century led to
a drastic change in war strategy: the wide expansion of war zones to include indiscriminate attacks on civilians.

Aerial bombing of civilians was first conducted by German planes
against Parisians in August 1914—eleven years after the Wright brothers
successfully flew the first aircraft in 1903. By the end of 1914, the Allies
were also making serial air raids into German territories. Thus, by the
time World War I ended in 1918, both sides had engaged in indiscriminate
bombing, killing or injuring several thousand civilians.

Shortly after World War I, planes from the British Royal Air Force
(RAF) were sent to the Middle East to engage in a new type of operation—
the bombing of what an RAF document refers to as "rebels of uncivilised
tribes" who refused to submit to British rule. Over several years from 1920
onward, the RAF attacked rebel groups in Iraq—for which Britain was
the trustee nation at the time—by dropping bombs, including incendiary
bombs, on remote villages and tent encampments. The same technique of
indiscriminate bombing was also used in other territories of the British
Empire, such as India and South Africa. Yet British administrators recommended this use of airpower as "outstandingly effective, extremely economical and undoubtedly humane in the long run."

As in World War I, at the beginning of World War II, both Britain and
Germany initially refrained from aerial attacks on civilians. However, in a
repeat scenario, both sides deliberately increased their revenge bombing of
civilian quarters in major cities following inaccurate bombings of military
targets. The German forces conducted Operation Blitz for almost nine
months from September 1940, attacking London, Coventry, Birmingham,
Manchester, and many other English cities, killing 60,000 civilians and destroying more than 2 million houses. On September 11, 1940, Joseph
Goebbels wrote in his diary that this aerial bombing operation would be
decisive in forcing the British government to surrender.

In revenge, the RAF started night raids on industrial cites in the Ruhr region in October 1940. However, aerial attacks on German civilians really expanded in February 1942 when Arthur Harris took over the RAF Bomber Command. Lübeck, a cultural city with no military importance, became the first target of Harris's new strategy, "area bombing." Cologne was then attacked by more than 1,000 planes. Other cities, such as Essen, Kiel, Stuttgart, Mannheim, Rostock, and Berlin, were also targeted. In February 1943, Harris pronounced that the morale of the German population in the bombed areas had reached an all-time low and that, if the RAF continued bombing, surrender could be expected in the very near future. Night raids continued on many German cites, including Hamburg, where 7,000 tons of bombs were dropped and about 45,000 people were killed. Yet there was no sign of surrender by the Nazi regime.

The RAF then began to target Berlin, bombing the city sixteen times between November 1943 and March 1944, while continuing to bomb other German cities. Still Harris's expectation of Nazi surrender was not fulfilled. On the contrary, the Germans started employing new weapons of indiscriminate killing—V-1 and V-2 rockets. More than 9,500 V-1 rockets were launched killing about 6,200 people. About 1,100 V-2 rockets reached various parts of England, killing 2,700 and injuring 6,500 people. Claiming again that the Germans were on the verge of a collapse in morale, Harris stepped up aerial attacks. In February 1945, the Bomber Command flew 17,500 sorties and dropped 45,750 tons on German cities. Between February 13 and 15, Dresden was heavily bombed for the first time by the RAF, this time together with the U.S. Army Air Force (USAAF). During the fourteen-hour raid, massive quantities of incendiaries burned large areas of this city, which housed no military facility, and killed an estimated 25,000 to 30,000 people.

The USAAF, led by Ira Eaker, entered the bombing campaign in Europe in August 1942. Despite repeated RAF requests to join it in low-altitude night bombing, the USAAF adhered to its traditional strategy, i.e., so-called precision bombing in daylight from a high altitude, using the Norden bombsight. In reality, "precision bombing" was a euphemism, as the bombs regularly fell at least a quarter mile from the target. It is not surprising, therefore, that the USAAF killed not only German civilians, but also many Allied civilians of German-occupied cities such as Paris, Nantes, Lille, Lorient, and Amsterdam. From November 1943, U.S. bombers started "blind bombing," by which was meant that advances in radar

technology would enable even a blind bombardier to accurately hit the desired target. In fact, due to technical limitations, the bombing became yet
more random and indiscriminate. Eaker shared the optimism of Arthur
Harris that the British and U.S. cooperative bombing campaign was destroying German morale. Dissatisfied with the results of precision bombing by the 8th U.S. Bomber command, however, General Henry Arnold
reorganized the USAAF in Europe and set up the United States Strategic
Air Forces in December 1943. Eaker was demoted, and Carl Spaatz became head of the USSF.

U.S. strategy moved steadily from precision to blind bombing throughout the years 1943 to 1945, i.e., to bombing that was increasingly indiscriminate in practice. In the four months between September 1 and December
31, 1944, the USSF dropped more than 140,000 tons of bombs on "major
targets," 60 percent of them in blind bombing. Only 674 tons were used for
precision bombing in the strict sense. Blind bombing increased to 80 percent of the entire U.S. bombing campaign between October 1944 and the
end of the war in Europe in May 1945. In February 1945, U.S. forces, together with the RAF, conducted Operation Clarion, in which numerous
German towns and villages were bombed from a low altitude in order to
demoralize the populace. It was an operation totally devoid of tactical
value. In short, U.S. air attacks in Europe had become mostly "area bombing," with no serious attempt to limit damage to military targets. The fact
that the USAAF leaders abandoned precision bombing in reality but
maintained it as a meaningless official principle is evident in the counter-
plan against V-1 and V-2 rockets advocated by General Arnold. That was
to fly 500 unmanned, radar-controlled, fully loaded B-17 bombers and
crash them into enemy-held cities. Fortunately this plan was never put
into practice.

Nevertheless, by the end of the war, 131 German towns and cities had
been bombed, and approximately 600,000 German civilians had been
killed by "strategic bombing."

It was against this background that the USAAF began the bombing
campaign of Japan in late 1944. According to Henry Arnold and Curtis
LeMay, bombing civilians was essential in order to break Japanese morale,
and this was the quickest way to force them to surrender. At the same
time, it was the most efficient method to minimize casualties to their own
men. In this sense, Arnold, LeMay, and other U.S. military leaders inherited the idea of strategic bombing originally advocated by RAF leaders in

World War I. According to this concept, the killing of enemy civilians is justifiable, no matter how cruel the method; indeed it is indispensable to hastening surrender. U.S. leaders, however, in their public pronouncements, continued to insist that their bombs were directed toward military targets. Consider, for example, President Harry Truman's announcement immediately after the bombing of Hiroshima: "The world will note that the first atomic bomb was dropped on Hiroshima, a military base. That was because we wished in this first attack to avoid, in so far as possible, the killing of civilians." Truman made this statement immediately following the instant killing of 70,000 to 80,000 civilian residents of Hiroshima. By the end of 1945, 140,000 residents of that city died from the bomb. In the end, more than 100 Japanese cities were destroyed by firebombing, and two by atomic bombing, causing one million casualties, including more than half a million deaths, the majority being civilians, particularly women and children.

Immediately after the war, the U.S. government created the myth that it was the atomic bombing of Hiroshima and Nagasaki that finally brought an end to the long and bloody war in the Asia-Pacific region, thus justifying the mass killing of civilians. Yet this myth, which the U.S. government has stubbornly maintained for more than sixty years since the end of the war, does not really correspond to the historical facts. The Japanese government did not concede to the Allies immediately after the atomic bombing of Hiroshima and Nagasaki, and U.S. bombing of other Japanese cities continued every day up until August 14, the day before Japan officially surrendered. Clearly, other important issues, in particular, the future fate of Hirohito and the monarchy, as well as the Soviet Union's entry into the war against Japan, must be considered factors critical in ending the war.

The United States was not, of course, alone in indiscriminate bombing in the Pacific War. The Japanese Imperial Navy engaged in the first indiscriminate bombing in the Asia-Pacific region with the January 1932 attack on civilians on Shanghai. Thereafter, Japanese bombers targeted civilians in Nanjing, Wuhan, Chongqing and other cities. Chongqing, in particular, was targeted in more than 200 air raids over three years from the end of 1938, bringing the total death toll up to 12,000. Here, too, the Japanese were not targeting a military facility, but sought to destroy the Guomindang's center of power and demoralize the civilians who supported this regime.

In the Korean War, U.S. forces bombed and destroyed two large irrigation dams, causing enormous flood damage in North Korea. As a result, North Korea's agricultural economy was ruined. In the Vietnam War, napalm, cluster bombs (with a high failure rate), daisy-cutter bombs (so-called earthquake bombs), and Agent Orange (a chemical defoliant) were widely used. These weapons resulted in long-term damage to the environment and the people, bringing suffering and death to countless civilians well after the actual bombing.

While bloody wars were being fought in Korea and Vietnam and many civilians from these countries became the target of heavy aerial bombings, the United States and the Soviet Union engaged in a cold war. Both nations devoted themselves vigorously to developing new and ever more destructive nuclear arms in order to annihilate each other's citizens. In the process, they produced a total of more than 69,000 nuclear warheads, conducted more than 1,700 nuclear tests between 1945 and 1998, and created a large number of victims of radioactive fallout.

Due to the widespread use of depleted-uranium weapons in both Gulf Wars and the increasing possibility that tactical nuclear arms may be used, as well as the availability of super-large daisy-cutter bombs and mother bombs, the distinction between conventional and nuclear weapons is rapidly disappearing. The number of countries seeking to equip themselves with weapons of mass destruction is increasing as nuclear powers like the United States and Britain attempt to subjugate so-called rogue nations by the use of military might.

The September 11 attack was unquestionably an act of terrorism, for it killed thousands of civilians indiscriminately. This act, perpetrated by an al Qaeda group, can be seen as a variation of indiscriminate bombing using civilian instead of military planes. Certainly al Qaeda would have used bombers if that had been an option. Whether such an attack is carried out by an unofficial armed group or by military forces, it is clearly an act of terrorism from the viewpoint of the civilian targets.

The majority of victims of strategic bombing are civilians—in particular, women and children. In plain language, "strategic bombing" of civilians is an act of terrorism. Is there any moral justification for killing tens of thousands of noncombatants under the rationale that it will force a swift surrender? It is important to remember that no war has ever been brought to an end by bombing civilians. Indeed, such a strategy typically strengthens resistance.

In assessing specific cases of indiscriminate bombing, we must remember the history of its justification and practice, which we have dated from World War I. In World War II, the British, the Germans, the Japanese, and the Americans all engaged in strategic bombing with heavy tolls in civilian lives, allegedly in the belief that it would demoralize the enemy and speed up surrender. We must be careful not to get bogged down in arguing whether or not the firebombing of Tokyo and the bombing of Hiroshima and Nagasaki were strategically justifiable. The fundamental question is why this theory of mass murder has persisted for so long, even after the atomic bombings. Why was the strategy applied during the Korean and Vietnam wars, and why are variants of it still used to justify the "collateral damage" of "precision bombing" in wars such as those in Afghanistan, Kosovo, and Iraq? The fact is that killing civilians is a crime against humanity regardless of the asserted military justification, a crime that should be punished on the basis of the Nuremberg and Geneva principles.

1

BRITISH "HUMANE BOMBING" IN IRAQ DURING THE INTERWAR ERA

Yuki Tanaka

Historical Background

On November 21, 1783, the world's first man-carrying hot-air balloon floated in the sky above the outskirts of Paris. Eleven years later, the French revolutionary government set up a corps of balloonists, whose task was to locate the size and position of enemy forces and to direct artillery fire against them. Thereafter, hot-air balloons were used in several conflicts to carry out similar tasks. A much smaller-scale hot-air balloon carrying a bomb was also invented and used by the Austrian forces to attack the city of Venice in 1849 during the First Italian War of Independence. The bomb was designed to explode on impact with any sharp object. Altogether, some 200 balloons were released for this purpose; they were not very effective, partly due to unpredictable weather conditions and partly due to the weak explosive power of the bomb itself. Yet this was probably the world's first indiscriminate aerial attack.[1]

In the latter half of the nineteenth century, when the industrial revolution was well under way in Europe, much science fiction predicting future aerial bombing was published and widely read. For example, in *Three Hundred Years Hence*, by William Hay, a European air fleet attacks and destroys Asian armies and devastates their lands. In 1886 Jules Verne, the popular French writer known as the author of *Around the World in Eighty Days*, published a novel, *Clipper of the Clouds*, in which he predicted that flying machines would be the major weapon in future wars. The story line in the novel *The Last War; Or, Triumph of the English Tongue*, by S.W. Odell, published in 1898, is of English-speaking people who win the war against inferior races by showering them with incendiary bombs, thereby bringing civilization to barbaric Asian and Russian lands and imposing the English language upon them. Many of these popular novels were likewise based on great expectations of modern technology as well as social Darwinism, i.e., the ideology justifying European colonialism with racial prejudice against non-European races and cultures.[2]

The "flying machines" imagined in such futuristic novels came closer to reality when the Wright brothers successfully flew the first aircraft in 1903. Within the next decade or so, aircraft technology made significant advances, and by 1909 planes were successfully produced in Germany and Austria, too. In fact, as early as June 1910, an experiment of dropping bombs from a biplane onto a battleship-shaped target was conducted in New York. In 1908, H.G. Wells, one of the most sophisticated science fiction writers, wrote *The War in the Air*, in which he predicted the devastating effects of aerial bombing upon the bodies and minds of enemies. He warned that the development of technology would outstrip the political and moral means to control it, and that modern civilization would be destroyed by bombers, creating chaos, famine, and political disorder.[3] His prediction of moral corruption as a result of aerial bombing was particularly prescient, as history subsequently proved.

It was around this time that a retired German army officer, Ferdinand von Zeppelin, started producing airships. In 1906 and 1907, Zeppelin successfully flew the airship LZ3 several times, and he subsequently produced many airships for the Imperial German Army and Navy. Beginning shortly before 1910, the military forces of each major European nation began purchasing planes and airships, and by the outbreak of World War I in 1914, Germany possessed 246 planes and 11 airships, England had 110 planes and 6 airships, France owned 169 planes and 4 airships, while Russia had 300 planes and 11 airships.[4]

Indeed, it was predicted already in the late nineteenth century that aerial bombing could become a major war strategy in the near future. Consequently, at the first Peace Conference, which was held at the Hague in 1899, Russia proposed a declaration to *permanently* prohibit discharging "any kind of projectile or explosive from balloons, or by other methods of similar nature," in particular, poisonous gas. Ultimately, however, this declaration was adopted for a term of just five years—a term that the

United States proposed. The Americans argued that, if aerial bombing technology developed further, it could shorten military campaigns and thus end wars quickly.[5] In other words, the United States claimed that aerial bombing could be humane and morally justifiable because it would cause fewer casualties. This was, to put it mildly, an excessively optimistic view, but it is still prevalent in certain circles, particularly among militarists.

This optimistic view was held not only by American politicians but by some contemporary writers. For example, in 1862, Victor Hugo argued that the popularization of the airplane would lead to a "peaceful revolution" by eliminating national borders throughout the world and thereby ending conflicts and wars among different nations. In 1894, Octave Chanute also claimed that, as any part of the world could become a target of aerial bombing, more rational and peaceful methods than warfare should be adopted for settling international disputes.[6] Toward the end of World War I, it is claimed that Orville Wright said no nation was likely to initiate war again, because of the dreadful consequences that airplanes had brought about.

Wars had been even more frequent than usual in Europe and the United States for more than a half century. These included the U.S. war against Mexico of 1846–48, the First Italian Independence War of 1848–49, the Crimean War of 1854–56, the Second Italian Independence War in 1859, the American Civil War of 1861–65, the Austro-Prussian War and the Third Italian Independence War in 1866, the Franco-Prussian War of 1870–71, the Second Russo-Turkish War of 1877–78, the First Boer War of 1880–81, the Serbo-Bulgarian War of 1885–86, the Second Boer War of 1899–1902, the Spanish-American War in 1898, the Russo-Japanese War of 1904–5, the Italian-Turkish War of 1911–12, and the First Balkan War of 1912–13. It is not surprising, therefore, that many people hoped that the invention of a flying machine could fundamentally change the way of conducting war, so that it would become difficult for any nation to go to war in haste.

In 1907, three years after the Declaration on the Launching of Projectiles from Balloons had expired, the same declaration was again signed and ratified by fifteen nations at the Second Peace Conference at the Hague. However, this amounted to only one third of the nations participating in the conference; many others, including France, Germany, Italy, Russia, and Japan, refused to sign or ratify the agreement. For example,

France claimed that it would be far more rational to permit aerial bombing strictly aimed at military targets.[7] In other words, justification of so-called precision bombing was already advocated just a few years after the world's first successful flight by the Wright brothers. France, next door to Germany and its powerful military force, thought it crucial to keep open the option to conduct aerial attacks on its potential enemy.

Italy, which did not sign the declaration, conducted aerial bombing in November 1911. When a military conflict occurred with Turkey over the dominium of Tripolitania (now a Libyan territory), Italy sent nine planes and two airships, dropping hand grenades upon a Turkish camp. The bombing of Turkish forces continued, using much larger bombs and incendiaries, until the war ended in October 1912. In the same year, France also conducted aerial bombing against "rebel bands" in its colony of Morocco. The French authorities ordered a large number of small bombs specially designed by a Danish inventor as suitable for dropping from the air. French pilots bombed not only "rebel bands" but also villages and markets indiscriminately. They also used incendiary fléchettes, fire-darts designed to shoot down zeppelins and set grain fields ablaze. In the Balkan wars of 1912 and 1913, Bulgarian forces hired French and British pilots to bomb their enemies.[8] Clearly, then, aerial bombing had already been conducted in a number of places a few years before the start of World War I, virtually invalidating the Declaration on the Launching of Projectiles from Balloons.

Indiscriminate bombing of civilians during major warfare was first conducted by both the German and the Allied forces during World War I. Initially, both sides refrained from targeting civilians or residential areas, but due to the rudimentary nature of their aircraft and aerial bombing techniques, bombs inevitably went astray. For example, in August 1914, a German plane dropped five bombs in an attempt to destroy a railway station in Paris, taking the life of a woman in a street nearby. By the end of the war, about 500 Parisians had been killed by German aerial bombing. In December 1914, the French army bombed the railway station of Freiburg, but the bombs missed their target and many civilians were killed.[9]

From early 1915, "revenge bombing" by both sides gradually escalated. Between 1915 and 1918, the Germans dropped 300 tons of bombs on London and English coastal towns, killing more than 1,400 people and injuring about 3,400, most of whom were civilians. In the final year of the war alone, various cities in western Germany were bombed 657 times by the Allied forces, who dropped a total of 8,000 bombs, which killed approximately 1,200 people. From May 1917, the Germans started to use a number of new large twin-engine bombers, Gotha G.IVs, to attack England. These were capable of carrying up to 1,000 pounds of bombs. The RAF also started producing a similar type of bomber plane, the Handley-Page 0/400, in order to reach inland German cities. If the war had continued, the number of civilian victims would have increased dramatically.[10]

World War I was a watershed in both the increased quantity and the technological improvement of warplanes. For example, by November 1918 the British forces possessed almost 23,000 planes, having entered the war with only 110. A total of about 100,000 warplanes were produced in France and England during the war.[11] Most importantly, it was at this time that the idea of strategic bombing was conceived and to a certain extent put into practice. Militarists on both sides argued that the "moral effect" of aerial bombing on civilians, i.e., popular fear, disillusion, and demoralization leading to lost working hours, lowered production, and perhaps political upheaval, would force the enemy nation to surrender quickly. In fact, this theory, which has remained robust in airpower circles ever since, was simply a myth that has never been proven. Its leading proponent was the Italian officer and strategist Giulio Douhet, author of *Command of the Air*, published in 1921, who claimed that the quickest way to win a war was to terrorize enemy civilians with intensive aerial bombing, combining three different types of bombs—explosives, incendiaries, and poison gas.[12]

In fact, some British generals entertained similar ideas during the war, although those ideas have never been systematically analyzed. Toward the end of World War I, in April 1918, the British government established the Royal Air Force, the first independent air force in the world. Combining its Naval Air Service and Army Flying Corps, the move sought to strengthen the British airborne and bombing capability at a time when London had come under repeated attacks by German airships and bombers.

The main task of RAF strategic bombing was to strike military targets as well as densely populated industrial centers in Germany and occupied areas. The bombing of industrial centers aimed not only to destroy military arsenals, but also to break the morale of German workers. For example, Lord Tiverton, a staff officer of the RAF, advocated the use of any method to demoralize German workers, including dropping planeloads of Colorado beetles on farmland in order to devastate potato crops.[13] General Hugh Trenchard, who led the Independent Force (the British bomber force), claimed that the "moral effect of bombing stands undoubtedly to the material effect in proportion of 20 to 1, and therefore it was necessary to create the greatest moral effect possible."[14] After the war, General Trenchard and other leaders of the RAF claimed that British bombing had made a great contribution to ending the war by demoralizing German civilians. None of the postwar surveys conducted by the British, French, and U.S. forces, however, found evidence to support Trenchard's claim.[15]

The Use of Airpower in the Immediate Postwar Era

Although Britain won World War I, the war consumed enormous amounts of funds and resources, leaving the management of the colonies in disarray and providing a milieu in which anticolonial sentiment and organization rapidly advanced. The British Empire faced a serious crisis immediately after the war, encountering popular revolts and violent political demonstrations throughout the colonies and mandated territories. British airpower was immediately utilized to suppress them.

Britain's first extensive use of planes for bombing outside Europe after World War I was in Afghanistan. Britain, i.e., India's colonial master, and Afghanistan, backed by Russia, had often been in conflict since the early nineteenth century. In May 1919, newly crowned Afghan king Amanullah suddenly attacked the British troops stationed in India, calling the attack a Jihad. This was the beginning of the Third Afghan War. In retaliation, the RAF's Thirty-first Squadron bombed the city of Jalālābād (now in Kyrgyzstan) on May 17, 20, and 24. The bombings destroyed much of the military zone of the city, but an extensive area of the civilian quarter was also burned down, forcing many people to flee the town in fear of further raids. The RAF also attacked the Afghan capital, Kabul, sending two Handley-Page bombers stationed in India. During World War I, Britain produced three of these bombers, two of which were sent to India immediately after the war in order to demonstrate the power of the British Empire to the Indians. Only one appeared in the sky over Kabul on May 24, as the other one could not reach the target due to a heavy sandstorm. The bomber dropped four 112-pound bombs and sixteen 20-pound bombs on palatial and government buildings but did not cause much damage. This exercise seemed intended more to demoralize the

Afghanis than to cause extensive damage. Although it is difficult to assess the contribution of these bombings, the war ended in two months with a British victory.[16]

Around the same time, bombings were conducted to suppress political uprisings in various places under British rule. For example, in March 1919, British planes attacked rioting Bedouins and demonstrators of the WAFD nationalist movement in Egypt, who demanded an end to martial law and censorship. RAF aircraft were also used to suppress similar political uprisings in Punjab in India, Yemen, and remote regions of Mesopotamia. Among them, the longest operation took place over one and a half months from mid-November 1919, in Punjab, the North West Frontier province of India. The targets of the RAF's bombing were the Mahsud and Wazir, two tribal groups who had been inspired by the Afghan War to rise against British colonial rule. During this time, about twenty-five planes dropped between 2.5 and 7 tons of bombs daily upon the tribesmen, who hid in the shadow of rocks and fired at planes with their rifles. As a result, the RAF lost several machines and the effect of the bombing did not match their expectations. The poor performance caused contention between the army and the RAF over the effectiveness of aerial bombing in suppressing revolts. The army claimed that airpower should be used in the front line of the battlefield, principally in the role of supporting ground forces, and that the air force should therefore be put back under the control of the army as in the early stages of World War I.[17]

Bombing of Somaliland

The bombing campaign in Somaliland from the end of January 1920 was widely publicized by the RAF as a great success in suppressing a political uprising, in order to brush off criticism from the army.

Somaliland, with a population of 300,000, was at that time under British trusteeship and had been since 1884. From the late 1890s, the British authorities in Somaliland became troubled by the armed resistance group led by the powerful religious figure Mohammed bin Abdulla Hassan. The British called him the Mad Mullah. Beginning around 1910, this movement gained strength, and between 1916 and 1917 (i.e., in the latter half of World War I) Abdulla Hassan managed, with German support, to import a large quantity of arms and ammunition from overseas and came to command over 6,000 warriors. In May 1915, the colonial secretary Lord Alfred

Milner asked General Trenchard, who had assumed the position of chief of air staff in February of that year, whether the RAF could crush the Mad Mullah cheaply without throwing more army troops into Somaliland. Winston Churchill, then minister for war and air, also backed the employment of a small bomber squadron for this purpose and rejected the request from the army to increase the number of dispatched troops. The cabinet approved Churchill's plan.[18]

Consequently, a small force called Z Unit, with eight aircraft and thirty-five members, was sent to Somaliland and began to engage in a bombing operation on January 21, 1920. Their operations were of two different kinds—one was the bombing operation, conducted solely by Z Unit, and the other was to support the land operations of army troops composed of colonial soldiers from India. The aerial photos that Z Unit took during the operation clearly show that the bombing destroyed not only the fortress of the militiamen but also private dwellings nearby. The British forces also captured a large number of camels and goats belonging to the people of villages targeted by Z Unit, in which Abdulla Hassan's warriors were supposedly hiding.[19] Such aggressive action must have been devastating to the villagers. Eventually Abdulla Hassan's men dispersed, and he fled to Ethiopia, dying there in 1921.

The money that the British government spent on the destruction of Abdulla Hassan's force of militiamen was £150,000 in total, including £70,000 for operating Z Unit. Indeed, this was considerably more economical than sending a large contingent of armed forces to Somaliland over a long period, yet the defeat of Abdulla Hassan cannot simply be attributed to the use of planes. Toward the end of World War I, it became difficult for Abdulla Hassan to secure arms and ammunition, and furthermore, his leadership rapidly declined due to internal political problems and tribal frictions that arose during the long rebellion. In addition, in the last few years of his struggle, his men lost their mobility as a guerrilla force because they moved into fortresses. Thus they were compelled to defend themselves at fixed locations, and this strategic error also contributed to the loss.[20]

However, the RAF senior officers dismissed such internal factors and praised their own aerial operations in Somaliland. One of the Z Unit reports claimed that "*Opportunity was taken to test the theory that the moral effect of the new arm*, with its power to carry out, without warning, a form of attack against which no counter measures could avail. *This object was at-*

tained in full"[21] (emphases added). Z Unit members strongly claimed that their operations in Somaliland proved the theory of "the moral effect of aerial bombing," i.e., the justification of indiscriminate bombing formulated during World War I.

A Demand for the Expansion of Aerial Bombing in Iraq and a Temporary Setback

Beginning around the spring of 1920, encouraged by the results of aerial operations in Somaliland, Churchill and Trenchard began proposing to the cabinet that "air policing" be utilized in the Middle East, where many revolts were also occurring. In order to defy the challenge from the army and navy to break up the RAF, senior RAF officers set out to further demonstrate the effectiveness of aerial bombing, particularly in areas where the army was having trouble controlling local uprisings.

Iraq was under the rule of the Ottoman Empire until 1914, being divided into three regions—Mosul in the north, Baghdad in the center, and Basra in the south. Shortly after war broke out between Britain and Turkey in October 1914, British forces landed in Basra from the Persian Gulf and occupied this region. In March 1917, the British conquered the Baghdad region, and when World War I ended in November 1918, Britain occupied the Mosul region as well. In 1921, Britain established the kingdom of Iraq by consolidating these three regions. This new state, with a population of 2.5 million, was placed under British trusteeship, and the Hashemite Amir Faisal was installed as king. One of the important aims of British rule of Iraq was to secure its rich oil reserves. Throughout the kingdom, however, many powerful tribal groups defied the new central government, among them some who adamantly refused to pay tax and even resorted to force of arms. In particular, some Shia Muslims in the south and the Kurds in the north strongly opposed British rule. In addition, the Turks often assembled troops near the border, seeking an opportunity to invade Iraq, at the same time supporting the Kurdish militiamen engaged in guerrilla activities against British troops.[22]

In 1919, in order to suppress rebels, Britain maintained 25,000 British soldiers together with 80,000 Indian soldiers in Iraq. By the end of 1920, there were 17,000 British and 85,000 Indian soldiers. Despite such large forces, controlling the vast area of Iraq was a difficult task, in particular in

the mountainous northeast and the extensive desert in the west and southwest. Sending troops to these regions alone was time consuming and
costly. Furthermore, to transport sick and wounded soldiers from these remote areas to a hospital in a large town was also laborious work. Britain
was spending about £30 million each year just in maintaining its troops in
Iraq. The British government had accumulated a huge deficit during
World War I and was striving to set its finances in order by cutting down
extensively on military expenditures. The constant demand from the army
and navy to abolish the RAF was thus closely related to the political problem of how to divide the reduced military budget between them. Hence
the RAF, a new and still small force, had to demonstrate its "merit" and
"efficiency" in order to survive this straitened postwar era.

It was in this political context that Churchill, who served as secretary of
state for war and air between 1919 and 1921, asked General Trenchard in
February 1920 if the RAF was prepared to take the ultimate responsibility
for suppressing Iraqi uprisings. He also suggested appointing an RAF officer as commander in chief of all British forces in Iraq in return for an increase to the RAF's annual budget by between £5 million and £6 million.
Churchill's plan was that the RAF would use gas bombs, but that the
number of British soldiers would be decreased to 4,000 and that of Indian
soldiers to 10,000. In response to Churchill's idea, Trenchard drew up a
proposal that the RAF would station ten squadrons in Baghdad and that
the army troops would be engaged mainly in protecting the RAF's air
bases. Trenchard suggested that only in some special cases would the army
conduct a joint operation with the RAF. In May 1920, Churchill submitted
this proposal to the cabinet. However, Maurice Hankey, the secretary to
the cabinet and the chairman of the Committee of Imperial Defense, was
skeptical about the effectiveness of this plan. Influenced by Hankey, Prime
Minister Lloyd George eventually decided against it. Churchill also faced
severe criticism from the army, which he headed. In July, he withdrew this
proposal.[23]

However, in the same month, a riot occurred in Rumaitha, a town
halfway between Baghdad and Basra, in opposition to the tax system introduced by the British government. This triggered uprisings that spread
quickly throughout the southwest. British troops were attacked by rebels
and were unable to defeat them. In August, the rebellion began spreading
toward Baghdad. In concert with this revolt, in the north, over 130,000

Kurdish tribesmen armed with rifles took a stand against British rule. By bringing in a large contingent of Indian soldiers, the British government managed to gain control of the situation by October. In addition, utilizing a small number of the RAF planes—which were available in Iraq even before this large-scale revolt occurred—Kurdish tribesmen were restrained through repeated bombing, conducted until spring 1921. The attacks on the Kurds were often conducted in conjunction with army troops, and these eventually succeeded in suppressing the revolt in the north, as well.[24]

Full-Scale Bombing in Iraq

In December 1920, the British government decided to set up a new Middle Eastern Department under the Colonial Office in order to confront the serious security problems in the Middle East, in particular, in Iraq and Palestine. However, Colonial Secretary Lord Alfred Milner did not want to be responsible for such arduous duties and resigned. In February 1921, Churchill took over the position of colonial secretary.

Taking advantage of his new position, Churchill moved swiftly to implement his previous plan of extensive bombing of Iraq. In March 1921, he traveled to Cairo, accompanied by Trenchard, and conferred with the British authorities in the Middle Eastern Mandates to review existing policy and make new proposals. The conference, which lasted over two weeks, approved the RAF's "air control scheme," i.e., the bombing of rebels, as well as the Air Staff scheme to make the RAF responsible for the maintenance of order in some areas of the Middle East. Naturally the army was opposed to this new plan, but this time Churchill gained strong support from other cabinet members by assuring them that a lot of money would be saved through the extensive use of bombers. Churchill's proposal was approved by the cabinet in August, and full-scale bombing operations in Iraq began in the middle of the following year with eight squadrons.[25]

Let us closely examine the RAF's "air policing" in Iraq by studying various official reports, such as the "General Resume and Daily Summary of Operations," prepared by the RAF headquarters in Baghdad.

For example, in the bombing operations conducted near Kirkuk in northern Iraq at the end of June 1922, "six raids were made and nine villages attacked." Throughout July, "the pursuit of Kerim Fattah Beg and his followers was energetically carried out . . . , and any village which gave shelter or assistance to the rebels was immediately bombed by aircraft." In December, twelve raids were made in which twenty-seven villages were bombed.[26] It is clear from this record that, as time passed, the number of targeted villages increased due to the expanding activities of the rebel group led by Kerim Fattah Beg.

In the attack on Rowanduz in northern Iraq, conducted by a formation of nineteen planes on July 10, 1922, 400 gallons of gasoline were first scattered about, then incendiary and delayed bombs were dropped. Gasoline was used to increase the incendiary effect of the bombs, and the delayed bombs, which would explode some time after being dropped on the ground, were intended to kill any person who might come close to the fire to try to extinguish it. On the following day, a second attack was made by nine planes, and further raids were carried out on July 18 and 21. In these four attacks, a total of five tons of bombs was dropped on the town of Rowanduz.[27]

The attack on Samawah on November 30–December 1, 1923, was conducted on a much larger scale. Forty planes were dispatched from four different squadrons. They dropped twenty-five tons of bombs and 8,600 incendiary bombs as well as showering the area with 15,000 rounds of ammunition in two days. Bomb raids were carried out more or less continuously during these two days. In this case, the term "warfare" rather than "air policing" was more appropriate to describe the actual operation, although the "warfare" in this case was essentially unilateral action. On December 4, the police force sent to Samawah found that the town had been completely demolished.[28]

Bombing targets were not limited to towns and villages; even the nomadic Bedouins were attacked. For example, at the end of August 1923, RAF planes attacked a Bedouin group led by the chief Yusuf al Mansur, who were camping thirteen kilometers from Shiaiba, a town southwest of Basra near the border between Iraq and Kuwait. Yusuf's group refused to pay tax on cattle to a man named Hamud, of the Dhafir tribe. Hamud was responsible for collecting animal tax from tribes within the Iraqi border. Due to this dispute, a feud had been smoldering for a long time between the two groups, and eventually Yusuf's men assaulted Hamud's tribe, which in turn brought on an aerial attack by the RAF. In this operation, four planes made two raids on Yusuf's camp, which consisted of about fifty tents. On one evening, the planes dropped 104 bombs and 250 small incendiary bombs and fired nearly 3,000 rounds of ammunition from a low alti-

A Chabaish village under heavy bombardment in 1924. THE NATIONAL
ARCHIVES OF THE UK

tude. Yusuf's group fled and moved camp, but on the following day, an
early reconnaissance located the camp, and five planes again attacked, this
time dropping 72 bombs and firing 700 rounds of ammunition. The RAF's
report records that the first day's operation produced a "good effect," and
on the second day, "direct hits were obtained on some of the tents and
many camels were killed."[29] The report does not refer to any human casualties, but it is presumed that not only rebels but also some women and
children living in the tents were victims of these aerial attacks.

The following extracts from a report[30] written by the commander of the
Forty-fifth Squadron clearly shows how indiscriminate the "air policing"
operations really were.

> They [i.e., the Arabs and the Kurds] now know what real bombing means, in
> casualties and damage; they now know that within 45 minutes a full sized vil-
> lage, vide attached photos of Kushan-Al-Ajaza, can be practically wiped out
> and a third of its inhabitants killed or injured by four or five machines which
> offer them no real target, no opportunity for glory as warriors, no effective

means of escape, and little chance of retaliation or loot such as an infantry col-
umn would afford them in producing a similar result.

Night bombing is necessary to avoid a safe period intervening between daylight operations, when they return to inspect damage, eat, sleep, evacuate personnel and material, and graze their herds. Dark night work has always been
carried out whenever practicable to impress upon them that aircraft are independent of daylight or moonlight.

It may often be impossible to find a target on a dark night, but the mere presence of a machine in the vicinity, and a few lucky "finds" on dark nights will
amply repay unavoidable failures whilst if a target can be got alight with B.I.
Bombs on a dark night, the ensuing H.E. bombs can be placed with just as
much accuracy and ease as in daylight.

This commander also proudly notes in the same report that the bombing did not simply cause "a purely moral effect" but also "real casualties,
and material damage that produce a real [effect]." This officer, Arthur
Harris, became the RAF's Bomber Command Chief in World War II and
commanded the extremely destructive bombings of various German cities,
including Hamburg and Dresden.

In addition to human casualties and the destruction of houses, this kind
of indiscriminate bombing by the RAF in Iraq seriously affected the lives
of the local people over a long period of time, as their indispensable crops,
fuel, and cattle were also destroyed. The following extract from a secret
report written in 1924 by the RAF air officer commanding in Iraq, Air
Marshall John Salmond, clearly indicates his awareness of the real effects
of the indiscriminate bombing that his men conducted on the local population.

> It can knock the roofs of huts about and prevent their repair, a considerable
> inconvenience in winter-time. It can seriously interfere with ploughing or
> harvesting—a vital matter; or burn up the stores of fuel laboriously piled up
> and garnered for the winter; by attack on livestock, which is the main form of
> capital and source of wealth to the less settled tribes, it can impose in effect a
> considerable fine, or seriously interfere with the actual food source of the
> tribe—and in the end the tribesman finds it is much the best to obey [the]
> Government.[31]

There is no doubt that Salmond knew that even if people had survived
a direct hit, it was quite possible that many of them might suffer from star-

vation over a long period and eventually die. Furthermore, he saw this slow and painful death as punishment for disobeying British rule and did not regard indiscriminate bombing as unjust at all.

Some aerial photos taken from RAF planes, now housed in the British National Archives in London, show the attacked towns and villages suffering from extensive fires producing clouds of smoke.[32] From these photos one can easily assume that the damage to both people and houses must have been devastating and extensive. As many houses in Iraq at that time were made of reed matting, they were easily burned and destroyed by incendiary bombs. In cases where the target was a Bedouin camp in a flat desert without obstacles such as trees and buildings, planes usually made an attack with bombs and machine guns from a low altitude, thus causing more casualties and material damage. If the target was easily reached by army troops, the target was totally demolished by armed men dispatched shortly after the aerial attack. Despite the fact that "air policing" caused such intensive physical damage on many people and their dwellings in various places in Iraq, senior officers at the RAF's headquarters in Baghdad insisted that their operations were "calculated to have a moral effect more than to inflict actual damage."[33]

As briefly mentioned before, in February 1920, Churchill proposed the discharge of poison gas from RAF planes in Iraq. The gas that he suggested for use was a "non-lethal" asphyxiating gas that would cause "discomfort or illness but not death." In fact, however, it could permanently damage the eyesight of a normal, healthy person and could "even kill children and sickly persons, more especially as the people against whom we intend to use it have no medical knowledge with which to supply antidotes."[34] This was proposed only a few years after World War I, in which a massive amount of gas weapons had been used, killing well over 90,000 and injuring tens of thousands of soldiers. Thus, understandably, Europeans viewed the use of any gas weapon negatively, hence the British government did not allow the RAF to use such controversial chemical weapons. Yet it is said that Churchill still persisted in using them in Iraq, claiming that gas bombs were "a scientific expedient for sparing life" and that their use should not be prevented "by the prejudice of those who do not think clearly."[35] The RAF in Iraq never actually used gas bombs, but the army used gas shells against rebels during the latter half of 1920s.

Racial prejudice against the people of the Middle East, which can be detected in Churchill's attitude, is also strongly pronounced in various parts of official reports prepared by RAF officers in Iraq. They often described local Iraqis by using arrogant expressions such as "uncivilised tribes," asserting that the only way to obtain obedience from these "savage people" is through bombing. However, it is interesting to note that one officer tries to justify the indiscriminate bombing in his report in the following manner:

> People who have no knowledge of the country or war against uncivilized tribes when reading this report may form a very erroneous idea as to the action taken in this instance in the preliminary measures to bring these tribes to heel, and I feel that if this report as it stands were to get into the hands of undesirable people, harm might be done not only to the Air Force but to the Government.[36]

It is said that about 9,000 people were killed as the result of "air policing" within the first nine months after its official commencement in the middle of 1922. However, there are no reliable figures documenting how many people became the victims of all the RAF's bombing operations in Iraq, which lasted almost ten years.

Internal Criticism of Indiscriminate Bombing, and the RAF Responses

Nonetheless, some in the RAF felt uneasy about "air policing" in Iraq. Air Commodore Lionel Charlton arrived in Baghdad in February 1923 and assumed the position of senior air staff officer. Shortly after his arrival, he went on a tour of inspection to Diwaniya in southern Iraq and visited a local hospital in that town during his trip. He was shocked by the scenes in that hospital, which he later detailed in his autobiography, published in 1931. He wrote:

> Here he [Lionel Charlton; he wrote his autobiography in the third person] experienced something of a shock. In addition to the ordinary cases, male and female, of eye trouble, stone in the bladder, burns and injuries, he discovered that several beds were occupied by patients who were being treated for bomb injuries, the result of a recent punitive flight from Baghdad. It seemed to him a most cold-blooded proceeding and a grave reflection on the ends of justice, that at one moment people were so harmful as to deserve sudden and terrifying death, and the next so harmless that no expense was spared in patching up their injuries. He was aghast to learn on further inquiry that an air bomb in Iraq

was, more or less, the equivalent of a police truncheon at home. It was a horrible idea and, in his private opinion, work in which no one with a moral standard should be asked to engage. In declared war or in the case of open rebellion no objection could possibly be advanced, but the indiscriminate bombing of a populace without power of selecting the real culprits, and with the liability of killing women and children, was the nearest thing to wanton slaughter which he had come across since the massacre at Dijon in 1914.[37]

In his book, Charlton also pointed out that the accuracy of bombs dropped from a height of three or four thousand feet on a selected target could not be guaranteed, and in the case of the bombing of as-Sulaymānīyah, for example, bombs were dropped in the midst of a market gathering, killing many women and children. He also condemned the bombing of incorrect targets due to the slackness of the RAF's intelligence activities, as well as bombing without prior warning, both of which seemed frequent occurrences. His detailed description of the unnecessary agony endured by camels attacked by bombs also demonstrates well the cruelty of indiscriminate bombing.[38]

Although initially Charlton was cautious not to express himself too forcefully on this matter, eventually he could not help voicing his concerns to his senior, Air Marshall John Salmond. Salmond showed no sympathy, however, and soon the relationship between these two top officers in the Baghdad headquarters became painfully strained. Charlton asked to be relieved of his duties within less than a year of his arrival in Iraq, and subsequently General Trenchard recalled him to London. After long and relentless examinations of his complaints and statements, he was reprimanded and his salary was halved.[39] In 1928, he was disgracefully forced to resign from the RAF. By this time, the theory of the moral effect of bombing espoused by General Trenchard had infiltrated deeply and widely into the RAF. Humanitarianism like Charlton's was seen as an old-fashioned idea that was no longer relevant to modern technological warfare and thus must be eliminated.

Yet the RAF could not completely cover up Charlton's whistle-blowing from inside their own organization. In February 1924, the issue of "heavy casualties caused by air policing" was raised in Parliament under the first Labour government in British history. J.H. Thomas, the new colonial secretary, instructed Henry Dobbs, the high commissioner for Iraq, to report on what kind of policy was actually being implemented in the RAF's air policing operations. In response to this request, in consultation with John Salmond, Dobbs drew up a report entitled *Note on the Method of Employment of the Air Arm in Iraq*, and submitted it to the government and to Parliament on August 1, 1924.

According to this report, the decision to bomb a particular location was a last resort, only after three stages of careful examination were completed: (1) A local British civil adviser assisting local Iraqi administration would examine the situation of rebel activities in his district and request an air policing operation from the minister of interior in the Iraq government. (2) The minister of interior and his British adviser would study the request and recommend that the high commissioner take appropriate action. (3) The high commissioner would make the final decision and request the air officer commanding to draw a plan of the effective operation and swiftly carry it out.[40]

This report further elaborates on the cautious decision-making process of the high commissioner by explaining that special service officers with knowledge of local conditions, together with the Iraqi governor of the district, his British adviser, the local commandant of police, and the British police inspector of the area, would be taken by air to Baghdad for consultation with the air officer commanding, who himself also would make a reconnaissance of the whole district from the air at a low altitude. Based on the most reliable information thus gathered, the high commissioner would make the final decision. In other words, the target was clearly identified after studying the insurgent situation thoroughly. The report also claimed that "bombing is only resorted to in answer to open and armed defiance persisted in after warning of the consequence of defiance has been given and explicit notice issued that air action will be taken unless submission is yielded."[41] The usual method of giving an "explicit notice" was to drop warning letters or leaflets from the air.

In this report, Dobbs and Salmond tried to give British politicians the impression that the bombings were being conducted based upon a carefully organized and comprehensive plan that specifically targeted rebel forces and were far from random and indiscriminate attacks. They also stressed that the aim of the use of air arms rested "more on the damage to morale and on the interruption to the normal life of the tribes than upon the number of actual casualties."[42] Salmond claimed that bombing was a "merciful act" that would reduce "casualties to both sides and long-remaining misery in the area visited" by the bomber planes.[43] In December 1923, he proudly wrote in his report to the Air Ministry that the bombing "operation has proved *outstandingly effective, extremely economical and undoubtedly humane* in the long run" (emphasis added).[44]

However, one can hardly find any official RAF documents prepared in Iraq before August 1924 that clearly confirm that this three-stage system was actually observed and implemented. In the above-mentioned case of the attack on Samawah in late 1923, for example, first a series of large-scale bombings was conducted, causing many casualties and the destruction of buildings, and then, ten days later, the minister of the interior, accompanied by British military officers, summoned local tribal chiefs and ordered them to surrender.[45] In other words, the actual procedure was the reverse of that officially claimed by Dobbs. Furthermore, among the RAF's operation reports or war diaries, one can find cases in which the pilot decided on his own judgment, without any permission from headquarters, to assault a group of local people that he happened to locate from the air.[46]

Indeed, in his secret memo, Salmond himself wrote the following statement, which clearly contradicts the official policy to which he claimed to adhere.

> Of course there cannot always be time to go so thoroughly as this into the details of every outbreak. Rapid action by Government, to give waverers the right lead, and show that defiance will not be tolerated, is sometimes essential and is then, beyond all argument, the most merciful course to take. To temporise is only to have in the end a larger disturbance, and a more stubborn one, to quell. This is where, because of its rapidity, air action is so much more humane than a column.[47]

Regarding an "explicit warning notice" in the form of letters or leaflets dropped from the air, Salmond doubtless conveyed his real opinion in the same secret memo as follows:

> Iraq is as yet far from the stage in which it can be influenced by the written advertisement, the pamphlet or the tract. Written material produces nothing like the result to be had from a personal visit. Moreover, in the tribal areas it is most commonly the case that not even the Shaikh himself can read; and any written matter is handled for him by a scribe, if he has one. Broadcasting of pamphlets in such an area is obviously quite hopeless.[48]

He was clearly aware that dropping letters or leaflets was quite a vain effort, because most Iraqis in those days were illiterate. He even described a case in which a sheikh, i.e., a tribal chief, "circulated a garbled version [of a letter] by which he was successful in convincing his people that he had now established satisfactory relationship with Government and that the letter had conveyed him the offer of a Government appointment!"[49]

Judging from these official and secret documents and Lionel Charlton's autobiography, it seems almost certain that "the official policy of three-staged examinations" was a quick improvisation on the part of Salmond and Dobbs, in order to avoid public criticism back in England. Clearly their report, *Note on the Method of Employment of the Air Arm in Iraq*, was drawn up to dispel criticism regarding the "heavy casualties caused by air policing" from British cabinet members and parliamentarians. Naturally the senior officers of the RAF feared that politicians would discover that similar indiscriminate attacks were being carried out in many other British territories in the Middle East, Asia, and Africa, too. This is evidenced in the following letter, seemingly written by the secretary of General Trenchard, chief of air staff, to one of his colleagues on July 24, 1924, a week before the *Note*, which this secretary called "a White Paper," was submitted.

> I have undertaken to lay before Parliament a White Paper summarizing the policy pursued as regards [to] air action in Iraq, which I hope will do something to allay the present crop of questions being put down on the subject. . . .
>
> To avoid complication and the need of consultation with departments other than the Colonial Office, *the paper should be confined to the principles governing air action in Iraq i.e. no mention should be made of the other theaters* in which resort has been had to air action in the course of the last year or two, such as the North-West frontier of India [emphasis added].[50]

In other words, he advised saying nothing more than what they had been asked to answer, at the risk of exposing their misconduct. Indeed, in India, for example, RAF planes bombed terraced fields and irrigation channels without prior warning even after August 1, 1924. In Yemen, most of the population of the largest town, Sana, was forced to move out due to heavy bombings in the summer of 1928.[51] It is also interesting to note that the word "theaters" is used in the above letter, which indicates that, in the eyes of the RAF officers, bombings were conducted in the war zones of the British territories—an idea far from the official name and concept of air policing.

It is clear that the policy of air policing described in *Note on the Method of Employment of the Air Arm in Iraq* was simply a formality disregarded in practice. Yet the RAF consistently maintained its theory of the "moral effect of aerial bombing," both in actual operations and in its formal policy. Although RAF officers attempted to cover up their practice of indiscriminate bombing, they justified it by its "damage to the morale" of rebels and their people. However, a superficial change in this justification occurred after August 1924 when the *Note* was submitted. Until then, the RAF's doctrine was to quickly destroy the enemy civilians' morale by materially damaging them as much as possible. Of course, it was tacitly accepted that human casualties could not be avoided. After August 1924, the doctrine was changed to destroy morale through "interruption to the normal life" of the people. As I have already explained, this change occurred due to political attempts to escape criticism regarding the "heavy casualties" caused by air policing, which was in reality indiscriminate bombing. The expression "interruption to normal life," however, conveys the impression that bombing was not conducted simply for the purpose of destroying houses and killing or injuring people. But without causing human and material damage, "interruption to normal life" was not at all feasible. In other words, no fundamental changes actually occurred in the RAF's doctrine of strategic bombing before or after the *Note on the Method of Employment of the Air Arm in Iraq*. Nevertheless, it is also true that the RAF's actual method of "air policing" was altered to some extent to fit the formal policy. In particular, from the early 1930s on, a warning of imminent bombing was always issued a few days before the aerial attack was conducted.

Many official and secret documents of the RAF, and other relevant publications, indicate that, through their experience of indiscriminately bombing Iraq and other territories and sacrificing many indigenous lives, RAF leaders came to believe in so-called Trenchardian tactics, based on the "moral effect of aerial bombing." At the same time, politicians also appreciated the merit of "air policing" as a low-cost method of revitalizing the power and authority of the British Empire, which had been considerably weakened during the war. This imperious self-confidence in the effect of strategic bombing that had been built up in the late 1920s and 1930s eventually led the RAF to commit the unprecedented large-scale mass killing of civilians through a series of indiscriminate bombings of many German cities toward the end of World War II.

Britain was not, however, the only European power that conducted extensive aerial bombing prior to World War II for the purpose of suppressing anticolonial resistance in occupied territories. During the Second Italo-Ethiopian War, between October 1935 and May 1936, Italian forces air-dropped a large number of conventional bombs, as well as bombs loaded with mustard gas, on enemy troops, villages, crossroads, valleys, river crossings, and other such places. It was a war of aggression that Italian dictator Benito Mussolini conducted out of a desire to colonize Ethiopia as a part of his grand plan to establish a new Italian Empire. According to one semiofficial Italian report, between the end of December 1935 and the end of March 1936, "Chemical Bombing Operations" were conducted 132 times, dropping 972 chemical bombs, a total of 272 tons. Especially in the Battle of Enderta in mid-February 1936 and the Battle of Maych'ew at the end of March 1936, Italian forces, under the command of General Pietro Badoglio, conducted intense aerial bombing, using conventional bombs, including firebombs, as well as chemical bombs. In some cases, Red Cross camps and ambulances became targets of such attacks. Italians also targeted civilians deliberately as part of their attempt to terrorize the local population.[52]

In this way, indiscriminate bombing was frequently conducted outside Europe by certain Western imperial nations in the 1920s and 1930s, and in the Western world it became tacitly accepted as a most effective strategy with which to terrorize enemy civilians. "Enemy civilians" were people in non-European countries whom Western political and military leaders saw as "inferior" and "uncivilized races." This racist element undoubtedly enabled the British and Italians to feel less hesitant about dropping the bombs. Yet this practice of indiscriminate bombing of "uncivilized people" clearly trail-blazed the advent of "strategic bombing" among "civilized nations" during World War II.

2

THE BOMBING CAMPAIGNS IN WORLD WAR II: THE EUROPEAN THEATER

Ronald Schaffer

While the belligerent powers in the European theater engaged in tactical as well as strategic bombing, what we mostly remember when we think of bombing in World War II are the air raids on such places as London and Berlin, Hamburg and Dresden. This chapter examines the development and employment of both types of aerial bombardment, though its emphasis will be on the kinds of attacks that left cities in ruins and brought catastrophe to their inhabitants. The chapter discusses the origins of the theory that underlay those attacks, shows how widespread its application rapidly became, and examines the weaknesses exposed in the theory when contending air forces sought to put it into practice, at enormous cost to all the parties involved. It will also pose a series of practical and ethical questions arising from the way bombers were employed over Europe from 1939 through 1945.

Strategic Bombing Theory

The experience of World War I gave rise to a theory of aerial warfare that informed the air campaigns of World War II. Officers like the Englishmen Hugh Trenchard and Lord Tiverton, the American Billy Mitchell, and the Italian Giulio Douhet had observed how young men from all parts of the world had died by the hundreds of thousands in battles on the western front to secure small amounts of territory, rarely achieving any important military purpose. They believed that in the next war, bombers would fly beyond the battle lines to destroy an enemy's will and ability to resist and make war again an effective instrument of national power. Some of them envisioned fleets of warplanes heading toward the vital centers of enemy nations to paralyze and destroy them with poison gas, incendiary bombs, and high explosives, terrorizing civilians until they begged their governments to surrender. Some imagined that aircraft would demolish the economic structures on which armies and navies depended.[1] Implicit in such theories was a trade-off of civilian for military lives, possibly on a massive, unprecedented scale.

Strategic Bombing in World War II: The Luftwaffe

On September 1, 1939, the German air force began World War II with a series of air attacks all over Poland. It may have appeared to onlookers that strategic air warfare, with all the horrors that had been depicted by air-power theorists like Douhet and by playwrights, and authors, and film-makers of the previous decades was about to begin. Yet at that moment, Germany considered the untried weapon of the strategic bomber chiefly a deterrent—against strategic air attacks on its own territory and people. This was the view of other governments, which proclaimed and mostly adhered to a no-first-use policy. Just before the attack on Poland, Hitler had announced that Germany would limit bombing to military targets, and his government informed the British that the Luftwaffe would make no attack on the British civilian population. British prime minister Neville Chamberlain had compelled the Royal Air Force, which had begun developing optimistic plans to devastate enemy strategic objectives, to limit itself to "legitimate military targets" and only to those that could be identified. The French had no plan whatsoever for using bombers against Germany's industrial centers or against targets far behind a potential enemy's battle lines.

Several considerations reinforced this system of mutual deterrence. Fearing that bombers would overcome whatever barriers were created to stop them, all the European powers rushed to prepare their peoples for bombing, including chemical and biological warfare. Shelters were built and civil defense cadres established. For a while, with certain exceptions, even the German armed forces limited themselves to essentially military targets, such as airfields.[2]

These limitations on strategic bombing arose, in the case of the Nazis, from technological weaknesses, especially in engines. They also reflected miscalculations—by Hitler, who considered medium bombers more effective than they actually were, and by German planners, who thought Hitler really did not intend to attack England and that true long-range heavy bombers would not be needed if war occurred. While German aircraft had done serious damage, including the killing of civilians, when they were sent to assist General Franco in the Spanish Civil War, German bombers had found it hard to strike Spanish Republican targets from high altitude.[3] In September 1939 during the invasion of Poland, the Luftwaffe secured air supremacy and assisted German ground forces by attacking Polish mobilization centers, march routes, and supply centers; where feasible, it gave them direct air support.[4]

These initial combined-force attacks demoralized Polish troops and disrupted Polish resistance. To impede movements of Polish troops, German aircraft bombed and strafed road traffic, terrorizing and killing fleeing civilians. In an exception to the no-first-use policy, the German air force also attacked Warsaw. German aircraft poured hundreds of high-explosive and incendiary bombs on the city, destroying a tenth of its buildings, devastating the city's historic center.[5]

By the end of the month, German objectives in Poland were achieved. The Polish nation had been swallowed up by the victors and by Hitler's temporary ally the Soviet Union. After a period of quiet, Germany again went on the attack in western Europe with what the press called *blitzkrieg* or "lightning-war" tactics, killing 800 people in Rotterdam in an air raid that destroyed the center of that city while negotiations for its surrender were under way.[6] As Nazi armies broke through French defenses, JU-87 Stuka dive-bombers helped smash the morale of combatants and civilians. After France capitulated, the Luftwaffe was directed to mount a massive offensive against England, in preparation for the conquest of the British Isles.

In August 1940, the German air force began a series of systematic attacks, intended first to defeat the British defensive fighter force and then, with precision daylight raids, to destroy the British aircraft industry. With control of the air, it would strike at British cities, whose inhabitants, high

Luftwaffe officials had long imagined, were not as tough as German civilians and would crack first in a terror war. The Luftwaffe plan, undertaken with slow bombers and inferior fighters, was thwarted. The Royal Air Force gained an intelligence advantage over the Germans and was able to anticipate enemy operations and tactics. After suffering severe losses to RAF fighter command, the Luftwaffe concentrated its efforts against London, targeting first the city's docks, then its commercial and financial center, and attacking other British cities, resorting to extremely inaccurate night attacks. It failed to achieve the air supremacy needed for a successful invasion and actually increased British will to resist.[7]

Inadequate as it was, the Nazi bombing campaign against England inflicted terrible damage, as illustrated by the assault on Coventry, an ancient cathedral city with more than 320,000 inhabitants, a center of light manufacturing that produced cars, airplane engines, and munitions. On the evening of November 14, 1940, a small group of pathfinder aircraft, guided by intersecting radio beams, dropped parachute flares and incendiary canisters filled with phosphorus on a designated target area. Next came hundreds of medium bombers dropping high-explosive bombs intended to destroy the telephone and electrical systems and disrupt the water supply. These bombs smashed and cratered roads, railroads, and streets, blocking fire equipment from the city center, where a stream of bombers dumped magnesium and petroleum incendiary bombs. The raid lasted more than eleven hours, including time for bombers to return to base, rearm, and bomb some more. It destroyed or damaged nearly 60,000 buildings, including the Coventry cathedral, and killed 568 civilians— fewer than the numbers estimated to have died in Warsaw and Rotterdam and a minuscule figure compared to what was to come.[8]

In the spring of 1941, the German blitz against Great Britain diminished, a failure. That was far from the end of German bombing against England, however. From April through the following June, Nazi bombers launched a series of what were essentially morale attacks on English towns known more for their beauty and cultural significance than for their military or industrial importance, and in 1944 unmanned German V-1 devices and V-2 rockets fell indiscriminately on London.[9]

The focus of the German air effort, meanwhile, had turned to other strategic objectives: to choke off shipping to the British Isles, to fasten Nazi control over eastern Europe, and to conquer the Soviet Union. As part of a thrust into the Balkans, the German air force bombed Yugoslavia in the spring of 1941. A series of high-explosive/incendiary attacks against Belgrade, which the Yugoslavs had declared an open city, claimed an estimated 17,000 lives. Then, on June 22, Germany began an invasion of the USSR with an air assault that crippled the Russian air force in European Russia, destroying 1,200 Soviet aircraft in eight and a half hours. In the ensuing campaigns, marked by the utmost ruthlessness, the Luftwaffe supported ground units, but also launched repeated attacks on cities, including Moscow, Stalingrad, and Leningrad. At Stalingrad, with virtually unchallenged air supremacy, it flew 1,600 sorties in a single day, August 23, 1942, dropping 1,000 tons of bombs, chiefly incendiaries, almost completely gutting the city's residential area. Over Leningrad, it served as an instrument of siege warfare, cutting off exit routes and incinerating food supplies in the city's warehouses. In addition to the several thousand civilians it killed directly in aerial attacks, the Luftwaffe contributed indirectly to the death by starvation of hundreds of thousands of Leningraders.[10]

RAF Bomber Command: Early Operations

With the European continent dominated by Nazi armies, the British could do little to hurt their would-be conquerors. Their primary offensive weapon, the RAF Bomber Command, was virtually impotent at first, capable of little more than dropping propaganda leaflets on German citizens and making pinprick attacks on enemy shipping. On the first day of the war, twenty-seven RAF medium bombers were dispatched to search for German vessels near Denmark. They did not find any. On the second day, twenty-nine bombers went to attack warships in the vicinity of Wilhelmshaven. Seven aircrews were lost. Ten failed to strike their targets. Those that did caused little harm.[11] For months afterward, British policy makers and planners floundered.

Before the war, airpower theorists had argued that somehow the bomber would always get through to its target. This hypothesis turned out to be highly dubious for the RAF as it confronted the reality of bad weather, insufficient training, inadequate navigation aids, and an enemy that resisted with antiaircraft fire, interceptor fighters, and deception. In the early months of the war, neither daylight "precision" raids nor nighttime mass attacks proved effective. It was hard to locate a target area smaller than a city, and sometimes even that was too difficult. At the be-

ginning of October 1941, RAF bombers sent to attack Stuttgart and Karls-
ruhe flew instead over twenty-seven other cities. On a 1941 raid on Berlin,
British aircrews dropped forty-three times more high explosives and
forty-seven times more incendiaries on a dummy target than on the Nazi
capital. A government inquiry into the effectiveness of night bombing
concluded that, of planes recorded as hitting the target, only one third had
gotten within three miles—one fourth for German targets, one tenth in
the Ruhr industrial region. Undeterred, the Bomber Command launched
attacks deeper in Germany, with minimum effectiveness and increasing
losses of aircraft and crew members. Then, on November 13, 1941, it
halted its long-range attacks. They had been no more effective than German air raids on England.[12]

Adversity produced new methods for employing British bombers. On
St. Valentine's Day 1942 the British Air Ministry directed Bomber Command to resume intensive night bombing—not precision attacks but "area
bombing" against cities or urban areas, with inevitable high civilian casualties. If it was impossible to destroy German war factories, bombers could
destroy the homes of the men and women who worked in those factories
and, above all (at least theoretically), their willingness to continue the war.
The primary target of the Bomber Command now became the morale of
the German civilian population, especially of industrial workers.[13]

A week later, Bomber Command acquired a new commander, Air
Chief Marshal Sir Arthur Harris, known as "Bomber Harris" or "Butcher
Harris," an officer deeply dedicated to destroying through area attacks
Germany's ability and willingness to make war. Bomber Command also
acquired thousands of more potent aircraft, including the Lancaster heavy
bombers, and better navigational and bomb-aiming devices and techniques. And Great Britain, meanwhile, had additional allies, the USSR and
the United States, both with the potential to do terrible damage, through
bombing and other means, to Germany and its European satellites.[14]

The USAAF and the Combined Bomber Offensive

The U.S. Army Air Forces differed in significant ways from Bomber
Command. The AAF had evolved, by the time it arrived in Europe, with
a technology and philosophy that lent themselves to precision bombing
rather than night area attacks. They had developed heavily armed and ar-

mored long-range bombers, equipped with advanced bombsights, that they expected to use against vital centers in Germany and in German-occupied areas. The British wanted to throw the arriving American forces into area-bombing raids against Germany, but the American air force leaders, supported by their government, resisted. They believed their bombers were unsuited to night attacks and that they could overcome the obstacles that had forced Bomber Command to change its tactics. Furthermore, some of the American air generals considered it extremely imprudent to use their weapons against primarily civilian targets. Unlike the RAF, the American air forces that arrived in Europe were part of a larger military organization, the United States Army. Several of those generals wanted eventually to create an independent arm. They believed they could demonstrate its value by defeating the German air force and, through selective daylight bombing of German vital centers, eliminating both Germany's ability to fight and its will to resist. If American bombers became known for attacking the kinds of civilian targets that the RAF now aimed at, this could cause problems with the American Congress and with the American public, who did not appear to have the stomach for annihilating ordinary Germans. The outcome was an agreement that each of the Allied air forces would bomb in its own way, the Americans hitting German targets in daytime and the RAF continuing to attack at night.[15]

The RAF Bomber Command launched increasingly devastating attacks on German cities, including a series of raids in late July and early August 1943 against Hamburg. In this assault, British bombers, with some participation by Americans, employed target marking and bombing techniques similar to those used against Coventry, though on a much larger scale. The result was a vast, self-perpetuating firestorm in which hurricane-force winds uprooted large trees and hurled unprotected persons into seething flames. Thousands of incendiaries ignited flammable structures, and convection currents raised temperatures high enough to melt metal utensils and destroy bricks. People who had reached underground shelters were roasted alive or died of suffocation as the flames sucked away oxygen and generated carbon monoxide and other toxic gases. An estimated 44,600 civilians died in these raids.[16]

The Americans, after some modest successes, increasingly encountered some of the problems that had caused the British to limit their own efforts at precision daylight bombing. On August 17, 1943, they launched simultaneous attacks on Regensburg and on the ball-bearing factories of Schweinfurt deep inside Germany, enduring heavy losses. These attacks and additional raids on Stuttgart and Schweinfurt virtually crippled the Eighth U.S. Air Force for weeks. The essential problem for the AAF was a flaw in doctrine, originally shared by the RAF—a belief that heavy bombers, if flown correctly in massed formations, could defend themselves against German interceptors.[17]

By the end of February 1944, the Allies had largely overcome this problem, dispatching new long-range fighters with disposable fuel tanks to their strategic air forces in Europe. These fighters were able to engage the Luftwaffe hundreds of miles from their bases in England and Italy. Together with attacks on German installations, and with increasing Luftwaffe attrition in encounters with a reviving Soviet air arm, the air war over Germany wore down Germany's ability to resist Allied bombing campaigns.[18]

For a while, Allied leaders and their advisers debated their next steps. Allied armies were making their way toward the German heartland from the south, in difficult campaigns in Italy. Yet the outcome of the war in the west would soon depend on the success of an invasion of western Europe. The air battles of 1943–1944, combined with enormous increases in the size of the Allied air forces, promised to give the Allies command of the air over the landing area. The question was which target systems to hit in preparing for the invasion. Would it be wisest to attack German fuel supplies; to focus on transportation systems, blocking German access to the landing sites; or to concentrate, through area bombing, on what remained of German industrial power? After weeks of discussion, it was decided to do all three, an indication of the air-war resources the Allies now had available. Officially, the U.S. Army Air Forces were to hit oil targets. Unofficially, they engaged in dual-objective attacks, in which a certain number of bombs intended for fuel-production facilities were expected to go astray, landing on rail installations.[19]

Anglo-American Air Attacks in Southeastern Europe: The Issue of "Collateral Damage"

Dual-objective attacks became standard in the Balkans. American and British bombers attacked Bucharest, Budapest, and Sofia in 1943 and 1944. The ostensible, and partly the actual, aim of the American forces was to damage transportation targets. But the inhabitants were terrorized. In

November 1943, for example, when 91 B-25 medium bombers blasted marshaling yards and airfields in Sofia, the inhabitants, not hardened like Berliners or Londoners to continuing air raids, panicked and tried to flee the city. The result was chaos. A daylight attack by 143 B-17s, followed by a night area raid by British bombers, smashed electrical and water connections, destroyed residential and other buildings, and killed thousands of people. Fires broke out all over the city. Desperate inhabitants thronged the roads and jammed the railroad terminal, carrying whatever possessions they could. It took a week before public employees were willing to return to work and restore public services. On March 29, hundreds of American and British aircraft created a firestorm in Sofia, destroying the national theater, the city arsenal, and the Holy Synod building of the Bulgarian Orthodox Church. On April 4, 1944, 300 American heavy bombers attacked the Sofia marshaling yards, destroying some 1,400 railroad cars and many buildings. The highest concentration of bombs landed on the city of Sofia, not the rail facilities.[20]

Some of the American officers involved in the Balkan raids, operating under British command, did not like the role they were playing. American planners felt these raids would not force Bulgaria out of the war. Moreover, the Nazis were using them to foment hostility against the Western allies and the Jews. And there were reports that these de facto terror raids were turning even middle- and upper-class citizens toward the USSR, which ordinarily did not bomb European cities, for the main mission of the Red Air Force was direct and indirect support of the Red Army.[21] The Roosevelt administration, with the concurrence of the American Joint Chiefs of Staff, agreed to recommend that bombing in satellite countries be limited to targets of military importance, with due consideration of the probable number of incidental casualties. The British and American Combined Chiefs of Staff accepted this position. Nevertheless, as late as November 27, 1944, with the Soviet army approaching Budapest, the U.S. Fifteenth Air Force dropped sixty tons of bombs on the center of the city.[22]

"Collateral Damage" in the West: Bombing Friendly Civilians in France and the Low Countries

As the scheduled time for an Allied landing on the European continent approached, the political and, for some, ethical issue of bombing civilians in occupied countries that had appeared in Eastern Europe intensified in the West. Raids intended to destroy military and industrial objectives in Paris, Nantes, Lille, Rouen, Lorient, Amsterdam, and elsewhere since the early days of the air war had killed thousands of inhabitants, severely undermined the morale of friendly civilians, provoked vehement complaints from governments in exile, and, as in Eastern Europe, provided material for Nazi propagandists. In 1944, as part of the effort to disrupt enemy defenses and ensure the planting of Allied armies in France and the Low Countries, the Allies would be bombing transportation and other targets in the whole region behind German lines. Were the American and British air forces to risk massive casualties among French, Dutch, and Belgian civilians or to allow the Germans to use those civilians as human shields against Allied attack?

These questions troubled British prime minister Winston Churchill and the British War Cabinet, who feared that bombs intended for railroad cars and marshaling yards would kill as many as 40,000 French and Belgian civilians and injure 120,000 more. However, General Dwight D. Eisenhower, who assumed control of Allied strategic air forces before the invasion, approved the plan to focus on enemy transportation in occupied countries and elsewhere as more likely than the alternatives to affect German resistance seriously before D-day. Churchill urged President Franklin D. Roosevelt to intervene to mitigate what he predicted would be "French slaughters," but Roosevelt refused, leaving General Eisenhower to make his own decision. He explained to the prime minister that he shared his distress at loss of life among the French populace and felt no possibility should be overlooked for "alleviating adverse French opinion," provided it did not interfere with military success. Yet he would not limit military action that, in the commanders' opinion, might aid the invasion or prevent additional Allied losses.

Thus on General Eisenhower but also on the president lay the responsibility for preinvasion air operations, which contributed substantially to the Allied return to the European continent but also killed some 12,000 civilians in the occupied Western countries. On May 15, 1944, General Carl Spaatz, commander of U.S. Strategic Air Forces in Europe, sent the commander of the Fifteenth U.S. Air Force a list of transportation targets located in France. Explaining that these targets had been chosen to minimize civilian casualties, he noted, "This consideration does not apply in Germany."[23]

Thunderclap and Dresden

A few months earlier, the British Air Ministry conceived a plan, code-named Thunderclap, intended to do to the German capital what was being done to the Balkan cities, only on a much grander scale. This plan aimed at saturating the core of Berlin with so many bombs that the raid would utterly destroy the administrative center of Germany and at the same time make an indelible impression on millions of people nearby who would witness the attack, which was to be made in daylight. American aircraft, using precision bombsights, were to concentrate 5,000 tons of bombs in two hours in a two-and-a-half-mile area. This would be followed by a British area attack. Bomber Command expected the operation to kill or seriously injure about 275,000 persons and might even precipitate German collapse—or so it was hoped.[24]

The officer in charge of the American air forces that would do most of the job, General Carl Spaatz, had been pressured by the British Air Ministry to take part in morale raids and had thus far resisted, supported by the Supreme Allied Commander, General Dwight D. Eisenhower. The American air commanders, wary of the effects of such a catastrophic attack on American public opinion and therefore on the reputation of the U.S. air forces, believed that the British were trying to implicate them in an extraordinarily distasteful kind of warfare. Eisenhower, however, was changing his position. "While I have always insisted that U.S. Strategic Air forces be directed against precision targets, I am always prepared," he wrote, "to take part in anything that gives real promise to ending the war quickly." On September 9, he instructed General Spaatz to be ready to bomb Berlin at a moment's notice, whereupon Spaatz informed James Doolittle, commanding general of the Eighth Air Force, that "we would no longer plan to hit definite military objectives, but be ready to drop bombs indiscriminately on the town" when Eisenhower gave the order.

The Thunderclap proposal elicited considerable controversy among lower-ranking AAF officers in the United States Strategic Air Forces (USSTAF), especially among a group of intelligence officers who questioned the morality of what one of them called "baby-killing schemes." The president's military adviser Admiral William D. Leahy told the Joint Chiefs of Staff that it would be a mistake to "record" a decision to proceed with the plan. However, it was postponed for operational reasons, notably problems in assembling the required escort fighters.

On February 3, 1945, General Spaatz sent 900 B-17s to attack Berlin. In less than an hour, the AAF dropped more than 6,000 high-explosive bombs, 1,000 air mines, and about the same number of incendiary canisters. This raid killed somewhat fewer than 3,000 people, and it did not produce the result that Thunderclap's planners desired, for it did not push Germany over the brink. It did not become the best-remembered operation of the European war.[25] That distinction went to the fire raid on Dresden, capital of Saxony.

Dresden was a great cultural center with magnificent buildings and artworks, relatively undamaged by previous bombing. Like Coventry, it contained several military targets, including a Zeiss Ikon optical factory and numerous workshops scattered among its streets, many converted from civilian production, that manufactured items used in the German military machine. How aware the Allies were of these shops is uncertain but, whether the Allies knew it or not, Dresden's economy was woven into the Nazi system of war making and extermination.[26] What chiefly made it a target were its railroad installations, used by tens of thousands of citizens to escape the advance of the Soviet army. As Victor Klemperer, a Dresden resident, observed the previous October,

> It worries me greatly that our personal situation has become so very much altered by Hungary's elimination. Now Dresden may become a transport junction beyond the front which is most threatened, and that in a very short time. Then we shall get heavy air attacks. . . .[27]

On February 13–14, 1945, two waves of British planes, dropping hundreds of thousands of high-explosive and incendiary bombs, burned out the core of Dresden. They were followed by AAF bombers that sought to attack the marshaling yard, dropping 296 tons of incendiaries and nearly 475 tons of general-purpose bombs, often bombing blind through the smoke rising from the firestorm that had been created. Fire and explosions, flying debris, suffocation, and toxic gases killed tens of thousands of inhabitants, most of them women, children, and the elderly. While the number of deaths was nowhere near the numbers killed in Tokyo a few weeks later, or in Hiroshima or Nagasaki, the death toll was nearly as great as in Hamburg, although Hamburg's population had been much larger.[28]

The bombing of Dresden, known for its beauty and cultural monuments, proved highly embarrassing to people in the British and American governments. For some reason, the censors passed an Associated Press cable, based on a British press briefing, that described the February 13–14 fire raid as the result of a decision "to adopt deliberate terror bombing of great German population centers." A few weeks afterward, Prime Minister Churchill, who on January 25 had encouraged the RAF to "baste" the Germans fleeing the Russian offensive, tried to insert into the record on March 28 a document questioning area attacks and urging the British military chiefs to concentrate more precisely on military objectives "rather than on mere acts of terror and wanton destruction." Although he had clearly encouraged the area attacks against east German cities, Churchill argued in this note that "the destruction of Dresden remains a serious query against the conduct of Allied bombing."[29]

The prime minister was obviously aware of the way what happened at Dresden would be used by Nazi propagandists, who afterward issued reports that multiplied the number of recorded deaths in the city by roughly a factor of ten and pretended that Dresden had been entirely a center for art and culture, with only the slightest military significance. This line spread through neutral countries, was adopted during the Cold War by East German communists and neo-Nazis, and even by scholars of no particular political persuasion.[30]

The incineration of Dresden was intended as an act of terror. It represented in part an attitude that the German people needed to have the deepest horrors of war "brought home" to them, that they had not been sufficiently touched by the effects of World War I, which ended before ordinary Germans could experience what it was like to be invaded. This notion of impressing the German people was described very well by a high-level officer, Major General Frederick L. Anderson, formerly commanding general of the Eighth Bomber Command in Europe. Anderson was telling another general what he thought should be said to the press about Operation Clarion, a series of dual-purpose attacks on February 22 and 23, 1945, by the RAF and the AAF against transportation targets all over Germany. These attacks wrecked rail facilities, impeded military movements, and helped paralyze what was left of the German economy. They also struck "virgin targets," villages and towns that had never been hit before, mainly because they lacked military significance. General Anderson observed:

> It should be pointed out that such an operation was not expected in itself to shorten the war—no such optimistic attitude existed here. However, it is ex-

pected that the fact that Germany was struck all over will be passed on, from father to son, thence to grandson; that a deterrent for the initiation of future wars
will definitely result—a reluctance to participate in any organization that has
war as its primary aim certainly will result.[31]

General Anderson's unverified and perhaps unverifiable comment
poses one of several important questions raised by the strategic bombing of
Europe in World War II:

• Is it true that the bombing of civilian as well as military targets has
served to deter a third world war by affecting the minds of people who
might otherwise have followed a would-be Hitler?

• How valid was the argument that strategic bombing deserved much
of the credit, and so much of the resources, for the Allied defeat of Germany and its satellites?

• Could some of those resources have been better diverted to tactical
bombing or to an increase in the firepower of ground forces? In particular,
would it have been better to focus on oil, coal, transportation, or other target systems rather than expend so much effort, wealth, and blood in urban
area attacks? How much did bombing in general and area attacks in particular contribute to the success of the Allies by using up the enemy's more
limited military and economic resources and by forcing the enemy to dis-
perse production?

• To what extent did morale attacks affect the enemy's ability to fight?
In the face of evidence provided by civilians on both sides, was it possible
to break civilian morale in countries like England and Germany? What
made officials in each of those countries imagine that the other's civilians
would crack before their own? And given the power of government police
agencies like the Gestapo to control civilians whatever their feelings, did it
pay to try through violence to shape the way those civilians felt? What reasoning did British commanders use to support their idea that the morale
of German civilians would collapse under air attack when the morale of
English civilians had not?

Then there are a series of questions of a less material nature:

• Were the Allies right to join their enemies in making war against
civilians? If civilians were making war possible by producing supplies and

supporting the morale of armed forces, did either side have any choice except to bomb women, children, and the elderly?

• Could the Allies have used their warplanes to reduce the number of casualties without loss of military effect? Should they, for instance, have tried to use long-range aircraft to impede the killing of Jews, Russian POWs, Gypsies, homosexuals, and others?

• Would the Allies have lost the war or taken much heavier casualties if they had seriously considered the morality of what they were doing?

• Is there some way of verifying the claim by military leaders that all-out attacks on civilians and the infrastructure that supported them ended the war more quickly than it would have ended otherwise? Was the strategic bomber, to use the terminology of General Henry H. Arnold, the commanding general of the U.S. Army Air Forces, "the most humane of all weapons" when used with understanding in the "unspeakable" horror of war?[32]

• What were the long-term effects of area bombing on the crews that attacked such places as Leningrad or Coventry, Hamburg or Dresden?

Then there is the all-important question of why, in the absence of evidence, indeed in the face of evidence that tended to disprove their theories, air force commanders and national leaders invested so much in bombing intended to destroy enemy morale.

Tami Davis Biddle, in one of the key studies of air-warfare theory and practice, examines this last question. She believes that psychological and institutional factors led to situations in which British and American leaders acted on unproven theories and expended vast amounts of resources on air strategies that lacked evidentiary foundations or conflicted with the results of actual practice. American and British airpower experts, she notes, failed to analyze World War I bombing experience with sufficient rigor, underestimated the difficulty of locating and bombing targets, failed to appreciate the resiliency of enemy economies and societies, and greatly underestimated the vulnerability of their own aircraft under actual war conditions. When confronted with evidence that undermined their notions, they discounted it.[33]

In part, as she observed, information-processing failures distorted their thinking. Thus, when evidence emerged that conflicted with their beliefs, they were frequently unable to process it properly, and so they made it appear to support those beliefs—a common reaction to what psychologists call cognitive dissonance, a reaction that was likely to occur when they were being swamped with information under conditions of great stress. In addition, the air leaders had founded or were seeking to found organizations based on their air-warfare doctrines. To adjust or rebuild those institutions in the light of air-war realities was an enormous challenge to the psychic and material investments the leaders of those institutions had made.

Thus when AAF intelligence officers challenged the notion that bombing could break civilian morale, doubted that it made sense to carpet-bomb cities and towns to prevent a future conflict, or questioned whether it made a difference, in a country under tight control of the Gestapo, how enemy civilians felt about the war, the result appeared to be more bombing. If one level of escalation did not cause the enemy to break, escalate some more. By 1945, the Allies had so many bombers and so much ordnance that if bombing or terrorizing civilians didn't seem to be ending the war quickly enough, there were these huge air forces to bomb and terrorize some more.

Finally, there is the question of why, in general, leaders of military institutions learn so slowly from experience and so often end up repeating what seem, in retrospect, like obvious errors.

3

THE BOMBING WAR IN GERMANY, 2005–1940: BACK TO THE FUTURE?

Robert G. Moeller

My mother-in-law was born in Belleville, Illinois, in 1924. At the age of seventy-eight, she decided to start seeing Europe, and she's now traveled through much more of it than I have, so I was happy when in September 2004 she finally opted for a trip to *terra* that at least for me is a bit more *cognita*—a cruise on the Mosel and the Rhine. For the most part, my mother-in-law's interest in my job has extended little beyond her concern that I provide adequately for her granddaughter, but before she left for Germany, she had many questions, and I looked forward to hearing her impressions when she returned.

My mother-in-law's first comment when she got back from her trip was: "They sure do like to talk about how they were bombed in World War II. Well, I guess they were. But you know, I have a different memory of the war. I remember how many people I knew didn't come home. I remember how many of our boys died." My mother-in-law and I had plenty to talk about. It is no surprise that in the fall of 2004 as she traveled through Germany, she heard a lot about the bombs that fell on Germany in the Second World War. In remarkable ways, as Germans prepared to commemorate the sixtieth anniversary of the war's end, many seemed intent on reliving it—in illustrated magazines, television documentaries, the feature sections of their newspapers, big-box-office films, big fat books with many footnotes and still others packed with pictures. The Second World War was "in."[1]

Perhaps more than any other single book, *Der Brand: Deutschland im Bombenkrieg 1940–1945* (*The Fire: The Bombing of Germany, 1940–1945*) by Jörg Friedrich, a freelance historian who was already well known for works on the postwar failure to bring Nazi criminals to justice and on the Holocaust, initiated a national discussion of the bombing war. Serialized in the mass circulation *Bild-Zeitung* before it was published as a book, *Der Brand* has been a runaway bestseller, widely discussed in the press. Columbia University Press has paid for an English translation.[2] Because it has attracted so much attention and claimed a space as *the* history of the bombing war, read by more Germans than any other, I want to look at it in some detail. But it's far from the only new book about the bombing war. You can read more than one book about the bombing of Hamburg, one of the most destructive raids, but there are also books devoted to the bombing of many other German cities. Books flooded the market as part of the sixtieth anniversary of the "year of catastrophe"—1943, when the bombing was significantly intensified—and of 1944, "the inferno of autumn."[3] In 2005, things went into even higher gear as another round of commemorative publications hit the bookshops.

If you want to read still more, you don't have to go far to find it. A very interesting Web site, historicum.net, produced by historians at the Universities of Cologne and Munich, has devoted considerable space to the bombing war, including extensive guides to further reading.[4] And if you don't have that much time to read, you can go to Amazon.de and get *Firestorm: The Bombing War Against Germany*, a documentary produced by Spiegel TV and seen by some 5.5 million viewers when it first aired on German television. Bonus materials include an extensive interview with Friedrich.[5]

In 1997, the novelist W.G. Sebald, a German expatriate, at home in England since 1966 but intellectually and emotionally never far from the country of his origin, turned his attention to this same bombing war. In an essay in his collection *On the Natural History of Destruction*, Sebald commented that "the destruction, on a scale without historical precedent, entered the annals of the nation, as it set about rebuilding itself, only in the form of vague generalizations." He described "a kind of taboo like a shameful family secret, a secret that perhaps could not even be privately acknowledged," surrounding the "darkest aspects of the final act of destruction,

as experienced by the great majority of the German population."[6] Sebald
died in a car accident in December 2001. Had he lived, he might have
been pleased to see the extent to which many dark aspects have been
brought into the light of television documentaries, the press, and scholarly
publications . . . or he might have learned that you need to be careful what
you wish for.

What does this explosion, as it were, of interest in the bombing war
have to say about the intersection of the politics of the past with the politics of the present in contemporary Germany? In what follows, I will offer some answers. I first want to review the outlines of the bombing war.
Then I want to consider what variations on these themes Friedrich has
to offer. I want to suggest how Friedrich's book fits into the "memory
landscape"—to borrow Rudy Koshar's phrase[7]—of contemporary Germany. I want to say why I find *Der Brand* a very troubling book. And I
want to reflect on how the historical account of the bombing war that I'd
prefer might look.

First, some basics about the Allied bombing campaign against Germany:
American, British, and German scholars have focused more on how the
bombing war came about and was executed, not the details of its consequences, which Sebald sought in vain. They emphasize that the bombing
campaign against Germany emerged from preparations for total war that
dated back to before World War I, as strategists in advanced industrial
countries began to think about how to use airpower as a weapon. In at
least three important ways, planning for a war that would include aerial
bombardment, in the 1920s and 1930s, was a response to the First World
War. First, there was a widespread desire to avoid the kind of war of attrition that led to the death of hundreds of thousands of ground troops. Second, World War I was a total war in which the mobilization of the
industrial army at home was vitally linked to the fate of the army in uniform at the front. From this perspective, the boundary between civilians
and the military was blurred, and attacking the home front—destroying
the means of war production and disrupting the daily routines of those doing the producing—was part of a strategy to win the shooting war at the
front. Third, the experience of bomb warfare in World War I—however
limited compared to what would follow twenty or so years later—provided
the evidence that military planners should incorporate strategic bombing

into the blueprint for wars of the future. The bomber was the right weapon for a modern total war.[8]

Translating theory into practice was not easy, but twenty years earlier, British fliers, including Arthur Harris, who designed the British bombing campaign in the Second World War, were experimenting, dropping bombs on Turks who sought to challenge the British presence in Iraq. Winston Churchill, then colonial secretary, was more than ready to use airpower against "uncivilised tribes."[9] American military planners were no less captivated by the possibilities of aerial warfare, and they carefully assessed the impact on domestic morale of the Japanese bombing of Shanghai and the German bombing of Guernica.[10] Still, not all military strategists were convinced that aerial bombardment could achieve much more than the support of ground forces, and Britain and the United States were the only major powers that were convinced that strategic bombing could be a decisive part of a successful military strategy.[11]

However, once World War II began, it was not the British and Americans but the Germans who initiated the bombing war. Although the Germans had no long-range bomber fleet, Poland was close by and the war began with the bombing of Warsaw in September 1939. Historians agree that the subsequent German decision to bomb London provided British political and military leaders with the rationale they needed to "take the gloves off": to disregard the haziness of international law on the topic of aerial warfare and retaliate. As military historians emphasize, unlike the Americans and British, German military leaders never committed the resources required to develop the medium and heavy bombers that would have been required for a systematic campaign of strategic bombing. At least in the prewar period, German military planners believed that the Luftwaffe should primarily support initiatives on the ground. Late in the war, the Nazis attempted to develop long-range missiles that could hit British cities—the so-called V or *Vergeltung* (revenge) weapons—but until then, German military strategists used airpower primarily as a source of tactical support for ground troops.[12] The British, on the other hand, developed a bomber fleet that set out to do in Germany what British ground forces couldn't accomplish—destroy industrial capacity and undermine civilian morale. Even before the entry of the United States into the war, American industrial production supported this effort. The bombing campaign was also a way to assure the Soviets that in the absence of a second front on the ground in the west, a second front would fall from the skies.

The initial results of the British bombing campaign were mixed. Bombs made little dent in German industrial production, and the costs in downed planes and flight crews were extremely high. Among political leaders, public intellectuals, clerics, the general public, and even some military strategists, there were real concerns about the ethical implications of killing large numbers of civilians. Still, the bombing campaign continued. The uneven record of "precision" bombing led by early 1942 to an explicit commitment to area bombing, intended to destroy "the morale of the enemy civilian population, and in particular industrial workers."[13] "Bomber" Arthur Harris, who took over Bomber Command in late February, enthusiastically endorsed area bombing, which sought not just to hit industrial sites but to level entire cities. Harris favored not only area bombing, but also the use of the "concentrated incendiary method"— what he called "fireraising" bombs—rather than high-explosive bombs, because he believed they could cause maximum destruction.

British fliers were joined by Americans in 1942. At the Casablanca conference in January 1943, Churchill and Roosevelt agreed to give the highest priority to the bombing campaign. The "Combined Bomber Offensive" defined a division of labor that left Americans conducting "precision" bombing missions by day and British squadrons "carpeting" German cities with bombs at night. The explicit objective was to achieve "the progressive destruction and dislocation of the German military, industrial and economic system, and the undermining of the morale of the German people to a point where their capacity for armed resistance is fatally weakened."[14] Both British and American military leaders, with approval from the highest levels of the civilian political order, endorsed the view that bombing to undermine domestic morale was legitimate and that destroying housing—or "dehousing," as the British called it—achieved by using incendiary bombs was potentially as disruptive to industrial production as the leveling of factories.[15]

As the war progressed, Britain and America produced more and more heavy bombers and more effective fighter planes to provide defense for bomber squadrons. Engineers also designed more devastating bombs and more effective technical means to jam enemy radar. Better radar devices on board planes improved the chances that pilots would find their sites and bombardiers would hit their targets. The bombing campaign intensified throughout 1943. Although the Royal Air Force (RAF) and the United States Army Air Force (USAAF) continued to lose hundreds of planes and their crews, mainly to flak batteries, the bombing campaign accelerated in 1944, crescendoing to its high point in the last months of the war. In March 1945 alone, American and British fliers dropped more than 130,000 tons of bombs on Germany, more than the total for all of 1942.[16]

For the residents of German cities, survival "beneath the bombs" was a defining characteristic of the war. The war in the skies had erased the distinction between home and front, adding "air terror psychosis" and "bunker panic" to the German vocabulary. Urban dwellers could also claim "moments of a life at the front," in a war that had transformed Germany's cities into a "battlefield."[17] Although those most directly affected were the residents of cities of 40,000 or more—virtually all of which were bombed and suffered significant damage by the end of the war—no German could remain unaware of the consequences of the Allied bombing campaign. For soldiers at home on leave from the front, the consequences of the bombing war delivered powerful evidence of how incompletely the Third Reich was able to protect the friends and families they had left behind. The state intervened to remove two million or more school-aged children from big cities to group homes in the countryside out of harm's way, keeping secret the extent of these actions lest the population take such measures as one more indication of how bad things were.[18] Urban families also made informal arrangements with relatives to take in countless more children. Evacuees' hosts, however, frequently welcomed them only grudgingly. The clash of urban and rural lifestyles, cramped quarters, and increased strains on rationed goods generated conflict and resentment.

By late 1944 and early 1945, as Allied bomber squadrons searched for new targets, areas that had been safe havens were suddenly vulnerable, and evacuees found themselves on the move again. Joining these homeless masses were millions more Germans, fleeing the advancing Red Army as it pushed into parts of eastern Europe occupied by the Nazis and by early 1945 into Germany itself. As many as half a million had found their way to Dresden by February 1945, where they confronted another face of the war—the massive RAF and USAAF bomber attack that destroyed that city, killing countless thousands.[19]

Propaganda Minister Joseph Goebbels's duties expanded to include coordinating relief efforts in bombed-out cities. In the diary he kept throughout the war, the bombing war was a preoccupation, and he closely followed reports from Nazi officials and the secret police that registered public opinion. The Nazi welfare organization (Nationalsozialistische

Volkswohlfahrt or NSV) mobilized with impressive efficiency to meet the needs of those bombed out of their homes, but as the war continued, it became increasingly difficult to find food, shelter, clothing, and household goods for millions of Germans who were left with nothing. When, as one eyewitness reported in Berlin in February 1945, "there are no more coffins," the regime had difficulty orchestrating the burials of bombing victims as war heroes whose example should inspire others to a total commitment to the "total war." Hitler said British bomber pilots cleared out cities that were "poorly laid out, musty, and miserably built," and as late as August 1943, Hitler's master architect, Albert Speer, credited Allied bombers with achieving in quick order the first steps toward a program of urban renewal that would allow for the modernization of German cities, but this was a silver lining that few could see.[20]

The bombing war gave rise to gallows humor—recorded by the ever vigilant secret police—that offered one indication of how catastrophic many Germans believed the situation to be. The story circulated that a soldier condemned to death had been allowed to choose how he would be executed. He opted for a novel alternative—death by antiaircraft fire. The prisoner was placed in a tower, and three antiaircraft batteries let loose their fury. After three weeks, the gunners approached their target. They found the soldier dead—from starvation.[21] Another secret police report recorded the tale of two survivors of bomb attacks, one from Berlin, the other from Essen. The bombardment of Berlin had been so severe, reported the resident of that city, that five days after the attack, glass panes had continued to fall out of the window frames. Compared with Essen, retorted his comrade, that was nothing. There for fourteen days after a big attack, not glass but pictures of the Führer had flown out of the windows. And by the end of the war, the V-1 and V-2 rockets that had promised revenge (*Vergeltung*) were ruefully referred to as failures (*Versager*).[22]

However, tragedy, not farce, was the genre employed by most Germans to describe their experience of the bombing war. Their voices registered in the files of the secret police, the reports of local officials, diaries, and postwar memoirs. Indeed, survey data collected in West Germany in 1948 revealed that for more than one in four of the women interviewed, the bombs continued to fall in their dreams.[23] What emerges from first-person accounts and official sources is a picture of days and nights interrupted by air raid sirens, shelters filled with the elderly and mothers trying to comfort small children, and, for the survivors of bomb attacks, the exit from shelters into dramatically altered urban landscapes where familiar land-marks lay in rubble and dead bodies filled the streets.

The reports of the secret police—the barometer used to measure public opinion in most historical accounts of the war's impact on domestic morale—record growing indifference and, in some cases, even "hostile at-titudes" toward the Nazi leadership and the regime's eroding "monopoly on the truth." However, anger and skepticism did not translate into open opposition, and apathy triggered disengagement, not attempts to over-throw the regime. The bombs also brought cries for revenge, particularly against the British, and hopes that the weapons that promised *Vergeltung* would let the British know what it meant to live under the constant threat of death dropped from above. And at least some groups—particularly young people whose socialization had taken place all but entirely in the Third Reich, many frontline soldiers, and the "old fighters," party mem-bers who had been with Hitler from the early 1920s—continued to believe that a reversal of fortune was possible.[24]

By the end of the war, the bombs had killed over 400,000 Germans. According to the best available estimates, this total included some 360,000–370,000 who had lived within Germany's 1937 borders. The bal-ance was made up of Austrians, citizens of countries occupied by the Ger-mans, slave laborers, prisoners of war, and soldiers. Because so many men were at the front, women were overrepresented among the dead, as were infants. Older children did not die in numbers proportionate to their share of the population, because of the success of Nazi initiatives to evacuate young people from the cities. All casualty counts are estimates, because lo-cal officials were kept so busy tending to the living that they could not ac-curately count the dead. Hundreds of thousands more Germans were wounded. And in many big cities where as much as 70 percent of housing stock was destroyed, millions more were left homeless at the war's end.[25]

After the German surrender in May 1945, there was no consensus about whether aerial bombing hastened German defeat. Extensive postwar sur-veys by the British and Americans yielded no unequivocal evidence of what the bombing campaign had accomplished, and historians are also of no one opinion. On the one hand, money and resources committed to at-tempting to shoot down American and British fliers, clearing away rubble, putting out fires, and evacuating the civilian population could not be used elsewhere. Bombs also destroyed some of Germany's industrial capacity. On the other hand, strategic bombing failed to realize its most passionate advocates' predictions that it would demolish not only cities but morale, and there is some evidence that the Nazi party's ability to manage adversity so effectively raised its credibility with parts of the German population. The German war economy also continued to produce despite the bombing campaign. In May 1945, there was no disagreement that the war was ultimately won on the ground.[26]

The bombing campaign in the Second World War left a legacy of controversy about the legality of such military tactics. It is telling that at Nuremberg there was no mention of German bomb attacks as war crimes, an indication that the Allies were worried that any mention of Coventry and Rotterdam would be countered with mention of German cities devastated by Allied bombs.[27]

In *Der Brand*, Friedrich presents these themes with some variations in chapters entitled "Weapon" (Waffe), "Strategy" (Strategie) and "Protection" (Schutz), drawing on histories of the bombing war by German, British, and American historians, including Ronald Schaffer, a contributor to this volume. In his criticism of British advocates of carpet bombing, Friedrich echoes opinions expressed in Britain during the war.[28] Virtually all students of the air war would agree with Friedrich's conclusion that Germany was the first "nation to test [the impact] of the fury of war let loose from the skies," but not all would accept his speculation that because of the absence of alternative weapons, lack of an adequate land army, and the unstoppable momentum of British interwar strategic planning, the British bombing campaign might well "have happened anyway" (76).[29] And not everyone would accept Friedrich's judgment that the Americans were "humane," engaging in the bombing of civilians only once their troops were on the ground. Although American fliers played only a minor supporting role in such truly devastating attacks as that on Hamburg in the summer of 1943, USAAF commanders studied the results and speculated about what a similar bombing strategy might do to cities in Japan.

Had Friedrich cast a glance at what motivated American bombing tactics against the Japanese, he would have seen not "humane" attitudes but rather what John Dower describes as a "war without mercy" fueled by an unbridled racism that allowed a U.S. admiral to call for the "almost total elimination of the Japanese as a race" and legitimated a rhetoric in which "the only good Jap is a Jap who's been dead six months."[30] In the case of Germany, U.S. planners continued to distinguish between Hitler and those he'd led astray, but even though anti-German propaganda was largely free of the racism that defined attitudes toward the Japanese, falling bombs often proved unable to distinguish neatly between the Nazis and "good Germans."

American "precision bombing" was also hardly precise. As historian Michael Sherry, another contributor to this volume, concludes, by 1944 it was increasingly difficult to distinguish U.S. from British techniques as "Americans were beginning to loosen their definitions of precision bombing." Because American bomber squadrons relied increasingly on "blind bombing" for seventy-five percent of their missions, "terror became their inevitable consequence even when defined targets were the avowed objectives," another measure of the "slow erosion of the distinction between precision and area bombing."[31]

Friedrich is certainly correct to emphasize that bombing was never pursued as retribution for the German attempt to kill Europe's Jews.[32] But he tells us only in passing that the British bombing campaign was at least in part meant as a way to reassure Stalin and the Soviets that in the absence of a second front and a ground offensive in the west, the British promised to do what they could to distract the Germans. Thus, if the British answered the bombing of British cities with the bombing of German cities, they were also responding to the deaths of millions of Soviet civilians and Red Army soldiers (some of whom were Jews) who were being killed by Germans.[33] In addition, although *we* know that U.S. and British bombs were not retribution for what Germans were doing to Jews, Nazi propaganda connected Jews and bombs, attributing the "terror" campaign to the influence of Jews on decision makers in Whitehall and the White House, all part of what Goebbels called the "Jewish War."[34] This Nazi propaganda campaign appears only occasionally in the margins of *Brand*'s nearly 600 pages.[35]

Not surprisingly, historians who know far more than I do about military history and the RAF and USAAF bombing campaigns in World War II have weighed in on these topics. Their criticisms of *Der Brand* make it clear that those who want the full story of the bombing war in Germany would do well to have more than Friedrich on their reading lists.[36]

Still, Friedrich's accomplishment—and what Sebald was, I think, calling for—is to provide powerful descriptions of how Germans experienced the bombing campaign. "For a long time," Friedrich writes, "nothing has been written over the form of suffering" in the bombing war (543), and in almost all of the historical scholarship on the bombing war, the face of death is masked, cordoned off in accounts that reduce the "balance of destruction" to numbers—cubic meters of rubble, totals of lives lost, houses destroyed, and people displaced.[37] In his report on the firebombing of Hamburg, the city's chief of police concluded that "speech is impotent to portray the measure of horror, . . . the traces of which were written indelibly on the face of the city and its inhabitants."[38] Friedrich seeks to find the words and read the traces.

To the captivatingly dramatic prose of Der Brand, Friedrich adds Brandtstätten (Sites of Fire),[39] a volume of photographs that appeared soon after Der Brand, in which he amasses visual evidence of destruction—bodies piled high or lined up as they await burial in mass graves, human forms transformed into coal, scenes of extraordinary physical destruction, and glimpses of how the living attempted to survive in the rubble. In one of many interviews that he's given since Der Brand appeared, Friedrich emphasized that "Seventy percent of my book consists in describing realistically, very graphically, the true situations of people trapped in burning cities. The women, the old, the young, the babies, even the animals trapped in zoos. Nothing emotional, just plain description."[40] But of course confronting death in this form evokes strong emotions. In both books, Friedrich makes sure that the reader confronts human suffering, and this is an important achievement of his work. He delivers powerful reminders that bombs do not just target enemy defenses, destroy enemy factories, or level enemy cities. They kill human beings.

What forces have combined to open the space in Germany's "memory landscape" into which Friedrich has charged?

The end of the Cold War is a big part of the explanation. Until 1989–90 and German unification, stories of the Second World War were always told in the context of the ideological conflict that followed.[41] West Germans were not completely silent about the bombing war, but it was in the East that Dresden became the most important symbol of the destruction caused by "Anglo-American gangsters from the air," a prelude to the destruction imperialists dropped on North Koreans only five years after doing the same to Germans. In West Germany, although the bombing war was not forgotten, as I'll discuss below, the expulsion of Germans from eastern Europe and the parts of eastern Germany that were added to postwar Poland and the retention of POWs in Soviet hands took pride of place in public memory. The enemy who had brought devastation to Germany was the enemy who threatened to do the same after 1945. Thus, the division of the world into East and West colored public memory of the Second World War. But once the Wall came down, it was possible for Germans to reflect on what *all* Germans had suffered, reexamining parts of their past that had been subordinated to Cold War priorities. In Friedrich's account, the consequences of the bombing war become part of a unified German history, no longer refracted through the prism of the Cold War.[42]

If stories of German suffering join East and West, they also can create a basis for reconciliation between those who grew up after the war and those who lived through it. Friedrich presents himself as a radical sixty-eighter, part of the "1968" generation, whose members were too young to have any firsthand memories of the war and for whom political engagement included excoriating the generation of their parents either for their roles as perpetrators or for their passive support of National Socialism as bystanders. In Friedrich's words, "We broke the silence imposed by our fathers and conquered the memory of their crimes."[43] He claims a bit too much, for many others had already chipped away at the silence before 1968. Since the late 1950s, West German courts had brought some Nazi war criminals to justice. By the 1960s, many public intellectuals insisted that Germans acknowledge the legacy of Auschwitz. And Chancellor Willy Brandt, who had spent the war fighting Germans in the Norwegian resistance, publicly acknowledged the crimes of Germans against Poles and Jews.[44] The sixty-eighters, however, did contribute to the larger West German political mix that put in place a left-liberal consensus according to which silence about German loss—of life, territory, material property, honor—was the price to be paid for the crimes of National Socialism. Any mention of German suffering would be seen as a move toward apologia, a moral "settling of accounts" (*Aufrechnung*) that might lead to demands to lay the past to rest. Many sixty-eighters supported this view. *Der Brand*, thus, represents a change of heart, a sort of peace offering of rebellious sons to fathers (and mothers). Friedrich and others are now ready to make the suffering of their parents' generation part of the public memory of the Second World War.[45]

The readiness of many on the left-liberal side of the political spectrum to talk of German suffering also reflects their belief that the past of German crimes is an irrefutable part of the foundations of the Berlin Republic. Since 1990 in a unified Germany, it has been clear that the view that dominated the politics of the past in West Germany by the late 1970s and 1980s—defined by the acknowledgment of the centrality of the Holocaust— has continued to be the view that is dominant in a unified Germany.[46] The most significant symbolic expression of this view, the monument to the murdered Jews of Europe, was dedicated in May 2005 and serves as a powerful reminder that what joins Germans in the present is a past in which millions of other Germans enthusiastically supported a regime that sought to eliminate European Jewry. The dominance and broad acceptance of this view has made it possible to call for the remembrance of other deaths without fear that commemorating German victims will lead to attempts to dodge responsibility for the ways in which Germans victimized others.

The evocation of German fates in World War II has also become a point of reference in contemporary German politics. In a number of interviews, Friedrich maintained that Germans' rejection of the U.S. intervention in Iraq reflected their own firsthand experience of the horrors of "shock and awe." As he would have it, "the stance of the Germans and their spiritual place is since 1945 beneath the bombs and never in the bombers."[47]

Finally, decades are important markers for the public commemoration of important events. It is no accident that Friedrich's book began to appear in serialized form just as the run-up to the sixtieth anniversary of the end of the Second World War kicked into high gear, an important opening salvo in what Norbert Frei has called the "battle for memory" that remains a central part of German political culture over sixty years after the last bomb fell.[48]

Still, even though this conjuncture of events can explain why in the early twenty-first century there was a space in which it was possible to tell a different story of the bombing war, there is much that is troubling about the way Friedrich has chosen to fill it. Let me offer three objections.

First, in ways he does not deny, Friedrich uses language to describe the effects of bombing on German civilians that has also been used to describe the crimes of Germans against Jews and other civilians in the war. His prose is peppered with words that evoke comparisons of victims of Germans and German victims—those bombed out of their homes, POWs left in Soviet captivity, and ethnic Germans driven out of Eastern Europe— which characterized much of the public discourse of the 1950s. For

Friedrich, bomber squadrons become *Einsatzgruppen*, the special German killing squads that murdered countless civilians in the war on the eastern front, the bomb shelter is a crematorium, and when libraries go up in flames Allied bombs are responsible for the "biggest book burning of all time" (515)—bigger and thus even more pernicious, Friedrich implies, than the one staged by Goebbels in 1933.

Friedrich's response to his critics is that language cannot be deemed "contaminated" just because it has been used to describe the Holocaust, and he asks rhetorically what other terms are available.[49] The question is either naïve or disingenuous. By employing the terms without reflection or commentary, he lines himself up with those who argue for the moral equivalence of the suffering Germans caused others and the suffering others caused Germans, uncritically reproducing categories that can be traced back to the bombing war itself and that have been recycled repeatedly. He moves from arguing that Germans, too, were victims of war crimes to implying that what Germans suffered was *like* what Jews suffered.[50] Elsewhere, Friedrich refers to a "Mongolian hurricane of destruction from the air," eerily echoing language reserved in the Third Reich for the "Judeo-Bolshevik" threat (138), and he describes the "negro lips" of the burned corpses in Pforzheim (434). Rather than reflecting on the meanings such terms might have carried in the Third Reich, he simply reproduces them.

Second, Friedrich sets out to historicize the experience of the bombing war, but he makes no attempt to historicize how the bombing war has been incorporated into public memory in East and West Germany since 1945. My concern is that those who have not stopped to study *this* history may, as it were, be condemned to repeat it, constantly claiming to break a silence around German suffering, but has that silence ever really existed?

Particularly in the decade after the end of World War II, memories of the bombing war registered in many forms. Although of greater significance in the commemorative culture of the East, the public memory of the vertical aggression of U.S. and British bombers was hardly absent in the West.[51] Pictures of bombed out cities filled the illustrated press immediately after the war, and pictures of urban ruins joined photographs of expellees, captured German soldiers, and unseated Nazi officials among the iconic images that shaped collective memories of the war. Because Nazi censors had allowed only a selective view of destruction before the war's end, as historian Jens Jäger remarks, "in peace the language of images was even more gruesome than it had been in war." The rubble left by Allied bombers also defined an entire genre of *moving* pictures—so-called rubble films—made in the immediate postwar period. The legacy of falling bombs became part of local histories and school atlases, which carefully documented the extent of destruction, and monuments memorialized those whom the bombs had killed.[52] The "woman of the rubble" took on enormous importance as a symbol of survival and a new beginning immediately after the war's end, and she was most frequently depicted in the midst of what the bombs had wrought.[53]

The losses of bombing victims were also the stuff of annual ceremonies. When in August 1952 the president of the West German parliament, Hermann Ehlers, dedicated a memorial to those killed in the bombing of Hamburg, he acknowledged that "all regions of Germany have their share of the wounds that the air war inflicted on the property and blood of our entire nation."[54] Ties between the incendiary bombs dropped on Dresden and the atomic bombs dropped on Japan also registered in public opinion polls in the 1950s in which West Germans expressed fears of another war, opposed placement of nuclear weapons on German soil, and associated the United States with mass death and destruction.[55]

Compensation for victims of the bombs loomed large in social policy debates in the early postwar years. Restoring lives and rebuilding cities destroyed by the bombs was another path followed by Germans in both East and West to move from the status of victims to shapers of their own destinies, not a form of denial or silence but an act of renewal that acknowledged a destructive past.[56] The decision by municipal governments to leave in place the massive concrete bunkers that had saved some from the bombs represented a commitment to preserving "a memory in stone."[57] And well into the 1950s, West German cities sponsored "evacuee days" to sustain ties to those "citizens outside" (*Aussenbürger*), who left because of the bombs but were still not able to return to their hometowns.[58] Yet a closer look at the postwar years suggests that the silence surrounding the memory of the bombing war was nowhere near as complete as Friedrich would have us believe.

Even in the 1970s and 1980s, when a left-liberal consensus in West Germany made it more difficult to talk of German victims and the victims of Germans in the same breath, there was no absolute taboo on discussions of the bombing war, nor could stories of bombs be heard only at neo-Nazi rallies or around some family dinner tables and at the local pub. For example, the feminist film director Helma Sanders Brahms's *Deutschland, bleiche Mutter* (Germany, Pale Mother) told a mother-daughter story in which bombs drive the protagonists from Berlin. And in Alexander Kluge's 1979 movie *Die Patriotin* (The Patriot), a West German high school teacher "who has sympathy with the dead of the [Third] Reich" tries to find a way to locate them in a history that she can present to her students.[59]

In 1979, as West Germans approached the fortieth anniversary of the war's beginning and the run-up to the fortieth anniversary of its end, the bombing war was hardly pushed to the margins. State-owned television commemorated 1939 with broadcasts that documented "The British in the Second World War," offering an account in which the British "strategy of terror" against Germany was judged to be "England's moral mistake." In 1984, one TV documentary that sought to evoke memories of "back then, forty years ago" featured the bombing of Dresden, and a year later, another state-owned station offered its viewers a five-part series on the "War of the Bombers."[60]

Five years later, when Helmut Kohl came to Dresden to meet with East German president Hans Modrow in December 1989, he chose to address the public in front of the ruins of the Frauenkirche. It was no accident that Kohl selected this monument to those who died as the backdrop for his remarks. The effort to restore the church, leveled in the Allied bombing campaign, became a major symbol of how a unified Germany offered a new set of possibilities for coming to terms with the destructive legacy of World War II.[61] In 1995, the first major commemorative year after reunification, local papers all over Germany and television documentaries prefigured the types of stories that would be repeated a decade later and sometimes echoed the discourse of the 1950s.[62]

Why then do Friedrich and so many reviewers of his book insist that he is breaking a taboo? Michel Foucault's famous observations in his *History of Sexuality* suggests one explanation: "The question I would like to pose is not, Why are we repressed? But rather, Why do we say, with so much passion and so much resentment against our most recent past, against our present, and against ourselves, that we are repressed?" And as Foucault makes clear, this insistence on repression becomes an incitement to discourse. If the repression has been so great, it will require an enormous effort to overcome it.[63] In Friedrich's case, it's not Victorian morality that allegedly does the work of repression; rather, it's the memory of the Holocaust. It can't be displaced; it has taken concrete form in the center of Berlin. But in popular receptions of Friedrich's book that emphasize that he is breaking a silence, the subtext is that the Holocaust should not be permitted to prevent Germans from talking about the crimes that others committed against them. In the case of German suffering, however, I would argue that, like sex in the Victorian age, in both post-1945 Germanies, it was discussed all along. The context in which stories of German suffering are being told and the meanings these tales carry have changed in a post–Cold War world. But the insistence that a taboo has prevailed justifies telling the stories again . . . and again . . . and again and neglecting the other contexts in which they have been told in the past.

My third objection to Friedrich's approach is that, while he does not consider how the bombing war was represented in postwar West and East Germany, in other ways *Der Brand* offers a history that far exceeds the years 1940–1945 announced in its title. Friedrich's Third Reich begins only once the bombs begin to fall, not in 1933, but he takes his reader on an excursion through many other parts of the German past. When the German military strategists began a plan of retaliatory bombing against the British in 1942, they called it the "Baedeker Bombing Raids," because they vowed to bomb every city that had at least two stars in the famous guidebook. In the longest section of Friedrich's book, entitled *"Land"* (which can also mean "country"), fully 40 percent of this massive text, Friedrich provides a different sort of Baedeker, taking us on a tour through Germany, from north to west, from south to east, detailing what city after city endured— how many bombs, how much destruction, how many dead. But *"Land"* implies much more than physical location. Friedrich also wants us to know how much German history, embodied in buildings and architecture, the bombs obliterated. At each stop along the way, we learn much about a particular city's past, not a past that begins when the city turns brown under the Nazis but rather a past that dates back to a time when Romans and Huns ranged over German territory, invading Swedes fought wars of religion, and "Germany was the object of power politics of the far more powerful," not an aggressor (325).

The Germans who are bombed by the Allies in World War II are a "Wir" with a long, complex history that cannot be collapsed into the Third Reich. In Friedrich's account, this history is profoundly Christian. His guided tour through Germany is a pilgrimage to a series of "stations of the cross" (*Kreuzwege*) marked by the "fires, destruction, pillaging and massacre" that most German cities suffered not once but many times from 1940 to 1945 (177). Again and again, Friedrich's record of destruction begins with churches and cathedrals, the symbols, he implies, of a nation whose citizens believed in God, not the Führer, and in his descriptions of bombing raids, the religious calendar, not weather patterns, strategic objectives, or Allied estimates of German defenses, seems to determine the timing of bombing missions. The historian Horst Boog points out that RAF commanders were careful to avoid any suggestion to pilots that they might be dropping their bombs on cultural treasures. The commanders were fully aware of the limits to what they could include in "operational orders," even if pilots might well know that their targets—often rail transportation hubs at the center of cities—were in close proximity to buildings of no military significance.[64] But from Friedrich's account, it would seem that churches and cathedrals, symbols of a *Germania Sancta*,[65] were at the top of the target list.

Consider a few examples of how Friedrich chooses to tell the story. In an "inexplicable destructive drunkenness" in late March 1945, British bombers leveled every church in Danzig (189). In Münster, he tells us, the British ravaged the city on the celebration of the Festival of Mary, Mother of God, in 1943. Clemens August, Graf von Galen, the Catholic bishop who had been openly critical of the Nazis' euthanasia program, looks on as the cathedral in that city comes under attack (222). Friedrich's preamble to the bombing of Cologne includes the story of St. Ursula, killed at the end of the fourth century by barbaric Huns, "Asians," in her battle to protect the honor of 11,000 legendary virgins who had accompanied her from Britain. Their memory was consecrated by the building of a cathedral on their grave site. In Friedrich's canned "lives of the saints," the virgins are awakened from their heavenly slumbers on March 31, 1942, in April and October 1944, and in January and March 1945, as British bombs continued what the Huns had begun (257). The *real* Huns, Friedrich soberly explains, had been vanquished once and for all by Charlemagne. They were the "riders of the apocalypse, born war criminals. They swept through the land, destroying churches and chapels, treacherously murdering the faithful and carrying forth their women. In the area of the Mosel and the Pfalz, they burned all the cities." For readers who are still curious about where Friedrich will end this argument from analogy, he leaves nothing to the imagination. In the "modern period," the British would pin the name "Hun" on Kaiser Wilhelm II, and between "1940 and 1945, Churchill would sweep away the huns in Cologne, Berlin and Dresden." But for whom does Friedrich want to reserve the name once the bombs begin to fall (257–58)?[66]

Again and again, Friedrich reproduces a language of popular religiosity rather than reflecting on why Germans living through the bombing war would have reached to Christianity to describe and understand their experience, interpreting the bombs as a form of divine retribution, connecting bombed-out churches with synagogues torched in 1938, or crediting God's intervention when a church remained unscathed. Religious ritual also provided the model for the Nazi regime's attempts to transform victims of the bombs into heroic martyrs, who in Goebbels's words "died for the eternity of the Reich."[67] Missing as well in Friedrich's account is any analysis of how after 1945 in the western zones of occupation and West Germany, the Catholic and Protestant churches could explain German suffering during the war as part of a process of atonement and redemption, while avoiding any confrontation with their deeply compromised relationship with National Socialism.[68] Although Jews are not entirely absent from the version of the past Friedrich provides, they appear at best on the margins, and in a Germany so thoroughly Christian they cannot be at ease. The flames that consumed their sites of worship blazed not only from 1940 to 1945 but also in November 1938. About these flames, Friedrich has very little to say.

In a chapter entitled "Stein" (Stone), history again goes up in smoke, this time in the form of archives, libraries, and cultural treasures that could not be removed in time to be saved from the bombs or were simply immovable. The Allies apparently knew not only the religious calendar but also dates of key events in German culture. In 1944, they bomb the house where Goethe was born on the anniversary of his death. As bombing continued into 1945, Friedrich argues, the war of the "present" had long since been won. But Allied bombers continued to devastate Germany as part of a "war against the roots of the past that had given birth to disaster" (190).

In 1948, the United Nations defined genocide as "acts committed with intent to destroy, in whole or in part, a national, ethnical, racial or religious group, as such."[69] Friedrich does not charge British and American bombers with attempting the physical destruction of the German people, but in these two chapters, he comes close to suggesting that the bombing campaign was a form of historical and cultural genocide, the destruction of a bridge to an historical landscape, which, he somberly concludes, "no longer exists" (177). Setting out to rebuild that bridge to the past reduced to rubble by the Allies, Friedrich makes symbolic amends not only with the generation of his parents but also with the cohort of former chancellor Helmut Kohl. Kohl is older than Friedrich, but he also came of age after 1945. In the mid-1980s, he listened carefully to the advice of Michael Stürmer, a historian who emphasized how important it was for Germans to define a new sense of national identity grounded in an understanding of the past that did not collapse German history into the twelve years of the Third Reich. Friedrich agrees. However, achieving this goal is not easy, he suggests, because so much of German history was turned into ash and rubble by Allied bomber squadrons, sent on their missions by political leaders who believed that National Socialism was the culmination of German history and who believed a fresh start was possible if the past was obliterated.

In still other ways, I think Friedrich tends to echo some of the categories that dominated the politics of the past in the mid-1980s. The chapters that provide the most graphic accounts of life in the bomb shelters, and visions of bodies ripped apart, trapped in melting asphalt, and blackened beyond recognition are entitled "We" and "I." Friedrich's point of empathetic identification is explicit, and it is difficult not to hear overtones of Andreas Hillgruber's mid-1980s account of the "two demises"—"the destruction of the German Reich and the end of the European Jewry"—in which he advised his reader to

> identify himself with the concrete fate of the German population in the east and with the desperate and sacrificial exertions of the German army of the East and the German fleet in the Baltic, which sought to defend the population of the German east from the orgy of revenge of the Red Army, mass rapes, arbitrary killing, and compulsory deportations.[70]

Friedrich adds to this list the "concrete fate" of the German population who lived through the attacks of British and American bomber squadrons.

In short, Friedrich has broken no particular taboo, nor described a new location in the German "memory landscape." Rather, he has traveled a fairly familiar route and ended up stuck in a rut. In *Der Brand*, much that was old is allegedly new again.

. . .

How else might we imagine the story? Let me briefly suggest alternative approaches to a history of the bombing war that might manage to offer a different sort of account rather than simply recycling the past.

We could start by deconstructing the "Wir." In her perceptive history of Britain in World War II, Sonya Rose concludes: "like all collective identities—all definitions of who 'we' are—national identity and concepts of nationhood are fragile. Even as they are articulated, once they move beyond the generality that 'we are all in this together,' once who the 'we' is, and what 'together' means are specified, the singularity of that identity is exposed as being false."[71] From 1940 to 1945, Germans who had not fled into exile or who were not deported to ghettos or death camps were in the bombing war together, but this "we" had many different faces, and what divided Germans was sometimes as significant as what united them.[72]

Consider those Germans who were part of the "Wir" before 1933, then were forced outside the *Volksgemeinschaft* (national community/community of the people) after the Nazis came to power, but were still in Germany when the bombs began to fall. Can we imagine a history of the war in which these other victims—not those whose lives end in death camps, but those who were also dodging Allied bombs—get to add their stories? An attempt to historicize the experience of the bombing war might include the tale of Marianne Ellenbogen, a Jew who survived in Nazi Germany. Her story has been superbly detailed in Mark Roseman's *A Past in Hiding*. In September 1943, Ellenbogen was on the run from the Gestapo in Essen, the city where Friedrich grew up. She had eluded the secret police. Her family had not, and on September 9, they were loaded on a train for deportation eastward. Hidden in a former schoolhouse by members of the Bund, a left-wing circle that had gone underground in the Third Reich, Ellenbogen watched as an incendiary bomb flew through the window. She courageously picked up the "hissing bomb" and tossed it outside into the garden, where it exploded.[73]

What of the story of Victor Klemperer, the rabbi's son and World War I veteran, a professor of romance languages whose conversion from Judaism to Christianity and marriage to a gentile could not forever keep his name off deportation lists? Like many other Germans, Klemperer's fate was profoundly altered by the massive Allied attack on his native Dresden in February 1945. Much paper went up in smoke, "my books, the reference works, my own works," but in the wake of the Allies' destructive bombing of the city, Nazi officials had to turn their attention away from deportations to more pressing problems, allowing Klemperer to move about freely.[74] Could a history of the bombing war also capture the meanings that Dresden's demise had for him? Or imagine a history of the bombing war in which Anne Frank's heart soars as Allied bombers fly over Amsterdam, never knowing that the bombs they drop will leave her former school friends in Frankfurt dead in the rubble.

The victim of Nazi persecution who gets to speak in Friedrich's account is Martha Haarburger, who reports from the Nazi concentration camp in Theresienstadt that the deportees from Swabia were linked to their region of origin—the *Heimat*—sustained by their bonds with Württemberg and "a strong Swabian dialect," which allowed them to define unity in adversity. And a lawyer from Stuttgart, Emil Dessauer, who was killed at Auschwitz, died only after he sent greetings to his native Württemberg (338–39). But surely a more comprehensive history of the bombing war would include a greater range of stories in which the ties of concentration camp prisoners to Germany were more tenuous and in some cases stretched to the breaking point.

A more complicated history of the bombing war might also reveal that some Germans who lost homes and loved ones to the bombs were also among those who bought "Aryanized" businesses at reduced prices in the prewar years; who, after 1941, upgraded their furnishings with objects stolen from German Jews and sold at public auction; or who replaced items destroyed by the bombs with household goods expropriated from Jews in other parts of Nazi-occupied Europe. Others, bombed out of their homes by the Allies, quickly occupied houses and apartments vacated by German Jews deported to ghettos and killing facilities in the East, and some soldiers on leave from the battle at the front declared their willingness to kill any remaining Jews in order to secure housing for their families, driven from their homes by the bombs.[75]

Some of the workers in war-related industries, bombed out of their homes and factories, may also have exulted in climbing to a higher rung on the status hierarchy once they had a slave foreign labor force working next to them. We learn from Friedrich of women who fell victim to the bombs, but a more complicated account might also include the nearly half million women who provided auxiliary service to the Wehrmacht and who by the end of the war "manned" the air defense network throughout Germany, shattering any delusions that it was a man's job to defend women and children from Allied aggression. These women were celebrated in Nazi propaganda for their "self-control," "good morale," and "competence."[76] They were also part of the "Wir," remembered six months after the war's end in a woman's magazine, *Sie* (You), which recalled a young woman, just returned from an Allied POW camp: "There lay the street along which she had strode, one long year ago, cheerfully, confidently, even a bit proud of the uniform that revealed to all that she belonged to the German Anti-Aircraft Service . . . that was once the uniform that made every young girl so endlessly proud."[77] Why shouldn't the history of the bombing war include their stories as well as the stories of the women the bombs killed and the women who cleared away the rubble?

The "Wir" also disintegrates when we hear the voices of the Düsseldorf miners whose refrain was "Dear Tommy, please fly further on your way; spare us poor miners for today. Fly instead against those people in Berlin; they're the ones who voted Hitler in." Or the Cologne workers who did not reflect on the graves of the Ursuline virgins or share with intellectuals dismay over the destruction of architectural treasures, but rather commented: "Germany can live without [the] Cologne Cathedral, but not without its people."[78] And perhaps a study of the bombing war that interrogated whether the "Wir" ever existed rather than simply reproducing the category would ask whether the intensified bombing campaign in late 1944 and 1945 in any way impeded the smooth functioning of the Nazi "Peoples' Courts." Among those they sentenced to death in 1943 were 3 Germans charged with refusing to help "those damaged by the bombs" (*Bombengeschädigten*), 938 who had taken advantage of mandated blackouts to commit crimes, and 182 who allegedly had plundered houses hit by the bombs.[79] A full account of German society "under the bombs" might also pay more attention to the German resistance that *did* exist, rather than concluding, as Friedrich does, that any resistance was impossible for a "Wir" caught between bomber pilots, "lords of the unrestricted massacre" (293), and the Gestapo, leaving Germans no choice "but to try to save their own skin" (371).[80] Some Germans tried to save more.

The story of the war in the air should also include a much fuller consideration of the ground war on the eastern front. Key to Friedrich's argument is that the most devastating bombing of German cities came in the very last months of the war; the war, he implies, was already over when the worst destruction took place. Friedrich does describe the faltering advance of British and American troops eastward—in some cases, he argues, made more complicated because ruins created by the bombs provided better cover for German resistance—but any history of the war's end must also include the movement of Soviet troops westward. Friedrich cites the staggering figure of over a thousand German victims a day to the bombing war in the last four months before the cessation of hostilities (168). But during the same period, German military casualties were running about 10,000 a day, and between December 1944 and May 1945, more than a million German soldiers died in the "Final Battle" on the eastern front. We still have no accurate figures for Soviet losses at this time. If we lose track of the ferocity with which the Wehrmacht was attempting to slow down the Soviet advance, the fears of what Soviet occupation would entail, and the widely held perception that the longer the eastern front was kept in play the more time could be won for Germans fleeing the Soviets, we cannot fully comprehend the context in which the British and American Allies continued to pursue the bombing campaign, devastating cities whose contribution to the war effort was not always clear. Sixty years after the fact, we should debate whether this strategy hastened the war's end, and we should acknowledge the massive loss of civilian life that the bombs caused, but only by comprehending the fighting on the ground can we begin to understand fully why British and American fliers so aggressively continued to prosecute the war in the air.[81]

The Rashomon-like history that I propose, a historicized account of the bombing war told from many perspectives, would also include the "they"—non-Germans—on whom the bombs fell.[82] What if Ben Halfgott, a Polish Jew, transported from Buchenwald, where his father was killed, to the satellite camp of Schlieben near Dresden in December 1944, might also offer his perspective of the bombing of that city and the "huge red glow" that "was like heaven for us"?[83] What if the story of life in the bunkers included some of the workers who built them—POWs and slave workers who were denied entrance to what they'd constructed once the bombs began to fall? And what if the history of the bombing war reminded us that some of those detailed to remove unexploded bombs were concentration camp inmates, drawn to volunteer for these dangerous assignments by rumors of better treatment, hopes for some scraps of food amid the rubble, or even the possibility of release, though they would more likely be killed or maimed?[84] Any full account of the bombing war would also give voice to some of the 5,700,000 foreign "civilian workers" and the nearly 2,000,000 POWS who were still in Germany in August 1944, over half employed in industries located in the cities that were prime targets. They appear in the shadows of Friedrich's account, and he records that the British and Americans killed 42,000 of them, but could we tell a story of the bombing war that made them into more than numbers?[85]

"They" might even include those who dropped the bombs. Friedrich hooks his reader by beginning *Der Brand* with a dramatic vignette in which a British Lancaster bomber drops its deadly load on Germans in the Ruhr. In Wuppertal, where most firefighters have taken off for the weekend, a wedding couple celebrates with friends outside the city, enjoying songs and speeches, unaware of impending doom and oblivious to air raid sirens until the lights go off and they hurriedly seek cover. When the sirens sound in Barmen, Luise Rompf springs from her bed and takes her son Uli into the cellar that will serve as a bomb shelter. The devastation wrought by the bombs is described by an English woman, Sybill Bannister, and the horrifying injuries the bombs inflict are detailed by Dr. Elisabeth Stark. Victims have faces. Perpetrators do not. What of an account of this evening in which the bomber squadron includes a flier like the one in Randall Jarrell's "The Death of the Ball Turret Gunner," who tells this other story of the bombing war:

> From my mother's sleep I fell into the State,
> And I hunched in its belly till my wet fur froze.
> Six miles from earth, loosed from its dream of life,
> I woke to black flak and the nightmare fighters.
> When I died they washed me out of the turret with a hose.[86]

Jarrell reminds us that for British and American fliers, the real combat was between flight crews, in historian Conrad Crane's words, "marooned aloft in an aluminum capsule," and German fighter pilots in the air and the operators of antiaircraft guns on the ground.[87]

Estimates of American and British deaths in the air war vary. According to the figures provided in 1945 by the United States Strategic Bombing Survey for the War in Europe, "the number of men lost in air action was 79,265 American and 79,281 British." Other sources cite a figure of 140,000 American and British losses. Friedrich tells us of 55,000 dead British fliers, a figure found elsewhere in the literature. He compares these military losses with the 420,000–570,000 Germans he estimates were killed by the bombs the squadrons dropped, urban dwellers who "fought no one."[88] From another perspective, Allied losses represented a stunningly high percentage of the total military and civilian casualties on all fronts, including some 300,000 Americans and 400,000 British.[89] With the discovery of incendiary bombs, Friedrich concludes, "the Allies could feel like the gods, who hurled lightening bolts at the vileness of the enemy. Only God can send the plague, because he isn't subject to any law. He is the law" (102). Even granting Friedrich a measure of poetic license, a more complete story of the bombing war might include American and British fliers who had faces, families, fates, and bellies filled with fear.

Describing those who dropped the bombs might also include a far more detailed description than Friedrich provides of scenes of Germans who lynched pilots who fell from the skies and local officials who counseled that downed fliers should not be protected from the "rage of the people." Rather, the "Anglo-American gangsters in the sky" should "get what they deserve," and anyone who sought to protect these "gangster types" should be called to account for their actions. These stories of Germans as perpetrators, not victims, also are part of the history of the bombing war.[90]

"They" would also include the woman depicted on the dustcover of Sonya Rose's book, her hair tied up in a handkerchief as she waves to bombers flying overhead, doubtless on their way to Germany, in planes, the wartime poster suggests, that she helped to build, armed with bombs she helped to make. And what if "they" made room for "Rosie the Riveter," a symbol appropriated by the American feminist movement, whose rivets might have held together some of the planes that dropped bombs on Dresden?[91]

Finally, a history that included "them" would not shy away from some of what is most important to Friedrich—an analysis of the ideological, moral, political, and military context that added "dehouse" to the English vocabulary and resulted in the deaths of hundreds of thousands of civilians. Writing of the controversy surrounding Friedrich's book, Charles Maier notes: "Ultimately those of us who would accept the air war say that under certain conditions it may be necessary to burn babies."[92] My history of the "bombing war" would also include a full treatment of how "they" understood the conditions under which this was necessary.

To be sure, American and British historians have shown themselves fully able to celebrate brave men in uniform and societies that mobilized successfully to "fight the good fight" or win "the people's war," while pay-

ing little attention to the victims on the other side of the conflict. But like
Der Brand, such histories tell only part of the story. They promote a vision
of a "Wir" that never existed while all but completely omitting a multifac-
eted "they." They reproduce national memories and echo wartime propaganda appeals in which the world was altogether too neatly divided into
victims and perpetrators, innocent and guilty. More than sixty years after
the end of the war, historians have demonstrated that they can tell far
more complicated stories. A history that did not shy away from seeing the
past from many different perspectives could prevent us from drawing
facile conclusions or imposing ex post facto a set of moral categories in
which few of the people we are describing lived their lives. It could also
better explain how, after 1945, different interpretations of the war translated into different modes of commemoration and remembrance that produced many histor*ies*, not one single history.[93] It would be a history that
did more than repackage memories that have circulated in Germany for
more than six decades.

Culture, that bridge to the past that the bombs destroyed, is very important to Friedrich, and culture is important to me, too. Who wouldn't regret the destruction of the churches, architectural monuments, medieval
cathedrals, works of art, forty percent of German archival holdings, and
libraries that went up in flames? But I wonder if there aren't other stories
that relate bombs, buildings, books, culture, and German history that be-
long in an account of the destruction wrought by World War II but for
which *Der Brand* leaves no space. Let me offer only one example. As I
wrote this essay, I thought that perhaps the distinction between mourning
and melancholy—as discussed by Freud and as applied to postwar West
Germany in Alexander and Margarete Mitscherlich's classic *The Inability
to Mourn*—might help me make sense of how Friedrich was describing
the consequences of the Allied bombing campaign against Germany. Rejecting the advice I give students, I went not to the library's guides to online research but to my Web browser's search engine to see if Freud's work
was available in full text online. Freud's estate is being carefully preserved,
it turns out, and I was forced out of my study and into the actual, not the
virtual, library. Freud wasn't much help, anyway. He writes: "The distinguishing mental failures of melancholia are a profoundly painful dejec-

tion, cessation of interest in the outside world, loss of the capacity to love, inhibition of all activity, and a lowering of the self-regarding feelings to a degree that finds utterance in self-reproaches and self-revilings, and culminates in a delusional expectation of punishment."[94] I do not know Friedrich, and I am not a psychiatrist, but given his high visibility in the press, on TV, and at public forums, I would conclude that he has a very lively interest in the outside world, and Freud's description does not fit the author of a book that is filled with sadness and anger but also accusation, that sets out to settle accounts, not to invite punishment.

On my cybersearch for Freud, however, I also came across other references to melancholy, including one to Albrecht Dürer's famous etching *Melencolia*, which depicts an angel sitting next to a half-finished building surrounded by the tools of the craftsman, which would allow her to complete construction. She is, however, immobilized, scowling, as she gazes off into the distance, allowing time—depicted by an hourglass on the wall of the unfinished building—to run out. I am as little an art historian as I am a psychiatrist, and with my search engine ready for more action, I tried "Dürer Melencolia" to see what I'd find. In only a mouse click or two, I located a copy of the etching at the Metropolitan Museum of Art with references to a work by Fritz Saxl and Erwin Panofsky. Another couple of clicks let me determine that Saxl and Panofsky, both Jews, had left Germany when the Nazis came to power, and then led me to references that allowed me to pursue this trail a bit further in the library stacks.

Panofsky was in the United States, a visitor at New York University, in 1933 when he learned that he had been stripped of his professorship in Hamburg. He returned to Hamburg briefly to collect his family and say his good-byes to loyal students who were not ready to denounce their mentor. Then he moved permanently to the United States, where in 1935 he was invited to become a member of the newly created humanities faculty of the Institute for Advanced Study in Princeton.[95]

Before the Nazis came to power, Saxl, Viennese by birth, had ended up in Hamburg because of his relationship with Aby Warburg, the eccentric art historian and avid book collector. In the 1920s, Saxl had met Panofsky, and together in 1923 they published an extensive work on Dürer's print.[96] With financial backing from Warburg's brothers, all well-established businessmen, Saxl expanded Warburg's extraordinary collection, which focused on books about the influence of classical antiquity on Renaissance art, and photographs of artworks, and he transformed a private library into a research institute with close ties to the University of Hamburg, which named Saxl professor extraordinarius. In 1929, Warburg died, and Saxl became completely responsible for the institute and its holdings. In January 1933, Saxl severed his ties to the university and acted quickly to move the library—headed by a Jewish intellectual and financed by the philanthropy of Jewish bankers—out of Germany. Dürer would enter the pantheon of Nazi culture as a characteristically Aryan artist, and in 1941 Hitler would enrich his private collection with some drawings plundered from a museum in Lvov.[97] But those who had some of the deepest insights into this artist's work hurried into exile.

With support from the Warburg brothers and colleagues in England, Saxl and the Hamburg institute found a new home in London. By 1939, he became a citizen, adopting the country that had taken him in and given the institute a home. At the beginning of the war, the University of London, which had given the institute space, worked with Saxl to evacuate the library, lest it fall victim to the Blitz. With the institute staff, Saxl took the last 12,000 or so volumes to the countryside outside London for the duration. Saxl also worked with the National Buildings Record to provide detailed photographic records of architectural landmarks in London— the British Museum, No. 10 Downing Street, sculptures in Westminster Abbey—recording a history threatened by German bombing raids. Like Friedrich, he too was interested in ensuring that the past be remembered.[98]

Dürer's house in Nuremberg was severely damaged. It is depicted in Friedrich's *Brandstätten*, left a skeleton by the bombs. A picture on the next page documents that by 1951, the house had been completely restored. (In fact, restoration had been completed two years earlier.)[99] This is a story of devastation that fits in Friedrich's account. But Freud, Saxl, Panofsky, Warburg and the institute that bears his name, Jewish philanthropy, exile, the immeasurable enrichment of the intellectual life of England and the United States, and the loss to German culture do not. Friedrich tells only the story of bombs that fell on Germany—not those that destroyed parts of a German culture evacuated to England—and a "Wir" in which Saxl and Warburg have no place. This is the history of the bombing war's consequences for German culture that Friedrich has chosen to write, but it is not the one that I would wish to read if I wanted to understand the "form of suffering" that bombs—German, British, and American—caused Germans in World War II.

. . .

I plan to give my mother-in-law a copy of the English translation of *Der Brand*. When she learns that only a year or so before her trip Friedrich's book was a bestseller, she will better understand why she heard so much about bombs and the war. Horst Boog, born in 1928, thus closer to my mother-in-law's age than Friedrich's, was old enough in 1940 to have his own memories of the bombing war. He is part of a team of German historians who for years have been writing a comprehensive, multivolume history of the "German Reich in the Second World War." Boog's assignment includes the history of the bombing war. Sixteen years older than Friedrich, he seems to have come of age in a different country. In a contribution to a 1995 conference on "Bomber" Harris, he remarked: "Whenever Germans think of the Second World War, they mostly think of the bombing war, because it affected them directly and left an enduring impression on their minds."[100] In his review of Friedrich's book, Boog notes a number of errors of fact and calls Friedrich to task for failing to consider much relevant secondary literature. He concludes that he could applaud *Der Brand* if it bore the subtitle of novel or theatrical drama.[101] Perhaps it would be more accurately described as a National Registry of German Memories, a collection of those "enduring impressions" that have been around since the early 1940s.

When asked by an interviewer whether *Der Brand* is a history book, Friedrich responded, "No . . . because it is the first book that turns its attention to the bombing war against Germany and thus to the largest battlefield of the Second World War." His book, he explains, includes "thousands upon thousands of claims of fact" that come largely from information compiled in cities in the 1950s, and these claims must still be verified. Subjected to the critical "editorial review of the nation," *Der Brand* has also prompted an enormous reader response, providing Friedrich with still more information about a German history that "academic historical scholarship has persistently ignored." Telling the whole story of this "colossal event" exceeds the capacity of the lone researcher, and if his book "perhaps" has provided a "panorama," Friedrich comments in an interview with newsmagazine *Der Spiegel*, it still remains to "map out the depths."[102] "There is still much work for historians to do," Friedrich told another interviewer. "History has to be retold."[103] I would not accept Friedrich's assessment of the historiography; were it not so rich, he could not have written this book. And historians of the former Soviet Union and China might quibble about who can lay claim to the largest battlefield of the Second World War. But at least on one point Friedrich and I agree: *Der Brand* should not be the last word about the Allied bombing campaign against Germany, and history should be retold. He and I just have very different visions of what remains to be said.

4

A FORGOTTEN HOLOCAUST: U.S. BOMBING STRATEGY, THE DESTRUCTION OF JAPANESE CITIES, AND THE AMERICAN WAY OF WAR FROM THE PACIFIC WAR TO IRAQ

Mark Selden

World War II was a landmark in the development and deployment of technologies of mass destruction by airpower, notably the B-29 bomber, napalm, and the atomic bomb. The air war culminated in the area bombing, including atomic bombing, of major European and Japanese cities and devastated their populations. An estimated 50 to 70 million people died in the war, and in a sharp reversal of the pattern of World War I and of most earlier wars, a substantial majority of the dead were noncombatants.[1]

What is the logic and what have been the consequences—for victims, for subsequent global patterns of warfare, and for international law—of the new technologies of mass destruction via airpower? Above all, how have they shaped the American way of war over six decades in which the United States has been a major actor in important wars? The issues have particular salience in an epoch defined by the so-called war on terror, when the terror inflicted on civilians by the major powers is frequently neglected.

Strategic Bombing and International Law

Bombs had been dropped from the air as early as 1849 on Venice (from balloons) and 1911 in Libya (from planes). Major European powers attempted to use them in newly founded air forces during World War I. Though the impact on the outcomes was marginal, the advance of airpower alerted all nations to its potential significance in future wars.[2] A series of international conferences at the Hague beginning in 1899 set out principles for limiting air war and securing the protection of noncombatants from bombing and other attacks. The 1923 Hague conference crafted a sixty-two-article "Rules of Aerial Warfare," which prohibited "aerial bombardment for the purpose of terrorizing the civilian population, of destroying or damaging private property not of a military character, or of injuring non-combatants." It specifically limited bombardment to military objectives, prohibited "indiscriminate bombardment of the civilian population," and held violators liable to pay compensation.[3] Securing consensus and enforcing limits, however, proved extraordinarily elusive then and since.

Throughout the twentieth century, and particularly during and immediately after World War II, the inexorable advance of weapons technology went hand in hand with international efforts to place limits on the barbarism of war, particularly the killing of noncombatants in indiscriminate bombing raids.[4] This article considers the interplay between these weapons and attempts to curb their use against civilians, with particular reference to the United States.

The strategic and ethical implications of the nuclear bombing of Hiroshima and Nagasaki have generated a vast contentious literature, as have German and Japanese war crimes and atrocities. By contrast, the U.S. destruction of more than sixty Japanese cities prior to Hiroshima has been slighted, both in the scholarly literatures in English and Japanese and in popular consciousness throughout the world. It has been overshadowed by the atomic bombing and by heroic narratives of American conduct in the "Good War," an outcome related to the emergence of the United States as a superpower.[5] Arguably, however, the central technological, strategic, and ethical breakthroughs that would leave their stamp on subsequent wars occurred in area bombing of noncombatants prior to the atomic bombing of Hiroshima and Nagasaki. A.C. Grayling explains the different responses to firebombing and atomic bombing this way: ". . . the frisson of dread created by the thought of what atomic weaponry can do affects those who contemplate it more than those who actually suffer from it; for whether it is an atom bomb rather than tons of high explosives and incendiaries that does the damage, not a jot of suffering is added to its victims that the burned and buried, the dismembered and blinded, the dying and bereaved of Dresden or Hamburg did not feel."[6]

If others, notably Germany, England, and Japan led the way in area bombing, the targeting for destruction of entire cities with conventional weapons emerged in 1944–45 as the centerpiece of U.S. warfare. The United States perfected the science of what is best described as terror bombing, that is the ability to annihilate urban residents on an unprecedented scale. It was an approach that combined technological predominance with minimization of U.S. casualties in ways that would become the hallmark of the American way of war in campaigns from Korea and Indochina to the Gulf and Iraq Wars and, indeed, define the trajectory of major wars since the 1940s. The result would be the decimation of noncombatant populations and extraordinary "kill ratios" favoring the U.S. military. Yet for the United States, victory would prove extraordinarily elusive. This is one important reason why, six decades on, World War II retains its aura for Americans as the "Good War," and why Americans, complacent in their role as "freedom fighters," have yet to come to grips with questions of ethics and international law associated with their area bombing of Germany and Japan.

The twentieth century was notable for the contradiction between, on the one hand, international attempts to place limits on the destructiveness of war and to hold nations and their military leaders responsible for violations of international laws of war (the Nuremberg and Tokyo tribunals and successive Geneva conventions, particularly the 1949 convention protecting civilians and POWs) and, on the other, the systematic violation of those principles by the major powers.[7] For example, while the Nuremberg and Tokyo tribunals clearly articulated the principle of universality, they were both held in cities that had been obliterated by Allied bombing yet famously shielded the victorious powers. Above all, the United States accepted no responsibility for war crimes and crimes against humanity that were the product of terror bombing. This was true despite the fact that Telford Taylor, chief counsel for war crimes prosecution at Nuremberg, would make the point with specific reference to the bombing of cities a quarter century later.[8]

Because both sides had played the terrible game of urban destruction— the Allies far more successfully—there was no basis for criminal charges for it against Germans or Japanese, and in fact no such charges were brought. Aerial bombardment had been used so extensively and ruthlessly on the Allied side as well as the Axis side that at neither Nuremberg nor Tokyo was the issue made a part of the trials.

From 1932 to the early years of World War II, the United States was an outspoken critic of city bombing, notably but not exclusively German and Japanese bombing. President Franklin Roosevelt appealed to the warring nations in 1939 on the first day of World War II "under no circumstances [to] undertake the bombardment from the air of civilian populations or of unfortified cities."[9] Britain, France, and Germany agreed to limit bombing to strictly military objectives, but in the May 1940 German bombardment of Rotterdam a square mile of the central city was obliterated and forced the Dutch surrender. Up to this point, bombing of cities had been isolated, sporadic, and for the most part confined to the Axis powers. But in August 1940, after German bombers bombed London, Churchill ordered an attack on Berlin. The steady escalation of bombing targeting cities and their noncombatant populations followed.[10]

Strategic Bombing of Europe

After entering the war following Pearl Harbor, the United States continued to claim the moral high ground by abjuring civilian bombing. This stance was consistent with the prevailing view in the air force high command that the most efficient bombing strategies were those that pinpointed destruction of enemy forces and installations, factories, and railroads, not those designed to terrorize or kill noncombatants. Nevertheless, the United States collaborated with indiscriminate bombing at the Casablanca Conference in 1943, when a division of labor emerged in which the British conducted the indiscriminate bombing of cities and the United States sought to destroy military and industrial targets.[11] In the final years of the war, Max Hastings observed that Churchill and his bomber commander, Arthur Harris, set out to concentrate "all available forces for the progressive, systematic destruction of the urban areas of the Reich, city block by city block, factory by factory, until the enemy became a nation of troglodytes, scratching in the ruins."[12] British strategists were convinced that the destruction of cities by night area-bombing attacks would break the morale of German civilians while crippling war production. Beginning in 1942 with the bombing of Lübeck, followed by Cologne, Hamburg, and others, Harris pursued this strategy. The perfection of onslaught from the air is better understood, however, as a British-American joint venture.

Throughout 1942–44, as the air war in Europe swung ineluctably toward area bombing, the U.S. Air Force proclaimed its adherence to precision bombing. However, this approach failed not only to force surrender on either Germany or Japan, but even to inflict significant damage on their war-making capacity. With German artillery and interceptors taking a heavy toll on U.S. planes, pressure mounted for a strategic shift at a time of growing sophistication, numbers, and range of U.S. aircraft and the invention of napalm and the perfection of radar. Ironically, while radar could have paved the way for a reaffirmation of tactical bombing, now made feasible at night, in the context of the endgame of the war, what transpired was the massive assault on cities and their urban populations.

On February 13–14, 1945, British bombers with U.S. planes following up destroyed Dresden, a historic cultural center with no significant military industry or bases. By conservative estimate, 35,000 people were incinerated in a single raid.[13] The American writer Kurt Vonnegut, then a young POW in Dresden, provided the classic account:[14]

> They burnt the whole damn town down. . . . Every day we walked into the city and dug into basements and shelters to get the corpses out, as a sanitary measure. When we went into them, a typical shelter, an ordinary basement usually, looked like a streetcar full of people who'd simultaneously had heart failure. Just people sitting there in their chairs, all dead.

"Along with the Nazi extermination camps, the killing of Soviet and American prisoners, and other enemy atrocities," Ronald Schaffer observes, "Dresden became one of the moral causes célèbres of World War II."[15] Although far worse was in the offing in Japan, Dresden provoked the last significant public discussion of the bombing of women and children to take place during World War II, and the city became synonymous with terror bombing by the United States and Britain. Because the attack came in the wake of both the Hamburg and Munich bombings, the British government faced sharp questioning in parliament.[16] In the United States, debate was largely provoked not by the destruction wrought by the raids, but by a widely published Associated Press report stating explicitly that "the Allied air commanders have made the long-awaited decision to adopt deliberate terror bombing of the great German population centers as a ruthless expedient to hasten Hitler's doom." Secretary of War Henry Stimson stated, "Our policy never has been to inflict terror bombing on civilian populations," claiming that Dresden, as a major transportation hub, was of military significance.[17] In fact, U.S. public discussion, not to speak of protest, was minimal; in Britain there was more impassioned discussion, but with the smell of victory in the air the government easily quieted the storm. The bombing continued. Strategic bombing had passed its sternest test in the realm of public reaction in Britain and the United States.

Strategic Bombing of Japan

But it was in the Pacific theater, and specifically in Japan, that the full brunt of airpower would be felt. Between 1932 and 1945, Japan had bombed Shanghai, Nanjing, Chongqing, and other cities, testing chemical weapons in Ningbo and throughout Zhejiang and Hunan provinces.[18] In the early months of 1945, the United States gained the capacity to attack Japan from newly captured bases in Tinian and Guam. Throughout 1943–44, it had tested firebombing options against Japanese homes, finding that M-69 bombs were highly effective against the densely packed wooden structures.[19] In the final six months of the war, the United States threw the full weight of its airpower into campaigns to burn whole Japanese cities to the ground and terrorize, incapacitate, and kill their largely defenseless residents in an effort to force surrender.

Prophecy preceded practice in the destruction of Japanese cities, that is, well before planners undertook strategic bombing. Michael Sherry observes that "Walt Disney imagined an orgiastic destruction of Japan by air" in his 1943 animated feature *Victory Through Air Power*, while Cary Karacas notes that Unna Juzo, beginning in his early 1930s "air-defense novels," anticipated the destruction of Tokyo by bombing.[20]

Curtis LeMay was appointed commander of the Twenty-first Bomber Command in the Pacific on January 20, 1945. Capture of the Marianas, including Guam, Tinian, and Saipan, in summer 1944 had placed Japanese cities within effective range of the B-29 Superfortress bombers, while Japan's depleted air and naval power left it virtually defenseless against sustained air attack.[21]

LeMay was the primary architect, a strategic innovator, and most quotable spokesman for U.S. policies of putting enemy cities, and later villages and forests, to the torch, from Japan to Korea to Vietnam. In this, he was emblematic of the American way of war that emerged from World War II. Viewed from another angle, however, he was but a link in a chain of command that had begun to conduct area bombing in Europe. That chain of command extended upward through the Joint Chiefs to the president.[22]

The goal of the bombing assault that destroyed Japan's major cities in the period between May and August 1945, as officers of the U.S. Strategic Bombing Survey (SBS) explained, was "either to bring overwhelming pressure on her to surrender, or to reduce her capability of resisting invasion . . . [by destroying] the basic economic and social fabric of the country."[23] A proposal by the chief of staff of the Twentieth Air Force to target the imperial palace was rejected, but in the wake of successive failures to eliminate such key targets as the Nakajima Aircraft Factory west of Tokyo, the area bombing of Japanese cities was approved.[24]

The full fury of firebombing and napalm was unleashed on the night of March 9–10, 1945, when LeMay sent 334 B-29s low over Tokyo from the Marianas. Their mission was to reduce the city to rubble, kill its citizens, and instill terror in the survivors, with jellied gasoline and napalm that would create a sea of flames. Stripped of their guns to make more room for bombs, and flying at altitudes averaging 7,000 feet to evade detection, the bombers carried two kinds of incendiaries: M-47s, 100-pound oil gel bombs, 182 per aircraft, each capable of starting a major fire, followed by M-69s packing 6-pound gelled-gasoline bombs, 1,520 per aircraft, in addition to a few high explosives to deter firefighters.[25] The attack, on an area that the U.S. Strategic Bombing Survey estimated to be 84.7 percent residential, succeeded beyond the wildest dreams of air force planners. Whipped by fierce winds, flames generated by the bombs leaped across a fifteen-square-mile area of Tokyo, generating immense firestorms that killed scores of thousands of residents. We have come to measure the efficacy of bombing by throw weights and kill ratios, eliding the perspectives of their victims. But what of those who felt the wrath of the bombs?

Police cameraman Ishikawa Koyo described the streets of Tokyo as "rivers of fire . . . flaming pieces of furniture exploding in the heat, while the people themselves blazed like 'matchsticks' as their wood and paper homes exploded in flames. Under the wind and the gigantic breath of the fire, immense incandescent vortices rose in a number of places, swirling, flattening, sucking whole blocks of houses into their maelstrom of fire."

Father Flaujac, a French cleric, compared the firebombing to the Tokyo earthquake twenty-two years earlier, an event whose massive destruction, another form of prophecy, had alerted both Japanese science fiction writers and some of the original planners of the Tokyo holocaust:[26]

> In September 1923, during the great earthquake, I saw Tokyo burning for 5 days. I saw in Honjo a heap of 33,000 corpses of people who burned or suffocated at the beginning of the bombardment. . . . After the first quake there were 20-odd centers of fire, enough to destroy the capital. How could the conflagration be stopped when incendiary bombs in the dozens of thousands now dropped over the four corners of the district and with Japanese houses which are only match boxes? . . . Where could one fly? The fire was everywhere.

Nature reinforced man's handiwork in the form of *akakaze*, the red wind that swept with hurricane force across the Tokyo plain and propelled firestorms that drove temperatures up to 1,800 degrees Fahrenheit, creating superheated vapors that advanced ahead of the flames, killing or incapacitating their victims. "The mechanisms of death were so multiple and simultaneous—oxygen deficiency and carbon monoxide poisoning, radiant heat and direct flames, debris and the trampling feet of stampeding crowds—that causes of death were later hard to ascertain. . . ."[27]

The Strategic Bombing Survey, whose formation a few months earlier provided an important signal of Roosevelt's support for strategic bombing, provided a technical description of the firestorm and its effects on Tokyo:

> The chief characteristic of the conflagration . . . was the presence of a fire front, an extended wall of fire moving to leeward, preceded by a mass of pre-heated, turbid, burning vapors. . . . An extended fire swept over 15 square miles in 6 hours. . . . The area of the fire was nearly 100 percent burned; no structure or its contents escaped damage.

The survey concluded—plausibly, but only for events prior to August 6, 1945—that "probably more persons lost their lives by fire at Tokyo in a 6-hour period than at any time in the history of man. . . . The largest number of victims were the most vulnerable: women, children and the elderly."

How many people died on the night of March 9–10 in what flight commander General Thomas Power termed "the greatest single disaster incurred by any enemy in military history"? The Strategic Bombing Survey estimated that 87,793 people died in the raid, 40,918 were injured, and

1,008,005 people lost their homes. Robert Rhodes, estimating the dead at more than 100,000 men, women, and children, suggested that probably a million more were injured and another million were left homeless. The Tokyo Fire Department estimated 97,000 killed and 125,000 wounded. The Tokyo Police offered a figure of 124,711 killed and wounded and 286,358 buildings and homes destroyed. The figure of roughly 100,000 deaths, provided by Japanese and American authorities, both of whom may have had reasons of their own for minimizing the death toll, seems to me arguably low in light of population density, wind conditions, and survivors' accounts.[28] With an average of 103,000 inhabitants per square mile and peak levels as high as 135,000 per square mile, the highest density of any industrial city in the world, and with firefighting measures ludicrously inadequate to the task, 15.8 square miles of Tokyo were destroyed. An estimated 1.5 million people lived in the burned-out areas. Given a near total inability to fight fires of the magnitude produced by the bombs, it is possible to imagine that casualties may have been several times higher than the figures presented on both sides of the conflict. The single effective Japanese government measure taken to reduce the slaughter of U.S. bombing was the 1944 evacuation to the countryside of 400,000 children from major cities, 225, 000 of them from Tokyo.[29]

Following the attack, LeMay, never one to mince words, said that he wanted Tokyo "burned down—wiped right off the map" to "shorten the war." Tokyo did burn. Subsequent raids brought the devastated area of Tokyo to more than 56 square miles, provoking the flight of millions of refugees.

No previous or subsequent conventional bombing raid came close to generating the toll in death and destruction of the great Tokyo raid of March 9–10, but the airborne assault on Tokyo and other Japanese cities ground on relentlessly. According to Japanese police statistics, the sixty-five raids on Tokyo between December 6, 1944, and August 13, 1945, resulted in 137,582 casualties, 787,145 homes and buildings destroyed, and 2,625,279 people displaced.[30] The firebombing was extended nationwide. Beginning on March 9, in the next ten days, 9,373 tons of bombs destroyed 31 square miles of Tokyo, Nagoya, Osaka, and Kobe. Overall, bombing strikes destroyed 40 percent of the 66 Japanese cities targeted, with total tonnage dropped on Japan increasing from 13,800 tons in March to 42,700 tons in July.[31] If the bombing of Dresden produced a ripple of public debate in Europe, no discernible wave of revulsion, let alone protest, took place in the United States or Europe in the wake of the far greater destruction of Japanese cities and the slaughter of civilian populations on a scale that had no parallel in the history of bombing.

In July, U.S. planes blanketed the few Japanese cities that had been spared firebombing with an "Appeal to the People." It read: "As you know, America which stands for humanity, does not wish to injure the innocent people, so you had better evacuate these cities." Half the leafleted cities were firebombed within days of the warning. Overall, by one calculation, the U.S. firebombing campaign destroyed 180 square miles of sixty-seven cities, killed more than 300,000 people, and injured an additional 400,000, figures that exclude the atomic bombing of Hiroshima and Nagasaki.[32]

Between January and July 1945, the United States firebombed and destroyed all but five Japanese cities, deliberately sparing Kyoto, the ancient imperial capital, and four others. The destruction ranged from 50 to 60 percent of the urban area in some cities, including Kobe, Yokohama, and Tokyo, to 60 to 88 percent in seventeen cities, to 98.6 percent in the case of Toyama.[33] In the end, the Atomic Bomb Selection Committee chose Hiroshima, Kokura, Niigata, and Nagasaki as pristine targets to display the awesome power of the atomic bomb to Japan and the world and send a powerful message to the Soviet Union.

Michael Sherry has compellingly described the triumph of technological fanaticism as the hallmark of the air war that quintessentially shaped the American way of fighting and heavily stamped remembrances of the war ever after:

> The shared mentality of the fanatics of air war was their dedication to assembling and perfecting their methods of destruction, and . . . doing so overshadowed the original purposes justifying destruction. . . . The lack of a proclaimed intent to destroy, the sense of being driven by the twin demands of bureaucracy and technology, distinguished America's technological fanaticism from its enemies' ideological fanaticism.

Technological fanaticism served to conceal the larger purposes of power from military planners and the public. This suggestive formulation, however, conceals core ideological patterns at the heart of American strategic thought. Wartime technological fanaticism, in my view, is best understood as a means of operationalizing national goals. Taken for granted were the legitimacy and benevolence of American global power and a perception of the Japanese as both uniquely brutal and inherently inferior. Technology was harnessed to the driving force of American nationalism, which repeatedly came to the fore in times of war and was fashioned under wartime conditions, beginning with the conquest of the Philippines in 1898 and running through successive wars and police actions in Latin America and Asia that spanned the long twentieth century. In other words, technological fanaticism is inseparable from American nationalism and conceptions of a benevolent American-dominated global order. In contrast to British, Japanese, and other nationalisms associated with expansive powers, the American approach to the postwar order lay in a vision not of colonies but of a global network of military bases, of naval and air power, which only in recent years has begun to be understood as the American way of empire.[34]

Throughout the spring and summer of 1945, the air war in Japan reached an intensity that is still perhaps unrivaled in the magnitude of human slaughter.[35] That moment was a product of the combination of technological breakthroughs, American nationalism, and the erosion of moral and political scruples about killing of civilians, perhaps intensified by the racism that crystallized in the Pacific theater.[36]

Targeting entire populations for destruction, whether indigenous peoples, religious infidels, or others deemed inferior or evil, may be as old as human history, but the forms it takes are as new as the latest technologies of destruction, of which airpower, firebombing, and nuclear weapons are particularly notable.[37] The most important way in which World War II shaped the moral and technological tenor of mass destruction was the erosion of the stigma associated with the systematic slaughter of civilians from the air, and elimination of the constraints that for some years had restrained certain air powers from area bombing. What was new was both the scale of killing made possible by the new technologies and the routinization of mass killing or state terrorism.

If area bombing remained controversial throughout much of World War II, something to be concealed or denied by its practitioners, by the end it became the acknowledged centerpiece of war making, emblematic above all of the American way of war. For six decades the United States (and those fighting under its umbrella) has been virtually alone in fighting wars and police actions notable for their reliance on airpower and in deliberately targeting civilians and the infrastructure needed for their survival. Certainly in this epoch no others have bombed on a scale approaching that of the United States, but it has tried to conceal its intent with the fig leaf that Sahr Conway-Lanz calls the myth of collateral damage, that is, the claim, however systematic the slaughter of noncombatants, that the intent was elimination of military targets.

Concerted efforts to protect civilians from the ravages of war reached a peak in the aftermath of World War II in the founding of the United Nations, in the German and Japanese war crimes tribunals, and in the 1949 Geneva Accords and the 1977 Protocol. The Nuremberg indictment defined crimes against humanity as "murder, extermination, enslavement, deportation, and other inhumane acts committed against any civilian population, before or during the war," language that covers the area-bombing campaigns not only of Japan and Germany but of Britain and the United States.[38] These efforts have done little to stay the hand of power. While the atomic bomb left a deep imprint on the collective consciousness of the twentieth century, memory of the area bombings and firebombing of major cities soon disappeared from the consciousness of all but the victims.

The ability to destroy an entire city and annihilate its population in a single bombing campaign was not only far more efficient and less costly for the attacker than previous methods of warfare; it also sanitized slaughter. Airpower distanced executioners from victims, transforming the visual and tactile experience of killing. The bombardier never looks squarely into the eyes of the victim, never even sees the victim. The act of destruction has no physical immediacy for the perpetrator, as in decapitation by sword or even shooting with a machine gun. This may be particularly important when the principal targets are women, children, and the elderly.

So far, the atomic bombing of Hiroshima and Nagasaki was the worst case of annihilating civilian populations in the pursuit of military victory. President Truman claimed that the Hiroshima bomb targeted a naval base, but the decision to detonate the bombs about 1,800 feet above the centers of Hiroshima and Nagasaki was taken to maximize the killing of the inhabitants and the destruction of the built environment. It was calculated to demonstrate American omnipotence to the Japanese government and people, to the authorities in the Soviet Union, to other potential challengers of American preeminence, and to the people of the world—to show them the certain destruction that would be visited on any who defied the United States. The debate over the use of the atomic bomb at Hiroshima and Nagasaki has reverberated throughout the postwar era, cen-

tered on the killing of noncombatants and on its significance in ending
World War II and shaping the subsequent U.S.-Soviet conflict that defined postwar geopolitics.[39] In a sense, however, the very focus of that debate on the atomic bomb, and later on the development of the hydrogen
bomb, may have contributed to the silencing of the no less pressing issue of
killing noncombatants with ever more powerful conventional weapons.

The United States has not dropped atomic bombs on people again, although it repeatedly used its atomic preeminence to threaten annihilation
in Korea, in Vietnam, and elsewhere. But it systematically exterminated
civilians by bombing in the conventional wars it has waged. With area
bombing at the core of its strategic agenda, American attacks on cities and
noncombatants have included firebombs, napalm, cluster bombs, chemical
defoliants, depleted uranium weapons, and bunker-buster bombs in an
ever expanding circle of destruction.[40] Indiscriminate bombing of noncombatants has caused the greatest destruction and loss of life throughout
this epoch. For their part, American officers staunchly maintain that they
do not deliberately kill civilians, repeatedly deploying the collateral-damage
explanation to protect themselves against political criticism in the United
States, and above all from international criticism.

World War II remains unrivaled in the number of people killed and the
scale of mass destruction. However, it was not the bombing of cities but
Nazi genocide, the German invasion of the Soviet Union, and the Japanese
slaughter of rural Asians that exacted the heaviest price in human lives.
Each of these examples had its unique character and historical and ideological origins, but all rested on dehumanizing assumptions about the "other,"
which produced large-scale slaughter of noncombatant populations.

Japan's China war produced notable cases of atrocities that, then and
later, captured world attention. They included the Nanjing Massacre, the
bombings of Shanghai, Nanjing, Hankou, Chongqing, and other cities,
the enslavement of the comfort women, and the vivisection experiments
and biowarfare bombs of Unit 731. Less noted then and since were the systematic barbarities perpetrated against resistant villagers, though this produced the largest number of the estimated 10 to 30 million Chinese who
lost their lives in the war, a number that far surpasses the half million or
more Japanese noncombatants who died at the hands of U.S. bombing,
and may have exceeded Soviet losses to the Nazi invasion, conventionally
estimated at 20 million lives.[41] But in that and subsequent wars, it was the

signature barbarities—such as the Nanjing Massacre, the Bataan Death March, and the massacres at Nogunri and My Lai—rather than the systematic daily and hourly killing that have attracted sustained attention, sparked bitter controversy, and shaped historical memory.

The World War II dead in Europe alone, including the Soviet Union, have been estimated in the range of 30 to 40 million, fifty percent more than the toll in World War I. To this we must add 25 to 35 million Asian victims in the fifteen-year resistance war in China (1931–45), approximately 3 million Japanese, and millions more in Southeast Asia. Among the important instances of the killing of noncombatants in World War II, the U.S. destruction of Japanese cities is perhaps least known. In contrast to the fierce and continuing debate over the atomic bombing of Hiroshima and Nagasaki, the Nazi extermination of Jews and others, and the far smaller-scale Allied bombings of Dresden and Hamburg, and such Japanese atrocities as the Nanjing Massacre and the vivisection experiments of Unit 731, the U.S. firebombing of Japanese cities has virtually disappeared from international and even American and Japanese historical memory.

In World War I, ninety percent of the fatalities directly attributable to the war were military, nearly all of them Europeans and Americans. Most estimates place World War II casualties in Europe in the range of 50 to 60 percent noncombatants. In the case of Asia, when war-induced famine casualties are included, the noncombatant death toll was almost certainly substantially higher in both absolute and percentage terms.[42] The United States, its homeland untouched by war, suffered approximately 100,000 deaths in the entire Asian theater, a figure lower than that for the single Tokyo air raid of March 10, 1945, and well below the death toll at Hiroshima or in the Battle of Okinawa. Japan's 3 million war dead, while thirty times the number of U.S. dead, was still only a small fraction of the toll suffered by the Chinese who resisted the Japanese military juggernaut.

World War II remains indelibly engraved in American memory as the "Good War," and in important respects it was. In confronting the war machines of Nazi Germany and Imperial Japan, the United States played a large role in defeating aggressors and opening the way for a wave of decolonization that swept the globe in subsequent decades. It was also a war that catapulted the United States to global dominance and established the institutional foundations for the worldwide projection of American power in a network of military bases and unrivaled technological supremacy.

For most Americans, in retrospect, World War II has seemed a "Good War" in another sense: the United States entered and exited the war buoyed by absolute moral certainty borne of a mission to punish aggression in the form of a genocidal Nazi fascism and Japanese imperialism run amok. Moreover, Americans remember the generosity of U.S. aid, not only to war torn allies, but also to rebuild the societies of former adversaries Germany and Japan. Such an interpretation masks the extent to which Americans shared with their adversaries an abiding nationalism and expansionist urges. In contrast to earlier territorial empires, this took the form of new regional and global structures facilitating the exercise of American power. The victory, which propelled the United States to a hegemonic position with authority to condemn and punish war crimes committed by defeated nations, remains a major obstacle to assessing America's wartime conduct in general, and issues of mass destruction carried out by its forces in particular.

German and Japanese crimes have long been subjected to international criticism, from the war crimes tribunals of the 1940s to the present.[43] At Nuremberg and subsequent trials, more than 1,800 Germans were convicted of war crimes, and 294 were executed. At the Tokyo trials, 28 were indicted and 7 were sentenced to death. At subsequent A and B class trials conducted by the Allied powers between 1945 and 1951, 5,700 Japanese, Koreans, and Taiwanese were indicted, and 984 were initially sentenced to death; the sentences of 50 of these were commuted. Another 475 received life sentences, and 2,944 received limited prison terms. Defeat, occupation, and war crimes tribunals produced long, profound reflection and self-criticism by significant groups within both countries. In the case of Germany—but not yet Japan—there has been meaningful official recognition of the genocide and other barbaric policies, as well as appropriate restitution to victims in the form of public apology and substantial reparations. For its part, the Japanese state, with U.S. support, continues to reject official reparations claims to such war victims as Korean and Chinese forced laborers and the military comfort women (sexual slaves). The war remains a fiercely contested intellectual and political issue, as demonstrated by the decades-long conflicts over textbook treatments of colonialism and the war, over the Yasukuni shrine (the symbol of emperor-centered nationalist aggression), and over official apologies for atrocities like sexual enslavement and the Nanjing Massacre.[44]

In contrast, there has been virtually no awareness of, much less of critical reflection on, the U.S. bombing of Japanese civilians in the months prior to Hiroshima. The systematic bombing of Japanese noncombatants in the course of the destruction of Japanese cities must be added to a list of the horrific legacies of the war that includes Nazi genocide and Japanese war crimes against Asian peoples. Mass murder of civilians has been central to all subsequent U.S. wars, and only by engaging this issue can Americans begin to approach the Nuremberg ideal, which holds victors as well as vanquished to the same standards with respect to crimes against humanity, or the standard of the 1949 Geneva Accord, which requires the protection of civilians in time of war. The principle of universality enshrined at Nuremberg has been violated in practice by the United States and others beginning with the 1946 trials, which declared America immune from prosecution for war crimes.

In his opening address to the tribunal, Justice Robert Jackson, chief counsel for the United States, spoke eloquently on the principle of universality. "If certain acts of violation of treaties are crimes," he said, "they are crimes whether the United States does them or whether Germany does them, and we are not prepared to lay down a rule of criminal conduct against others which we would not be willing to have invoked against us. . . . We must never forget that the record on which we judge these defendants is the record on which history will judge us tomorrow. To pass these defendants a poisoned chalice is to put it to our own lips as well."[45]

Nevertheless, every president from Roosevelt to George W. Bush has endorsed in practice an approach to warfare that targets entire populations for annihilation, one that eliminates all distinction between combatant and noncombatant with deadly consequences. The awesome power of the atomic bomb has obscured the fact that this strategy came of age in the firebombing of Tokyo and became the centerpiece of U.S. war making from that time forward.

That poisoned chalice was put to American lips in the 1946 trials and all the more so in subsequent wars. Sahr Conway-Lanz rightly points to the deep divisions among Americans seeking to strike an appropriate balance between combat and atrocity, between war and genocide.[46] In the end, however, American self-conceptions of benevolence and justice have remained fixed not on the reality of killing civilians but on idealized intentions and past generosity in aiding postwar recovery in Germany and Japan.

Epilogue: Korea, Vietnam, Iraq, and the Uses of Airpower to Target Noncombatants

The strategy of killing noncombatants through airpower runs like a red line from the bombings of 1944–45 through the Korean and Indochinese wars to the Gulf, Afghanistan, and Iraq wars. In the six decades since the firebombing and atomic bombing of Japan, while important continuities are observable, such as the firebombing and napalming of cities, new, more powerful and versatile aircraft and weapons were also deployed.

General Curtis LeMay, the primary architect of the firebombing and atomic bombing of Japan, played a comparable role in Korea and Vietnam. Never one to pull punches or minimize the claimed impact of bombing, LeMay recalled of Korea:

> We slipped a note kind of under the door into the Pentagon and said, "Look, let us go up there . . . and burn down five of the biggest towns in North Korea— and they're not very big—and that ought to stop it." Well, the answer to that was four or five screams—"You'll kill a lot of non-combatants," and "It's too horrible." Yet over a period three years or so . . . we burned down *every* town in North Korea and South Korea, too. . . . Now, over a period of three years this is palatable, but to kill a few people to stop this from happening—a lot of people can't stomach it.[47]

In the course of three years, U.S./UN forces in Korea flew 1,040,708 sorties and dropped 386,037 tons of bombs and 32,357 tons of napalm. Counting all types of airborne ordnance, including rockets and machine-gun ammunition, the total tonnage comes to 698,000 tons. Marilyn Young estimates the death toll in Korea, most of it noncombatants, at 2 to 3 million, and in the South alone more than 5 million people had been displaced, according to UN estimates.[48]

One striking feature of these wars has been the extension of bombing from a predominantly urban phenomenon to the uses of airpower directed against rural areas of Korea and Vietnam. Beginning in Korea, U.S. bombing was extended from cities to the countryside with devastating effects. In what Bruce Cumings has called the "final act of this barbaric air war," in spring 1953, North Korea's main irrigation dams were destroyed shortly after the rice had been transplanted.[49]

Here we consider one particularly important element of the American bombing of Vietnam. In 1943, Franklin Roosevelt issued a statement that long stood as the clearest expression of U.S. policy on the use of chemical and biological weapons. In response to reports of Axis plans to use poison gases, Roosevelt stated "categorically that we shall under no circumstances resort to the use of such weapons unless they are first used by our enemies."[50] This principle of no first use was incorporated in U.S. Army Field Manual 27-10, Law of Land Warfare, issued in 1954. By 1956, that provision had disappeared, replaced by the assertion that the United States was party to no treaty in force "that prohibits or restricts the use in warfare of toxic or nontoxic gases, or smoke or incendiary materials or of bacteriological warfare." U.S. CBW research and procurement efforts, which began in the early 1950s, resulted in the use of chemical and biological weapons both against Vietnamese forces and nature, extending from the destruction of forest cover to the destruction of crops. As Seymour Hersh documents, the U.S. CBW program in Vietnam "gradually escalated from the use of leaf-killing defoliants to rice-killing herbicides and nausea-producing gases."[51] How widespread were the gas attacks in Vietnam? A 1967 Japanese study of American anticrop and defoliation attacks concluded that more than 3.8 million acres of arable land in South Vietnam had been ruined and more than 1,000 peasants and 13,000 livestock had been killed by then.[52] In the face of U.S. military claims that the gases were benign, Dr. Pham Duc Nam told Japanese investigators that a three-day attack near Da Nang from February 25 to 27, 1966, had poisoned both livestock and people, some of whom died. "Pregnant women gave birth to still-born or premature children. Most of the affected cattle died from serious diarrhea, and river fish floated on the surface of the water belly up, soon after the chemicals were spread."[53]

Before turning to Iraq, it is worth recalling President Nixon's comments on the bombing of Cambodia as preserved in the Kissinger tapes released in May 2004. In a burst of anger on December 9, 1970, Nixon exploded: "I want them to hit everything. I want them to use the big planes, the small planes, everything they can that will help out there, and let's start giving them a little shock." Here was an early warning signal of the "shock and awe" strategy of a generation later. Kissinger relayed the order: "A massive bombing campaign in Cambodia. Anything that flies on anything that moves."[54]

An important story of indiscriminate bombing in Cambodia came to light thirty-six years after the events. The new evidence makes clear that the bombing of Cambodia began not with Nixon in 1970 but on October 4, 1965. The records released in 2000 reveal that between October 4, 1965, to August 15 1973, the United States dropped far more ordnance on Cambodia than was previously known: 2,756,941 tons, dropped in 230,516 sorties on 113,716 sites. As Taylor Owen and Ben Kiernan argue persuasively, "Civilian casualties in Cambodia drove an enraged populace into the arms of an insurgency that had enjoyed relatively little support until the bombing began, setting in motion the expansion of the Vietnam War deeper into Cambodia, a coup d'état in 1970, the rapid rise of the Khmer Rouge, and ultimately the Cambodian genocide."[55]

Americans remember World War II above all as the crowning achievement of airpower, symbolized and mythologized by the atomic bombing of Hiroshima and Nagasaki; they remember the era of U.S.-Soviet confrontation above all as one of nuclear standoff; and they remember both Korea and Vietnam in no small part through images of American predominance in the air, as in the bombing of Hanoi and North Vietnam as well as the defoliation using Agent Orange via airpower. But, as Michael Sherry observes, airpower has largely receded from consciousness in the wake of the collapse of the Soviet Union and the shift in target from the other superpower to faceless terrorists associated with al Qaeda and Islamic militants. Sherry concludes that a sea change has occurred, a shift from prophecy to memory in which air power declines in American consciousness: "Bombers attacking Baghdad, B-52s over Belgrade, Russian planes hitting Grozny, rulers bombing their own peoples—the scale of those operations (however devastating for the locals) and the fact that they involved such unequal forces did not stir Americans' apocalyptic fears and fantasies." Where airpower did appear in American consciousness, he finds, "American bombing came across on U.S. television screens more as a fascinating video game than as a devastating onslaught." More important, he concludes, because of the attack on New York's Twin Towers and the Pentagon on 9/11, and because of the horrific images that it conjured, in contrast to the heroic images of air power in World War II, the prophecy associated with it "did not seem to last long or run deep."[56]

In thinking about the Iraq War and contemporary American consciousness, I would like to suggest an alternative scenario. First, I believe that the Twin Towers in flames remains the iconic image of our times in American consciousness. It is the central mobilizing image for U.S. war making and the primal scene that drives American fears of the future. Second, the U.S.

military, with the complicity of the press, while continuing to pursue massive bombing of Iraqi neighborhoods, has thrown a cloak of silence over
the air war.[57] Airpower remains among the major causes of death, destruction, dislocation, and division in contemporary Iraq in a war that had
taken approximately 655,000 lives by the summer of 2006 in the most authoritative study to date, published in *The Lancet*,[58] and created more than
2 million refugees abroad and an equal number displaced internally (one
in seven Iraqis are displaced). Despite the unchallenged air supremacy that
the United States has wielded in Iraq since 1991 and especially since 2003,
there is no end in sight to U.S. warfare and civil war in Iraq and throughout the region.[59]

We have shown the decisive impact of the final year of World War II in
setting in place the preeminence of strategic bombing as quintessential to
the American way of war, one that would characterize subsequent major
wars that have wreaked yet greater devastation on noncombatant populations. Yet for all the power unleashed by bombers, for all the millions of
victims, in the six decades since 1945, victory against successive predominantly Asian foes has proved extraordinarily elusive for the United States.

5

WERE THE ATOMIC BOMBINGS OF HIROSHIMA AND NAGASAKI JUSTIFIED?

Tsuyoshi Hasegawa

> In principle, the extermination camps where the Nazis incinerated over six million helpless Jews were no different from the urban crematoriums our air force improvised in its attacks by napalm bombs on Tokyo. . . . Our aims were different, but our methods were those of mankind's worst enemy.
>
> —Lewis Mumford (1959)[1]

On the sixtieth anniversary of the Dresden bombing, ambassadors from the United States, Russia, France, and Britain attended a wreath-laying ceremony. Clergy from Coventry Cathedral in England, destroyed by German bombing in 1940, presented a cross to Dresden's Frauenkirche. Chancellor Gerhardt Schröder spoke: "Today we grieve for the victims of war and the Nazi reign of terror in Dresden in Germany and in Europe." Despite this attempt at historic reconciliation, however, discordant views that separate the Germans from the Allies in historical memory have surfaced. Outside the anniversary ceremonial site in Dresden, neo-Nazi demonstrators marched with a slogan charging that the bombing of Dresden was a holocaust perpetrated by the Allies.[2] And, as Robert Moeller discusses in his chapter in this volume, the discourse in Germany touched off by Jörg Friedrich's *Der Brand* [*The Fire*] indicates that, despite the gathering of the Allied representatives in Dresden, the memory war in Europe is intensifying.

Nonetheless, the Allied representatives did attend the ceremony at Dresden. While in Europe the Germans and the Allies seem to have taken the first major step toward reconciliation in Europe, in Asia no such steps have yet taken place. Nor is it conceivable in the near future that an American president or an American ambassador, officially representing the United States government, would dedicate a wreath to the victims of Hiroshima and Nagasaki without provoking angry voices of protest from the American public. In the meantime, Japan's prime ministers routinely visit Yasukuni Shrine, which houses a museum exhibit that unabashedly glorifies Japan's involvement in the Pacific War.

Although postwar U.S.-Japanese relations have been founded on their close-knit alliance, mistrust lurks beneath the surface. American memories of Pearl Harbor, reinforced by Japanese brutality in treating POWs, and Japanese memories of Hiroshima, Nagasaki, and the firebombing of Japanese cities lie at the core of it. During the Cold War, their common security and economic interests concealed this mistrust, but the resurgence of nationalism in Japan after the end of the Cold War and of patriotic fever in the post-9/11 United States may resurrect it.[3]

In June 2007, Japan's defense minister Kyuma Fumio stated that the atomic bombings on Hiroshima and Nagasaki were justified because they prevented the Soviet Union from occupying Japan. This statement touched off an instant storm of protest in Japan. The progressive newspaper *Asahi Shimbun* editorialized that Kyuma's remarks "were not only insensitive to the feelings of atomic bomb survivors and victims, but also seriously undermine Japan's 'non-nuclear' stand." With a chorus of protest mounting not only from the opposition party but also from within the Komeito, a coalition partner in the ruling Liberal-Democratic Party, Kyuma was forced to resign. The new defense minister, Koike Yuriko, categorically stated that the atomic bombings by the United States should never be condoned.

Across the Pacific, asked about Kyuma's statement, Robert Joseph, President George W. Bush's neoconservative appointee as the special envoy for nonproliferation, justified the atomic bombing as the action that ended the Pacific War and saved not only a million Americans but also more Japanese. Asked about this opinion, Prime Minister Abe Shinzo replied, "I have not changed my view that we should never forgive the atomic bombings." Ozawa Ichiro, the head of the Democratic Party, the major opposition party, demanded that the government seek an apology from the United States for dropping the atomic bombs.[4]

Hiroshima and Nagasaki, Soviet Entry into the War, and Japan's Surrender

The literature on the end of the Pacific War has evolved in a truncated fashion along three distinct tracks. American historians have generally been preoccupied with the question of the American decision to drop the bombs on Hiroshima and Nagasaki. Japanese historians have focused on the political process through which Japan came to accept surrender. Least developed has been the Soviet role in ending the war, which has been treated as a sideshow by both American and Japanese historians. It is important, however, that Stalin be brought to center stage, because the Soviet Union played a crucial role in the American decision to drop the bomb and was the focus of Japan's diplomatic and military policy during the last months of the war. The atomic bombing of Hiroshima and Nagasaki must be understood in a broader context of international history by closely examining, first, how the atomic bombs influenced the Japanese decision-making process leading to their acceptance of surrender, second, how the Soviet factor influenced President Harry S. Truman's decision to drop the bombs, and third, how Soviet entry into the war influenced Japan's decision to surrender.

Looking at the end of the Pacific War from the international perspective, three important conclusions can be drawn. First, there was fierce competition between Truman and Stalin to force Japan to surrender: Truman wanted to end the war before the Soviet entry, and Stalin wanted to join the war before Japan surrendered. The atomic bomb played an important role in this race.

Second, there was a dispute in Japan among top policy makers about whether and on what terms they should end the war. Both for the peace party and for the war party, determining the role that the Soviet Union would play had the highest priority during the last months of the war. To the Japanese leaders, the specific definition of the *kokutai* (national polity) built on the emperor system became the most important issue, as both parties struggled to come up with acceptable conditions for ending the war. Rejecting the American demand for unconditional surrender and destruction of the *kokutai*, the peace party sought Moscow's mediation to preserve it. The war party insisted on the need to inflict decisive damage on the expected American invasion of the homeland in order to gain favorable peace terms and considered Soviet neutrality essential to wage such a battle. Both parties thus pinned their hopes for a satisfactory end to the war on the Soviet Union. Japan's policy, however, was exploited by Stalin to prolong the war long enough for the Soviet Union to join it.

Third, the widely held view in the United States that the atomic bombings were the most decisive factor that led to Japan's surrender must be rejected. Although the atomic bombing of Hiroshima on August 6 injected urgency among Japanese policy makers in their attempt to terminate the war, it did not result in a change in the official policy to achieve this goal through Soviet mediation. It was only after the Soviet entry into the war in the early hours of August 9 that the Japanese policy makers, for the first time, confronted the issue of whether or not they should accept the terms specified by the Potsdam Proclamation. Although the Soviet entry, like the atomic bomb on Hiroshima, did not lead to a prompt decision to surrender, the Soviet factor played a far more important role than the atomic bombings.

The Soviet entry into the war dashed any hope of bargaining for terms through Moscow's mediation, nullifying the policy that the Japanese rulers had pursued since the middle of June 1945 and continued even after they received the Potsdam ultimatum of July 26. Furthermore, in order to preserve the imperial house, the Japanese policy makers decided to gamble on the Americans rather than prolong the war and risk the danger of exposing Japan to the expanded influence of the Soviet Union.[5]

Truman's Dilemma

When Truman assumed the presidency in April 1945, he faced two dilemmas with regard to the Pacific War. The first was the danger of Soviet expansion in Asia. In February 1945, at the Yalta Conference, President Franklin D. Roosevelt had been eager to conclude the Yalta Secret Agreement, which gave Stalin a series of rewards, such as concessions to the railways and ports in Manchuria and occupation of southern Sakhalin and the Kurils held by the Japanese, in return for his pledge to enter the war against Japan after the defeat of Germany. The U.S. policy makers, both military and civilian, believed then that Soviet participation in the war against Japan would be the most important prerequisite for the successful American invasion of Japan's homeland, because this would pin down the Japanese forces in Manchuria and North China.

However, the political and military situation had drastically changed

since the Yalta Conference. By April there emerged a serious conflict between the Soviet Union and the Western Allies over Poland and Eastern
Europe. Led by W. Averell Harriman, the American ambassador to
Moscow, those advisers who had become concerned about Stalin's increasingly hostile attitude toward the West over Poland and Eastern Europe
came to advocate abandoning FDR's policy of conciliation with the Soviet
Union. Harriman was soon joined by Joseph Grew, the influential undersecretary of state, and former president Herbert Hoover, who were worried about the consequences of Soviet expansion in the Far East after it
entered the war. Navy Secretary James Forrestal and William Leahy, chief
of staff to the president, also joined this group.

By April, the military situation had developed favorably for the United
States to the extent that the Joint Chiefs of Staff no longer considered Soviet entry essential for an invasion of Japan. Nonetheless, Army Chief of
Staff General George C. Marshall, supported by Secretary of War Henry L.
Stimson, continued to believe that Soviet forces would be important to
bringing about Japan's surrender before the initiation of Operation
Olympic, the massive invasion of Kyushu, the southern part of Japan's
homeland, scheduled for November 1. Truman wanted to avoid Soviet
participation, as he became increasingly concerned with its consequences
in Asia, but in order to end the war quickly with a minimal cost in American lives, Soviet entry would still be necessary.[6]

Truman faced a second dilemma. He was committed to the unconditional surrender demand. This was not merely because he wanted to continue FDR's legacy, and not merely because he feared that revising this
demand would run counter to prevailing public opinion, which took a
harsh attitude toward the Japanese emperor, but because he himself firmly
believed that imposition of unconditional surrender represented just retribution for the humiliation inflicted on the Americans by Japan's dastardly
attack on Pearl Harbor. Since May, however, there had been a growing
voice within his administration, led by influential advisers such as Grew,
Stimson, Forrestal, and Leahy, among others, in favor of modifying the
unconditional surrender demand by promising the Japanese that they
could maintain the monarchy under the current dynasty. This group argued that in order to bring the war to a speedy conclusion, modification of
unconditional surrender would be necessary because this would induce
the Japanese moderate elements to accept surrender before the country
was completely destroyed. For Grew, Forrestal, and Leahy, this recom-

mendation was also connected to their concerns about Soviet expansion in Asia. Truman found himself unable to resolve these dilemmas before the Potsdam Conference.[7]

On June 18, the president summoned his military advisers to the White House. He wanted to know how many troops would be needed to invade Japan, how many U.S. casualties would be expected in the invasion, and whether Soviet entry into the war would be advisable to end the war. Taken aback by the casualty figures (killed and wounded) given by Army Chief of Staff George Marshall (63,000 out of 190,000 troops) in the Kyushu operation alone, the president approved only Operation Olympic (the Kyushu invasion scheduled for November 1) while postponing the decision on Operation Coronet, the invasion of the Kanto Plane (Japan's central heartland, which includes Tokyo) in March 1946. Although Admiral Ernest J. King did not consider Soviet participation in the war necessary, Marshall told the president that the American invasion of Japan's homeland, combined with Soviet entry into the war, would lead to Japanese capitulation.

At this White House conference, Stimson recommended that the United States revise the unconditional surrender demand in such a way that the moderate elements within the Japanese government would accept surrender before the American invasion of Kyushu. John J. McCloy went further than Stimson, recommending that the United States send the Japanese a strong communication demanding a full surrender with a proviso that Japan would be able to continue to exist as a nation and keep the emperor under a constitutional monarchy. If the Japanese rejected such an offer, then the United States should reveal that it possessed the atomic bomb.[8]

Two alternatives had thus been suggested to the president: (1) to welcome Soviet entry into the war and (2) to revise the unconditional surrender demand. Truman made no decision at that point, except for endorsing Operation Olympic. In the meantime, Churchill from London, and Harriman and Grew in Washington, on separate occasions urged Truman to hasten the convening of the Big Three meeting to forestall further Soviet expansion in Eastern Europe. Each time, Truman demurred, citing his obligations to Congress for budget matters, but the real reason was that he wanted to postpone the Potsdam Conference until the United States tested the first atomic bomb.

Stalin's Dilemma

Stalin also faced a dilemma. In April, the Soviet government notified the Japanese government that it did not intend to renew the Soviet-Japanese Neutrality Pact. The pact, signed in April 1941, stipulated that unless one party notified the other of its intention not to renew one year prior to its expiration, the pact would automatically be renewed for another five years. Thus despite the fact that the Soviets renounced the pact in April 1945, it should have been in force until April 1946. Stalin and the Soviet government took it for granted that their planned attack on the Japanese forces in Manchuria in the summer of 1945 would have to be launched in violation of the neutrality pact. Yet if they intended to violate the pact anyway, why did they renounce it in April, taking the risk of signaling to the Japanese that they might join the Allies in the war against Japan?

There are two possible reasons. First, by renouncing the pact, the Soviet government diminished the impact of the *political*, if not *legal*, implications of violating it, thus avoiding the inevitable comparison with the German violation of the Nazi-Soviet Non-Aggression Pact. In fact, after the war, the Soviet government and Soviet historians consistently took the position that the pact lost its force immediately when renounced.

But if no one but the Japanese cared about the violation of the pact and if the Western allies and the Chinese would not have considered Soviet entry into the war a violation of the pact—and they did not—why did the Soviets bother to renounce it? It is possible to interpret this as a signal to the United States that the Soviet Union intended to honor the commitment it had made at Yalta to enter the war against Japan. It appears that Stalin considered the Soviet commitment to enter the war against Japan to be important leverage with the United States. It was all the more important for Stalin to reaffirm this commitment when conflict between the United States and the Soviet Union over Poland and Eastern Europe emerged as a major discord in the Grand Alliance.[9]

Nevertheless, the renunciation of the neutrality pact was a risky move. It was a clear signal to the Japanese that the Soviet Union would very likely join the Western Allies in the war against Japan. This might even prompt the Japanese to launch a preemptive attack on the Soviet forces in the Far East before preparations for war were completed. To avoid this, Stalin placed the Far Eastern army on alert status just in case, while the commissar of foreign affairs, Viacheslav Molotov, told the Japanese that, despite the Soviet renunciation, the pact itself was in force until it fulfilled its term in April 1946. The Japanese, who desperately wanted Soviet neutrality, gullibly accepted this explanation, and this information was accurately conveyed to Stalin by the Soviet ambassador, Iakov Malik. Thus while, as Stalin later explained, "lulling the Japanese to sleep," Stalin began frantically transporting troops and equipment from Europe to the Far East. This policy, however, left one major problem for Stalin and the Soviet government. Although it satisfied the tactical problem of deceiving the Japanese into believing that the Soviet Union was to maintain neutrality, it created the strategic problem of how to justify the war against Japan in violation of the neutrality pact.

In this respect, the Harry Hopkins–Stalin meeting from May 26 to June 6 had major significance.[10] In the conversations dealing with the question about the war in Asia at the third meeting on May 28, Hopkins pledged that the question of issuing an ultimatum to Japan would be placed on the agenda of the forthcoming Potsdam Conference. The ultimatum, in which the Soviet Union would be invited to join, would justify the violation because the commitment to the Allies would supersede its commitment to the neutrality pact, which the Soviet government had already renounced. This was similar to the logic used by Japan's foreign minister Matsuoka Yosuke, who, although instrumental in negotiating the neutrality pact, had argued, after the German attack on the Soviet Union on June 22, 1941, that Japan should attack the Soviet Union in violation of the pact it had just concluded on the grounds that Japan's commitment to the Tripartite Pact should supersede its commitment to the neutrality pact. The only difference was that Matsuoka's argument did not prevail in 1941, while Stalin did attack Japan in 1945.

Two additional matters of significance were brought up at the Hopkins-Stalin meetings. First, Stalin reaffirmed the Soviet commitment to enter the war against Japan and told Hopkins that preparations would be completed by August 8. Although Stalin's statement should not be taken as a pledge to launch an attack precisely on August 8, as is often asserted, it is important to note that Stalin continued the policy to maintain the Yalta framework. His pledge to enter the war against Japan was meant to induce the U.S. government's continued adherence to the Yalta Agreement.

Second, he supported the U.S. policy to impose unconditional surrender on Japan. To Stalin the destruction of the emperor system would be necessary to eradicate the sources of Japanese militarism, but also, so long as the Japanese would resist unconditional surrender, it would serve as a convenient pretext to prolong the war long enough for the Soviet Union to join it.[11]

Japan's Dilemma

By June, Japan's policy makers came to the conclusion that the war was lost and that now it was time to contemplate how to end it. The army high command took the position that the best way to end the war was to wage a last decisive battle against the expected American attack in Kyushu (Ketsu-Go Operation) to secure surrender terms favorable for Japan. In contrast, the peace party considered it necessary to terminate the war as quickly as possible if Japan were to maintain its national sovereignty and territorial integrity without jeopardizing the *kokutai*. The most important change in June in the relations between the peace party and the war party was the emperor's change of mind from "the one-last-battle-before-surrender position" advocated by the war party to "immediate peace."[12]

It is important to stress two factors in Japan's policy to seek termination of the war. First, despite differences, both parties agreed on one thing: the minimal condition for surrender should be the preservation of the *kokutai*. Without it, they were prepared to continue the war to the bitter end. But oddly, the policy makers never clearly defined what specific values constituted the *kokutai*. Navy Chief of Staff Toyoda Soemu later testified, "Strangely enough, in spite of the fact that numerous arguments on the eve of surrender took place, concerning the question of 'safeguarding the National Polity' [*kokutai*] . . . , those arguments never included any discussion as to what was the meaning of the term 'National Polity' or what sort of conditions were involved in the word 'safeguarding.'"[13]

Within a small circle around Rear Admiral Takagi Sokichi, who served as the brain of the peace party, however, two ingredients of this concept—the emperor's political role and the preservation of the imperial house—were clearly delineated. Takagi himself was prepared to jettison the first to preserve the second as the minimum condition for surrender. This idea was also shared by the high officials within the Foreign Ministry as well as the former prime minister Konoe Fumimaro. There existed, therefore, a very important common ground between the Japanese peace party and those within the U.S. government who advocated the redefinition of unconditional surrender.[14]

Second, despite the differences between the war party and the peace party, they agreed on the importance of keeping the Soviet Union neutral, albeit for different reasons. For the war party, Soviet neutrality was the sine qua non without which the entire Ketsu-Go Operation would be impossible. For the peace party, Soviet mediation provided the only hope to end the war without accepting unconditional surrender, and, as far as the Foreign Ministry and Foreign Minister Togo Shigenori were concerned, they wished to use Moscow as a conduit to the Allies.[15]

As the military situation went from bad to worse, the Soviet Union occupied a more and more important position in Japan's foreign and military policy. In June the Foreign Ministry sent former prime minister Hirota Koki to Soviet ambassador Iakov Malik to explore the possibility of renegotiating the neutrality pact or even elevating Soviet-Japanese relations to a higher level of cooperation. While the Japanese wasted precious time in these futile negotiations, the Soviets exploited the Japanese overtures to make secret preparations for the war against Japan. When the Hirota-Malik negotiations failed, the Japanese government, with the tacit approval of the army minister and the army chief of staff, decided to seek Soviet mediation to end the war, sending Prince Konoe to Moscow as the emperor's special envoy. On July 12, five days before the Potsdam Conference began, Togo sent a telegram instructing Ambassador Sato Naotake in Moscow to request that the Soviet government mediate for the termination of the war and receive Prince Konoe as the emperor's special envoy for this purpose. Togo warned, however, that as long as the Allies adhered to unconditional surrender, Japan had no choice but to fight the war to the bitter end.[16] This telegram was intercepted by the American code-breaking operation called Magic, and buoyed the hopes of Stimson, McCloy, and Forrestal that the modification of the terms would hasten Japan's surrender.

The Potsdam Conference

The Potsdam Conference of the Big Three (Truman, Stalin, and Churchill—later replaced by Clement Attlee) was a decisive turning point for the outcome of the Pacific War. The successful detonation of the atomic bomb in New Mexico on July 16, one day before the opening of the conference, changed the dynamics of U.S.-Soviet relations with regard to the war against Japan. The atomic bomb provided Truman with the answer to the two dilemmas he had faced. First, it gave him the possibility of ending the war before the Soviets entered it. Second, it gave him the possibility of securing Japan's defeat without compromising the principle of unconditional surrender.[17]

On July 2, Stimson had already given Truman a draft proposal for a joint ultimatum to be issued to Japan at the Potsdam Conference. This draft contained two crucial points. First, it expected the Soviet Union to join the ultimatum. In fact, the Operation Division (OPD) of the U.S. Army General Staff, which was most responsible for writing this draft for Stimson, considered that the ultimatum would best be timed to coincide with Soviet participation in the war. The second important point of Stimson's draft was that it contained the provision in Paragraph 12 that allowed the Japanese to maintain "a constitutional monarchy under the present dynasty." In fact, as far as Stimson and the OPD were concerned, this provision was the linchpin of the ultimatum, since they believed that this promise would induce the moderate elements in Japan to accept surrender before the scheduled U.S. invasion of the Japanese homeland. On July 13, the OPD sent the following memo to the Joint Chiefs of Staff:

> The primary intention in issuing the proclamation is to induce Japan's surrender and thus avoid the heavy casualties implied in a fight to the finish. It is almost universally accepted that the basic point on which acceptance of surrender terms will hinge lies in the question of the disposition of the Emperor and his dynasty. Therefore, from the military point of view it seems necessary to state unequivocally what we intended to do with regard to the Emperor.[18]

Before the final Potsdam Proclamation was issued on July 26, however, Truman and Secretary of State James F. Byrnes made two revisions to Stimson's draft. First, they rejected Soviet participation in the joint ultimatum. In fact, while they consulted the British on the contents of the Potsdam Proclamation, they completely excluded the Soviet delegation from any deliberation on the joint ultimatum. Second, they dropped the passage that allowed the Japanese to maintain the constitutional monarchy. Thus, the final Potsdam Proclamation, signed by Truman, Churchill, and Chiang Kai-shek, but not by Stalin, failed to include any clarifications about the fate of the emperor and the imperial house.[19]

On his first meeting with Truman on July 17, Stalin had already demonstrated Soviet readiness to cooperate with the Western Allies by reaffirming the commitment to enter the war against Japan by the middle

of August, and on the following day he even revealed to Truman that the
Japanese government had requested Soviet mediation to end the war,
which he said he would ignore "to lull the Japanese to sleep." What Stalin
tried to impress upon Truman as a goodwill gesture was meant to secure
an American invitation to append Stalin's signature to the joint ultimatum, which would serve as the justification to violate the neutrality pact.

Did Truman welcome Stalin's pledge to join the war? Those who reject
the view that the Soviet factor played a role in Truman's decision to drop
the atomic bomb refer to Truman's own writings as evidence. Truman
wrote in his diary: "He [Stalin]'ll be in the Japan War on August 15th. Fini
Japs when that comes about." He also wrote in his memoirs: "There were
many reasons for my going to Potsdam, but the most urgent, to my mind,
was to get from Stalin a personal reaffirmation of Russia's entry into the
war against Japan, a matter which our military chiefs were most anxious
to clinch. This I was able to get from Stalin in the very first days of the conference." After the first day of the conference, he wrote to his wife, Bess:
"Stalin goes to war August 15th with no strings on it. I'll say that we'll end
the war a year sooner now, and think of the kids who won't be killed. That
is the important thing."[20]

Despite Truman's words, there is a substantial body of evidence that
Truman and Byrnes decided to drop the atomic bombs to end the war before Soviet entry. As early as July 17, Byrnes told Stimson that he and Tru-
man had worked out a "timetable."[21] After the war, Byrnes told historian
Herbert Feis: "having reached the conclusion that it would be a disaster
for the United States and China if the Soviet Union entered the Pacific
War. This led to the thought that it would be just as well, if not better, if
Stalin were not too fully aware of the potentialities of the atomic bomb, for
otherwise he might hasten Soviet entry into the war."[22] Forrestal wrote:
"Byrnes said he was anxious to get the Japanese affair over with before the
Russians got in with particular reference to Dairen and Port Arthur."[23]

Truman, too, indicated the use of the atomic bombs as a means to end
the war before the Soviets entered it. Stimson wrote in the diary about his
meeting with Truman on July 23:

> He [Truman] told me that he had the warning message which we prepared on
> his desk, and had accepted our most recent change in it, and that he proposed
> to shoot it out as soon as he heard the definite day of the operation [i.e., drop-
> ping the atomic bombs]. We had a brief discussion about Stalin's recent expan-

sions and he confirmed what I have heard. But he told me that the United States was standing firm and he was apparently relying greatly upon the information as to S-1 [the atomic bomb project].[24]

The following day, when Stimson brought the telegram from his assistant, George L. Harrison, about the timing of the atomic bomb deployment, the secretary of war noted in his diary, "I then showed him the telegram which had come last evening from Harrison giving the dates of the operations. He said that was just what he wanted, that he was highly delighted and that it gave him his cue for his warning [the Potsdam Proclamation]."[25]

These passages demonstrate that not only Byrnes but also Truman connected the timing of the Potsdam Proclamation and the timing of the atomic bomb, with the desire to prevent what they saw as Soviet expansionism.

Stalin's suspicion about the American motivation was first piqued by a half-truth that Truman told him about the atomic bomb, describing it nonchalantly as a "weapon of enormous destructive capacity" without specifically identifying it as the atomic bomb. Stalin knew then exactly what Truman was talking about, although the Soviet leader may not have expected that the United States would use the weapon so soon.

But the issuance of the joint ultimatum, without Stalin's signature and without any consultation with the Soviet delegation in violation of what Hopkins had promised in May, was a greater shock to Stalin. On July 26, Molotov asked Byrnes to delay the issuance of the ultimatum, but Byrnes rejected this request on the grounds that the proclamation had already been released to the press. Three days later, Stalin requested through Molotov that the United States, Britain, and China invite the Soviet government to join the joint ultimatum. Truman flatly refused. Stalin now realized that Truman was determined to secure Japan's surrender without the Soviet Union. The race between Truman and Stalin—and the race between the atomic bomb and the Soviet entry into the war—began in earnest.

When the Potsdam Proclamation was issued, the Japanese government immediately noticed two things. First, it said nothing about the fate of the emperor and the imperial institution. Second, Stalin did not sign it. The Japanese decided to "ignore" it for the time being, while continuing to seek Moscow's mediation for ending the war. Stalin's failure to get himself invited to sign the joint ultimatum served to prolong the war, thus ironically working in his favor.[26]

Hiroshima and Soviet Entry into the War

On July 16, one day before the Potsdam Conference began, Stalin asked Marshal Aleksandr Vasilevskii, commander of the Far Eastern Front, if it would be possible to move up the date of the Soviet offensive against the Japanese forces in Manchuria by ten days to August 1. Vasilevskii replied that "the concentration of the troops and the transportation of essential war supplies would not allow" a change in the date of attack. The large-scale Manchurian operation, in an area four times as large as France, had been carefully prepared, and it was supposed to be a surprise attack initiated simultaneously on all fronts. Vasilevskii's reluctance to comply with Stalin's request was understandable, and Stalin, for the time being, respected the view of his commander in chief.

On August 3, however, Vasilevskii proposed to hasten the attack by one or two days before the designated date of August 11. It is possible to speculate, although no documentary evidence exists to prove it, that this suggestion was prompted by Stalin's request, which he must have made from Potsdam. On the day that Truman rejected Stalin's request to sign the Potsdam Proclamation, Stalin reorganized the Far Eastern front and formally appointed Vasilevskii (not pseudonym Vasil'ev until then) as its commander. But the Stavka (Soviet general headquarters) ruled it unwise to change the date of attack so late in the game when all were carefully prepared to synchronize the attacks "on the same time on the same day on all three fronts."[27]

It was the United States that made the first successful move. On August 6, the B-29 bomber the *Enola Gay* dropped the atomic bomb on Hiroshima. Truman, who received the news on the USS *Augusta* off Newfoundland on his way back to the United States, was overjoyed. Having a hard time containing his excitement, he jubilantly declared, "This is the greatest thing in history." In contrast, Stalin, who returned to Moscow on August 5 to resume his frantic activities, retreated from the Kremlin, presumably depressed by the news. Stalin must have thought that he had lost the race, convinced that the atomic bomb would promptly force Japan to surrender before the Soviets entered the war.

But the atomic bombing of Hiroshima did not change Japan's policy of seeking Moscow's mediation, although it certainly injected a sense of urgency. On August 7, Togo sent a telegram to Sato in Moscow, instructing him to seek an appointment with Molotov as quickly as possible to find out

Moscow's answer to Japan's pending request to receive Prince Konoe. Sato contacted the commissariat of foreign affairs on that day to make an appointment with Molotov. This was the first reaction to the outside world by the Japanese government to the atomic bombing on Hiroshima.

This request must have made Stalin realize that Japan had not yet surrendered. He reacted swiftly. He immediately ordered the military to advance the date of attack by forty-eight hours, to midnight of August 9, Far Eastern time (6 P.M. of August 8, Moscow time). Molotov finally agreed to meet Sato and asked the Japanese ambassador to come to his office at 5 P.M. on August 8. When this news reached Japan, all policy makers' attention was focused on how Molotov would respond to Japan's request for mediation.

As soon as Sato entered his office at the designated time, Molotov immediately read the Soviet declaration of war against Japan. The declaration stated that because Japan rejected the Potsdam Proclamation (it did not), which the Allies had asked the Soviet government to join (they had not), the Soviet government would find itself in a state of war with Japan as of midnight on August 9. Within one hour after Sato received the declaration of war, Soviet tanks and airplanes crossed the Manchurian border. Stalin managed to join the war in the nick of time. Truman and Byrnes were disappointed by this news.[28]

In contrast to the atomic bombing on Hiroshima, the Soviet entry into the war prompted Japanese policy makers into immediate action. The Supreme War Council or the Big Six meeting, consisting of Prime Minister Suzuki Kantaro, Foreign Minister Togo Shigenori, Army Minister Anami Korechika, Navy Minister Yonai Mitsumasa, Army Chief of Staff Umezu Yoshijiro, and Navy Chief of Staff Toyoda Soemu, which had not been held for two days even after the atomic bombing of Hiroshima, was immediately summoned on the morning of August 9. Only after the Soviets entered the war did the Japanese government, for the first time, confront the question of whether it should terminate the war on the conditions stipulated by the Potsdam Proclamation. But if the atomic bombing of Hiroshima did not immediately lead to Japan's decision to surrender, neither did the Soviet entry into the war. The Big Six were hopelessly divided. Only Togo advocated acceptance of the Potsdam terms, with one condition: preservation of the imperial house. But Army Minister Anami, Army Chief of Staff Umezu, and Navy Chief of Staff Toyoda insisted on attaching three additional conditions with regard to war crimes trials, occupation, and disarmament.

It was during the intense debate on the surrender terms among the Japanese policy makers that for the first time they confronted the issue of how to define the *kokutai*. During the Big Six meeting, Togo attempted to define it as preservation of the imperial house. When Prime Minister Suzuki Kantaro reported in the early afternoon of August 9 to Privy Seal Marquis Kido Koichi, the emperor's trusted adviser, about the stalemate of the Big Six meeting, he told Kido that the Big Six majority were in favor of four conditions to terminate the war. Although this position was tantamount to rejecting the Potsdam terms, Kido at first accepted it, indicating strongly that Hirohito also shared this view. Pressured by Prince Konoe, former foreign minister Shigemitsu Mamoru, Prince Takamatsu, Hirohito's younger brother, and Takagi Sokichi's group, Kido finally changed his view and had an important meeting with the emperor. It was then that the scenario for the "emperor's sacred decision"—the imposition of the emperor's decision to surrender on the military and the nation—was hatched.

Although there is no record of what Hirohito and Kido talked about at this unusually long meeting that afternoon, it is possible to surmise that the emperor resisted the narrow definition of the *kokutai* as preservation of the imperial house and expanded it to include the emperor's political rule as defined by the Meiji Constitution. When the Big Six and their secretaries were summoned to the imperial conference held from 11:50 P.M. on August 9 to 2:30 A.M. on August 10, the participants saw on the table a printed copy of Togo's proposal to accept the Potsdam terms with one condition, but this condition was altered to "preservation of the status of the emperor within the national laws."

This condition changed again, due to the intervention of Baron Hiranuma Kiichiro, chairman of the Privy Council and an ultranationalist. Hiranuma argued that the *kokutai* was the national essence that transcended the national law; hence the condition to be attached for acceptance of the Potsdam terms should be changed to: "on the understanding that the Allied Proclamation would not comprise any demand which would prejudice the prerogatives of His Majesty as a Sovereign Ruler." No one, including the emperor himself, challenged the prevailing orthodoxy presented by Hiranuma, but this change made it impossible for the United States to accept Japan's reply. At the end of the conference Hirohito spoke and endorsed Togo's proposal with one condition as amended by Hiranuma. The first "sacred decision" was made.[29]

The Byrnes Note and the Emperor's Second Intervention

When Japan's conditional acceptance of the Potsdam Proclamation was relayed to Washington, the Truman cabinet was divided on whether the U.S. government should accept it. Although Stimson, Leahy, and Forrestal favored acceptance, Byrnes opposed it.[30] Truman supported Byrnes, and the Secretary of State composed the Byrnes Note, which stipulated that the emperor and the Japanese government would be subject to the Supreme Commander of the Allied Powers and that the ultimate form of government would be determined by the freely expressed will of the Japanese people.

The Byrnes Note provoked a counterattack by Japan's war party and nearly wrecked its surrender decision. Met with Anami's and Hiranuma's arguments that the Byrnes Note was tantamount to the rejection of the *kokutai*, Suzuki wavered. In the cabinet meeting on August 12, Togo was the only one who stood firm in favor of accepting the Byrnes Note, while his important ally Navy Minister Yonai kept silent. Hard-line staff officers in the Army General Staff began plotting a coup, with Army Minister Anami showing sympathy with the plotters. Togo himself was contemplating resignation. Japan's decision to surrender was in grave danger of being overturned.

Two factors intervened to turn the tide toward surrender. First, there was a concerted effort by the second-tier players within the peace party— Cabinet Secretary Sakomizu Hisatsune, Deputy Foreign Minister Matsumoto Shun'ichi, and Takagi Sokichi's circle of advisers—to regroup the peace party leaders and to pressure their superiors into arranging a second imperial conference. Second, Hirohito, assisted by Kido, asserted more active leadership for accepting the Byrnes Note. He convened the imperial household conference to attain unanimity among the imperial family for his decision, preventing any members of the imperial family from colluding with radical army officers to derail the surrender. Hirohito and Kido also heavily leaned on wavering Suzuki to stand firm to support the emperor's decision.

The second imperial conference was held on the morning of August 14, where Hirohito spoke in favor of unconditionally accepting the Byrnes Note. The army high command, under Army Chief of Staff Umezu, quickly unified the army to support the emperor's decision, thus isolating the coup plotters and Army Minister Anami. The coup engineered by the radical staff officers in the General Staff managed to occupy the Imperial Palace, virtually holding the emperor as a hostage, but without the crucial support of the army high command it fizzled out. At noon on August 15, Hirohito broadcast the imperial rescript on the termination of the war. The Pacific War was nearly over, but not completely.[31]

Truman, Stalin, and the Kurils

When Truman received the emperor's unconditional acceptance of the Byrnes Note, he said, "The guns are silenced." But this statement was premature, because the emperor's acceptance of surrender prompted Stalin to speed up the occupation of Manchuria, the northern half of Korea, southern Sakhalin, and, more important, to launch the Kuril-Hokkaido operation. Stalin's objective was to complete the physical occupation of the territories promised by the Yalta Agreement, and if possible beyond, before Japan formally signed the surrender documents. He accomplished almost all his objectives by ruthlessly combining military operations with skillful diplomatic maneuvers. Truman acceded to Stalin's demand to occupy the entire Kurils, including Shikotan and the Habomai groups that should have belonged to the American occupation zone, but he adamantly rejected Stalin's demands to transform the Supreme Commandership in Japan into a joint commandership headed by MacArthur and Vasilevskii, to occupy the northern half of Hokkaido, and to create a Soviet occupation zone in Tokyo.

The fierce maneuvering between the United States and the Soviet Union over Dairen, Korea, and especially the Kurils and Hokkaido—a final act in the drama of the ending of the Pacific War, an issue that has largely been ignored by historians—must be placed in the context of the "race" between the United States and the Soviet Union that preceded it.[32]

The Impact of the Atomic Bombs and the Soviet Entry on Japan's Decision to Surrender

Although challenged by revisionist historians, the standard American interpretation, supported by the widest segment of public opinion, has been that the atomic bombings of Hiroshima and Nagasaki ended the war. This is simply a myth that has little relationship to historical facts.[33]

Even after the atomic attack on Hiroshima on August 6, the Japanese government continued to seek the termination of the war through Moscow's mediation, that is to say, the government and the emperor continued to adhere to the policy that they had pursued since June and even after the Potsdam Proclamation. Nor is there any evidence to indicate that the cabinet made a decision to accept the Potsdam Proclamation immediately after the atomic bomb was dropped on Hiroshima, contrary to the contention advanced by some historians.[34] On August 7, Togo sent an urgent telegram to Sato instructing him to meet Molotov immediately to find out Moscow's answer to Japan's pending request for mediation to end the war.[35] Hasunuma Shigeru, the emperor's chief aide de camp, who accompanied the emperor like his shadow wherever he went, testified that the atomic bomb on Hiroshima did not influence the emperor's view.[36]

In contrast, the Soviet invasion of Manchuria on August 9 was a great shock to Japanese policy makers. It represented the bankruptcy of the policy to seek an end to the war through Moscow's mediation, and it punctured a gaping hole in the Ketsu-go strategy that the Japanese military had hoped to implement in anticipation of the American invasion of Kyushu. Only after the Soviet invasion did the Japanese government begin discussing seriously the possibility of accepting the Potsdam Proclamation. The Supreme War Council, which was not convened for two days after the atomic bombing of Hiroshima, was summoned hours after Soviet tanks crossed the Manchurian border.

To be sure, the Soviet entry into the war did not provide a knockout punch for Japan's surrender either. The Supreme War Council was hopelessly divided on the conditions to be attached for the acceptance of the Potsdam terms, although the Big Six for the first time decided to accept the termination of the war on the basis of the Potsdam Proclamation. Nevertheless, it was the Soviet entry, not the atomic bomb on Hiroshima, that immediately led the Big Six to accept the Potsdam Proclamation, albeit conditionally. The news of the atomic bombing on Nagasaki reached Tokyo late on the morning of August 9 but had little influence on the outcome of the discussion at the Supreme War Council.[37]

Some historians argue that because the military anticipated Soviet entry into the war, while the atomic bombs were totally unexpected, the atomic bombings were more of a shock.[38] This argument cannot be seriously entertained. Deputy Army Chief of Staff Kawabe Torashiro's diary entries on August 6 and August 9 make it clear that he was more shocked by the Soviet entry into the war than by the atomic bombing on Hiroshima, although his postwar statement to the GHQ interrogators gives equal weight to both. Arisue Seizo, chief of the intelligence division of the general staff, told the GHQ interrogators: "The Soviet participation in the war had the most direct impact on Japan's decision to surrender." Major General Amano Masakazu, chief of the operations department, remarked that although the army thought the Soviet entry was likely in early autumn, it had no way of resisting it if it happened. Navy chief of Staff Toyoda testified: "I believe the Russian participation in the war against Japan rather than the atomic bombs did more to hasten the surrender."[39]

The Soviet entry into the war derailed the Ketsu-go strategy, for which neutrality of the Soviet Union was a sine qua non. The argument advanced by Anami, Umezu, and Kawabe for the last-ditch defense suddenly lost conviction. Both Anami and Kawabe came to rely on the Yamato spirit without any strategic rationale to insist on continuing the war, while Umezu, and soon Kawabe, too, quietly resigned themselves to accepting the emperor's "sacred decision" to end the war.

Finally, the emperor and his advisers feared that Soviet power might eventually extend to Japan itself unless the war were stopped immediately. Prime Minister Suzuki stated on August 13: "If we miss today, the Soviet Union would take not only Manchuria, Korea, [and] Karafuto [Sakhalin Island], but also Hokkaido. This would destroy the foundation of Japan. We must end the war when we can deal with the United States."[40] If Soviet influence were to extend to the Allied occupation policy after Japan's defeat, the preservation of the monarchy could not be guaranteed. This is the reason why the emperor and his advisers decided to gamble on the Americans, whose Potsdam terms left open the possibility of preserving the monarchy.

Paths Not Chosen

American planners assumed that killing a massive number of civilians and destroying cities would shock Japan into accepting surrender, as in today's strategy of "shock and awe." This strategy failed because it was based on a false assumption. The Japanese leaders did not care about civilians; in fact, they were more than willing to sacrifice them to preserve what they cherished most: the *kokutai*. That's why they pinned their last hope on Moscow's mediation.

If the United States really had been interested in saving the lives of American soldiers, as the atomic bomb defenders argue, Truman and his advisers could have sought Stalin's signature to the Potsdam Proclamation and retained the passage that promised the Japanese the possibility of retaining a constitutional monarchy, as Stimson had proposed in his original draft. Had they done so, it is possible, though not certain, that Japan might have surrendered before the atomic bombings and the Soviet entry into the war. It was a conscious political choice on the part of Truman and Byrnes to remove these provisions.

Diplomacy and the Soviet invasion, not the atomic bombs, ended the war. As Michael S. Sherry puts it, "Hiroshima and Nagasaki mocked the fantasy that they seemed to fulfill. For the atomic bomb, like bombing in its other forms, had triumphed not as a weapon of shock that obviated a protracted struggle, but only as a climax to it."[41]

Incendiary Bombings and Atomic Bombings

Why did the American policy makers rush to use the atomic bombs when other alternatives were available?

In his recent book, historian Michael D. Gordin makes the point that until it was used, the atomic bomb was perceived by policy makers as an extension of conventional weapons. They believed that the only difference was that one atomic bomb could kill exponentially more people than one incendiary bomb, a difference perceived as merely quantitative, not qualitative. According to Gordin, that was the reason why the decision to drop the bomb on Hiroshima and Nagasaki was left to the military without presidential authorization, exactly in the same manner that the decision to carry out air raids on Japanese cities was left to the commander of the Army Air Force, more specifically the commander of the Twenty-first Bomber Command. Curtis LeMay, the architect of strategic bombings on Japanese cities, stated in his memoirs: "Nothing new about death, nothing new about deaths caused militarily. We scorched and boiled and baked to death more people in Tokyo on that night of March 9–10 than went up in vapor at Hiroshima and Nagasaki."[42]

Some historians, therefore, argue that the United Stated did not cross a moral divide when it used the atomic bombs, because it had already crossed it when it used incendiary bombs on cities. But how did the United States, which was once horrified by the German strategic bombings on Guernica and Rotterdam and the Japanese bombardment of Tsianjin, Nanjing, and Chongqing, come to accept its own strategic bombings on cities? In 1938 the State Department issued a statement condemning indiscriminate aerial bombing of civilians: "When the methods used in the conduct of these hostilities take the form of ruthless bombing of unfortified localities with the resultant slaughter of civilian populations, and in particular of women and children, public opinion in the United States regards such methods as barbarous." When the war began in Europe in 1939, President Roosevelt said, "The ruthless bombing from the air of civilians in unfortified centers of population during the course of the hostilities which have raged in various quarters of the earth during the past few years, which has resulted in the maiming and in the death of thousands of defenseless men, women and children has sickened the hearts of every civilized man and woman, and has profoundly shocked the conscience of humanity."[43]

This moral high ground began to erode when the Japanese attacked Pearl Harbor. "The shock of Pearl Harbor did not abruptly sweep away moral scruples against annihilation," Sherry argues, however. "What happened instead was a gradual descent into the hell of all-out air war, a descent made so incrementally that its flames and shadows were only dimly discerned."[44] It was President Roosevelt himself who first sanctioned an all-out assault on enemy cities by allowing the Army Air Force to carry out the Doolittle air raid on Tokyo in 1942. Japanese savagery on battlefields and in treatment of POWs helped the Americans overcome moral doubts about destroying cities.[45] Soon civilian deaths in incendiary bombings were not collateral damage, but rather civilians became the primary targets. In February 1944, when Henry H. ("Hap") Arnold, commander of the Army Air Force, recommended to Roosevelt a strategic bombing campaign against Japanese cities, creating "uncontrollable conflagrations," he added almost as an afterthought that the "urban areas are profitable targets, not only because they were greatly congested, but because they contain numerous war industries." Military targets became reduced to merely secondary objectives.[46]

In 1942 Alexander Kiralfly, a contributor to the *New Republic*, argued:

"The natural enemy of every American man, woman and child is the Japanese man, woman and child."[47] After the Japanese government called up all men from fifteen to sixty and all women from seventeen to forty for defense, the Fifth Air Force's intelligence officer declared on July 21, 1945, "The entire population of Japan is a proper target ... THERE ARE NO CIVILIANS IN JAPAN," a declaration that predicted U.S. bombing during the Korean War, and massacres like those at My Lai and Srebrenica. Yet there was a difference between the atrocities committed on the ground and those done from the air. Alexander de Seversky, the author of *Victory through Air Power* (1942), explained: "The kind of large-scale demolition which would be looked upon as horrifying vandalism when undertaken by soldiers on the ground can be passed off as a technical preparation or 'softening' [for invasion or occupation] when carried out by aerial bombing."[48] Soon even this rationale disappeared, and annihilation of cities from by bombing, targeting civilians, became the primary objective in itself.

Behind the justification for indiscriminate killing of Japanese civilians lurked latent racism. General George Kenney, commanding MacArthur's air force, maintained that the Japanese were "a low order of humanity," prey to "his Mongol liking for looting, arson, massacre and rape." Admiral William Halsey, commander of the South Pacific Force, compared the Germans and the Japanese: "Germans are misled, but at least they react like men. But the Japanese are like animals. . . . You have to get used to their animal stubbornness and tenacity. They take to the jungle as if they had been bred there, and like some beasts you never see them until they are dead." Such an enemy had to be exterminated, and strategic bombing was the ideal method. A navy representative to the first interdepartmental U.S. government committee that was to study how Japan should be treated after the war called for "the almost total elimination of the Japanese as a race," because this "was a question of which race was to survive, and white civilization was at stake."[49] Paul V. McNutt, chairman of the War Manpower Commission, advocated "the extermination of the Japanese in toto." The president's son Elliott Roosevelt did not go as far as McNutt, but wanted to bomb Japan until "half the Japanese civilian population" was destroyed. The U.S. Marine monthly called for the extermination of Japanese "pestilence," until "the breeding grounds around the Tokyo area were completely annihilated." The weekly *United States News* wrote in early 1945 that the proper question was not whether the Japanese should be exterminated, but rather "whether, in order to win unconditional surrender, the Allies will have to kill Japan's millions to the last man."[50]

These views that justified incendiary bombings on Japanese cities seem to validate Gordin's argument that there was no qualitative leap from the use of incendiary bombings to atomic bombings. The moral threshold had already been crossed, and the use of atomic bombs was not considered anything new that had not been attempted by incendiary bombings. As Sherry aptly observes, "The destructiveness of incendiary attacks invited attention to the bomb's psychological effect and obliterated any perceptible moral difference between bombing in its old and new forms."[51]

The continuity can be used in two ways. Some, like Sherry, Ronald Schaffer, and John Dower, condemned the incendiary bombings as the major moral descent that prepared the way for the atomic bombings. But to others, the continuity between the two serves to justify the atomic attack. Incendiary bombings killed more people than the atomic bombings; therefore, the argument goes, the use of atomic bombs was not so terrible.

Uniqueness of Atomic Weapons

Gordin's argument that the atomic bomb was considered merely an extension of incendiary bombs is an overstatement. Scientists, military strategists, and policy makers all knew the difference: the atomic bomb with its enormous destructive capacity—one bomb, one city—transformed warfare. The atomic bomb was intended to be used precisely for this new attribute: to shock the enemy in a way that incendiaries could not. More than anybody else, Major General Leslie Groves, commander of the Manhattan Project, and Secretary of War Stimson clearly understood that the atomic bomb was no conventional weapon.

In late April, Groves and Stimson presented the first full report on the atomic bomb to President Truman. The report revealed: "Within four months we shall in all probability have completed the most terrible weapon ever known in human history, one bomb of which could destroy a whole city." It further stated: "The world in its present state of moral advancement compared with its technical development would be eventually at the mercy of such a weapon. In other words, modern civilization might be completely destroyed."[52] No one had feared that incendiary bombs would destroy modern civilization. It is difficult to argue, therefore, that Truman did not know the difference between incendiary bombs and the atomic bomb. In fact, he wanted to have the Big Three summit postponed until the first atomic bomb test. Stimson concurred: it was not yet the time to talk about the atomic bomb with the Soviets, before the United States actually possessed a usable weapon, which he called "the royal straight flush."[53] Two pairs could trump lesser hands, but they were hardly a "royal straight flush."

The Target Committee was created within the Manhattan Project on April 27 and made the decision to use two bombs. "The logic was," Robert S. Norris, a biographer of Groves, notes, "that the first bomb was necessary to show what it could do, and the second would convince them that the United States would produce bombs in quantity. This would give them an excuse to surrender."[54] Needless to say, if the only purpose of using the atomic bombs was to destroy cities and kill civilians, as incendiary bombs had been doing, there was no need for demonstration, and the Target Committee could have chosen to drop them at night. Instead, it made it clear that the atomic bomb should be dropped during the daytime, aiming at the target visually, not directed by radar.

On May 31, the Interim Committee devoted part of its discussion to international control of the atomic bomb. Stimson opened the meeting by stressing the importance of the atomic bomb as "a revolutionary change in the relations of man to the universe." The new weapon could be "a Frankenstein which would eat us up" or it might secure world peace.[55] Stimson therefore reminded the members of the committee that they should discuss the implication of the new weapon "like statesmen and not like merely soldiers anxious to win the war at any cost." The momentous importance of the bomb was clear to them all.

That was why the Interim Committee discussed whether the United States should give a warning or have a demonstration before using the atomic bomb against Japan. In the end, it decided that the bomb should be used without prior warning. Because it was the general practice toward the end of the war to warn the Japanese before a firebombing, urging civilians to evacuate the cities targeted, the decision to give no warnings for the atomic bomb was meant to maximize the impact of surprise and the number of deaths. Here again, the policy makers were clearly aware of the difference between the atomic bomb and incendiary bombs.

When the news of the successful test detonation at Alamogordo was reported to Truman, the president was "evidently very greatly reinforced over the message," Stimson noted. "The President was tremendously pepped up by it and spoke to me of it again and again when I saw him. He said it gave him an entirely new feeling of confidence."[56] In his Potsdam diary, Truman marveled at the destructive power of the atomic bomb, which "caused the complete disintegration of a steel tower 60 feet high," and "knocked over a steel tower ½ mile away."[57] Churchill was delighted to hear the "earth-shaking news." To the prime minister, the news meant that the Allies would no longer need a costly homeland invasion against Japan. Instead of man-by-man and yard-by-yard combat, Churchill now had "the vision . . . of the end of the whole war in one or two violent shocks." Most important, Churchill concluded that with the possibility of using the atomic bombs, the United States would no longer need Soviet participation in the war.[58]

On July 23, General Carl Spaatz, commander of the Army Strategic Air Forces, who had left Europe and stopped by Washington on the way to his new command post in Guam, asked General Thomas Handy, Acting Army Chief of Staff, for a written order to use the atomic bombs. Spaatz recalled: he gave "notification that I would not drop an atomic bomb on verbal orders—they had to be written—and this was accomplished."[59] Had the atomic bomb been considered merely an extension of incendiary bombs, such an order would not have been necessary, because the use of incendiary bombs was left completely at the discretion of local commanders.

Clearly the atomic bomb was perceived by scientists and policy makers as a novel weapon with extraordinary destructive capacity, a weapon qualitatively different from the incendiary bomb and one that had the potential of revolutionizing future warfare. And it was precisely because of this quality, the policy makers hoped, that it would shock the Japanese into accepting surrender.

Denials and Self-Deceptions

In the ambiguous psychological realm between thinking of the atomic bomb as the extension of incendiary bombs and thinking of the bomb as a novel weapon, policy makers went back and forth, moving inexorably to the ultimate use of the bomb, suspending necessary moral judgment.

Stimson's intervention in reversing the Target Committee's decision to select Kyoto as the number-one target is too well known to be described in detail here. Needless to say, the Japanese and the world should be thankful for his courageous effort in saving this magnificent ancient city of temples, shrines, gardens, and artistic treasures. But even in his heroic act, an element of deception crept into Stimson's thinking. To save this ancient city, he directly appealed to Truman and argued that if the United States dropped the atomic bomb on Kyoto, the entire world would equate the action with Hitler's barbarism.[60]

On May 31 and June 1, the Interim Committee decided that the bomb must be used on Japan "as soon as possible, that it be used on a war plant surrounded by workers' homes, and that it be used without prior warning."[61] The decision to use it "on a war plant surrounded by workers' homes" was purposely inserted to quiet the conscience of those who had misgivings about targeting only the civilians. The truth is that the Target Committee had carefully discussed various options, including:

1. use as a tactical weapon to assist in the invasion of Japan,
2. use as a demonstration before observers,
3. use as a demonstration against a military target,
4. use against a military target without warning,
5. use against a city with warning, and
6. use against a city without warning.

Groves advocated the last option. Norris states: "In the course of the war Americans had gradually ceased to distinguish clearly between what was military and what was civilian. Military targets were few and hard to hit, civilian targets were many and easy; and cities were the easiest of all."[62] But the pretense inserted in the Interim Committee's decision, which the Target Committee was fully aware was merely a pretense, contributed to the self-deception of the president, as we shall see below.

On June 6, Stimson informed the president of the Interim Committee's decision. The secretary of war reported that he had had a hard time trying to hold the Army Air Force down to "precision bombing" rather than "area bombing." He was concerned about the continuing area bombings for two reasons. First, he did not want the United States to receive the reputation of outdoing Hitler's atrocities and, second, he feared that the "Air Force might have Japan so thoroughly bombed out that the new weapon would not have a fair background to show its strength." Stimson notes: "Truman laughed and said he understood."[63]

Neither Stimson nor Truman seems to be aware of the contradiction. If carpet bombings against civilians was comparable to Hitler's atrocities, why wouldn't the use of the atomic bomb on a city that had been left intact purposely to demonstrate its destructive capacity be equally barbaric? And why did the president laugh about this serious distinction if he really understood that what Stimson had just recommended was precisely the barbaric act that might earn the United States a Hitlerlike reputation?

After he received Groves's report on the successful detonation of the first atomic bomb in Alamogordo, Truman marveled at its destructive power but added, "This weapon is to be used against Japan between now and August 10th. I have told the Sec. of War, Mr. Stimson, to use it so that military objectives and soldiers and sailors are the target and not women and children. Even if the Japs are savages, ruthless and fanatic, we as the leaders of the world for the common welfare cannot drop this terrible bomb on the old capital or the new. . . . He and I are in accord. The target will be a purely military one." The Interim Committee's June 1 decision to use the bomb against workers' houses was now elevated in Truman's mind to a fantasy, as if a bomb that could disintegrate a sixty-foot steel tower would leave women and children unscathed. And his restraint for dropping this "new destructive weapon" was limited merely to the "old capital or the new." It would be acceptable to drop it on other cities.[64]

In contrast to the president, Stimson and Arnold had no illusions. On July 22, as Arnold recalled, "We talked about the killing of women and children, the destruction of surrounding communities, the effect on other nations, and the psychological reaction of the Japanese themselves."[65] Stimson and Arnold differed on the implications, however. When Marshall had told Groves and Arnold back in May that "we should guard against too much gratification over our success, because it undoubtedly involves a large number of Japanese casualties," Groves answered that he was not thinking so much about those casualties as he was about the men who had made the Bataan death march. When they got into the hall, Arnold slapped Groves on the back and said, "I am glad you said that—it's just the way I feel."[66]

Stimson, however, did not seem to relish the thought of "killing women and children." Probably more than anyone else involved in the leadership of the Manhattan Project, he was aware of the grave consequences of the atomic weapon and the nuclear arms race that was to ensue inevitably after the war, and the implications of the new weapon for the future of civilization. He had desperately tried to end the war quickly, modifying the unconditional surrender demand by promising the Japanese that they could retain the monarchical system under the current dynasty. But there was a strange disconnect between Stimson's profound understanding of the implications of the bomb and his willingness to use it on Japan. How should we understand the contradiction? First of all, Stimson was a faithful servant to the president. He knew where the president stood on the use of the atomic bomb. After he became aware through Magic of Togo's July 12 telegram to Sato, he rushed to the president and pleaded to include the provision modifying the unconditional surrender demand. But learning from Byrnes that the president and the secretary of state had already worked out a "timetable," which certainly meant the timing of the Potsdam ultimatum before Soviet entry into the war, the secretary of war bowed to the president's wish. After Stimson learned of Togo's other telegram on July 21, he made a last desperate plea to Truman. But met with Truman's rejection, Stimson signed off. He left Potsdam, and from then on he never attempted to intervene.[67]

Would Stimson have been completely happy if he had not had to use the atomic bomb? He had presided over the most expensive weapons project to date, which cost $20 billion of taxpayers' money. He was aware of the pressure coming from General Groves to use the weapon and, like everyone else, succumbed to the strong inertial force that was moving inexorably toward the use of the bomb. Perusing his diary entries after he left Potsdam for Washington, one sees the secretary of war immersing himself in the frantic effort to drop the bombs.[68] And later Stimson, like Truman, justified his decision: "The face of war is the face of death; death is an inevitable part of every order that a wartime leader gives. . . . But this deliberate premeditated destruction [the decision to use the atomic bomb] was our least abhorrent choice. The destruction of Hiroshima and Nagasaki put an end to the Japanese war. It stopped the fire raids, and the strangling blockade; it ended the ghastly specter of a clash of great land armies."[69]

Many historians—Bernstein, Frank, and Gordin, for instance—argue that no one in the Truman administration believed that one or two atomic bombs would be sufficient to persuade Japan to surrender, and when Japan surrendered on August 14 it came as a total surprise.[70] To be sure, there *were* influential policy makers and military leaders who did not believe that one or two atomic bombs would end the war. These include

Stimson, Marshall, Arnold, Groves, King, Leahy, and Nimitz. Marshall believed that the American invasion, coupled with the Soviet entry into the war, would be necessary. Arnold insisted on the continuation of conventional aerial bombardment to destroy all the cities in toto, while the navy men advocated the naval blockade, alarmed by the reinforcements of Japanese forces in Kyushu. Groves believed that additional atomic bombs would be necessary. Stimson, Marshall, Leahy, and Nimitz doubted that the bombs alone would lead to Japan's capitulation.

Nevertheless, what matters is the position taken by Truman and Byrnes, and there is enough evidence to indicate that they believed that one or two atomic bombs would be enough to convince the Japanese to surrender. On August 7, one day after the atomic bomb was dropped on Hiroshima, Grew wrote a memorandum to Byrnes that "the end of the Pacific War might come suddenly and unexpectedly," and recommended the names of political advisers to be attached to the Supreme Commander of the Allied Forces.[71] It is likely that this memorandum was written at Byrnes's original request to Grew to provide him with the names of political advisers for the occupation headquarters and, if so, Byrnes was preparing for the American occupation of Japan immediately after the atomic bombing on Hiroshima.

In fact, Byrnes's secretary, Walter Brown, wrote in the July 18 entry of his diary that Byrnes believed that the joint ultimatum without the Soviet Union would be issued and that since the "secret weapon will be ready by that time," Japan would surrender in two weeks. Furthermore, he wrote on July 24: "JFB [Byrnes] still hoping for time, believing after [the] atomic bomb Japan will surrender and Russia will not get in too much on the kill, thereby being in a position to press for claims against China."[72] Forrestal wrote: "Byrnes said he was most anxious to get the Japanese affairs over with before the Russians got in."[73] If Byrnes thought that the atomic bombs would finish off Japan before the Soviet entry into the war, the president must have also thought so; Byrnes was the president's closest and most influential adviser, and the two shared living quarters during the Potsdam Conference.

Stimson's diary for July 23 indicates that Truman instructed Stimson to have a conference with Marshall to find out whether the Russians were needed to end the war. This instruction was given after Truman requested "more definite information as to the time of operation from Harrison [about the availability of atomic bombs for use against Japan]." The implication seems clear: Truman wished to know whether Marshall considered it possible to end the war with the atomic bombs but without the Soviets. Although Marshall's answer was ambiguous, Stimson reported to Truman about Marshall's "feeling that the Russians were not needed."[74] It is possible to deduce from this that Truman was hopeful, if not absolutely certain, to be able to end the war with the atomic bombs before the Soviets entered the war around August 15. This explains the jubilance and excitement with which Truman received the news of the dropping of the atomic bomb on Hiroshima on August 6.

Immediately after the United States dropped the second bomb on Nagasaki, Truman announced in a radio address: "Having found the bomb we have used it. We have used it against those who attacked us without warning at Pearl Harbor, against those who have starved and beaten and executed American prisoners of war, and against those who have abandoned all pretense of obeying international law of warfare."[75] Truman's statement underscores one important motivation behind the use of the atomic bomb: revenge.

Truman's statement raises another important point. While accusing the Japanese of abandoning "all pretense of obeying international law of warfare," Truman never questioned the legality of the use of the atomic bomb in light of the existing international law of warfare. Here in the president's mind, the continuity between incendiary bombing and atomic bombing was taken for granted. If incendiary bombings were not a violation of international law, it followed that the atomic bombing would not violate international law, either.

But on the same day after he made this radio address, something important happened. In response to a letter written by Senator Richard Russell, who had urged the president to use more atomic bombs and incendiary bombs against the Japanese, Truman wrote:

> I know that Japan is a cruel and uncivilized nation in warfare, but I can't bring myself to believe that, because they are beasts, we should not ourselves act in the same manner. For myself, I certainly regret the necessity of wiping out whole populations because of the "pigheadedness" of the leaders of the nation and, for your information, I am not going to do it unless it is absolutely necessary. I also have a humane feeling for the women and children in Japan.[76]

Why this sudden change? According to the diary of Secretary of Commerce Henry Wallace, at the cabinet meeting on August 10, Truman announced that he had given an order to stop further atomic bombing without his authorization: "He said the thought of wiping out another 100,000 people was so horrible. He didn't like the idea of killing . . . 'all these kids.'" Leahy also noted in his diary that "information from Japan indicated that 80 percent of the city of Hiroshima had been destroyed and 100,000 people killed."[77] It appears that this report had a sobering effect on the president. For the first time, Truman realized the clear distinction between the atomic bomb and incendiary bombs. The dawn of the nuclear age began at that moment.

Nevertheless, one should not be too quick to conclude that the self-imposed ban on using more atomic bombs was firmly enshrined in U.S. policy at this moment. On August 11, only three days after he wrote this letter to Senator Russell, Truman replied to a prominent Protestant leader:

> Nobody is more disturbed over the use of Atomic bombs than I am but I was greatly disturbed by the unwarranted attack by the Japanese on Pearl Harbor and their murder of our prisoners of war. The only language they seem to understand is the one we have been using to bombard them.
>
> When you have to deal with a beast you have to treat him as a beast. It is most regrettable but nevertheless true.[78]

Contradicting his statement in his letter to Senator Russell, he reverted to revenge as the motivation for the atomic bombings. The pendulum between remorse and justification continued to the rest of Truman's life. Shortly before he left office, he replied to Atomic Energy commissioner Thomas Murray, who did not consider the use of the atomic bomb on Hiroshima and Nagasaki an immoral act. Truman wrote to Murray: "It [the use of the atomic bomb] is far worse than gas and biological warfare because it affects the civilian population and murders them by the wholesale."[79] Truman's schizophrenic approach to the nuclear weapon is a symbolic reflection of the two diametrically opposite U.S. nuclear strategies—deterrence and war fighting—that have continued to this day.[80]

Proposals Not to Use the Atomic Bomb

In 1947 Stimson wrote, "At no time, from 1941 to 1945, did I ever hear it suggested by the President, or by any other responsible member of the government, that atomic energy should not be used in the war."[81] No cabinet member may have suggested that the atomic bombs should not be used against Japan, but a number of influential scientists and government officials did express grave doubt about its use.

The most famous case is the petition brought by Leo Szilard and two associates (Walter Bartky and Harold Urey) to Byrnes, after their effort to see the president was rebuffed. In May 1945, they traveled to Spartanburg, South Carolina, to the future secretary of state's residence to present their argument that U.S. use of atomic bombs would provoke a dangerous nuclear arms race with the Soviet Union. Byrnes scornfully snubbed their plea. He was "much concerned about the spreading of Russian influence in Europe," and declared, "Our possessing and demonstrating the bomb would make Russia more manageable in Europe."[82] Stunned by this rude rebuff, Szilard went back to the University of Chicago's Metallurgical Laboratory, where a committee to study the political and social implications of the use of the atomic bomb produced what is known as the Franck Report. This report warned that the use of the atomic bomb in the form of a surprise attack would destroy all chances for international agreement "on total prevention of nuclear warfare."[83] Oswald K. Brewster, an engineer on the gas diffusion project, wrote a letter to Truman stating that since the threat of Germany was removed, "We must stop this project." Stimson intercepted his letter and brought it to the attention of Marshall and the president. [84]

Szilard was a scientist and Brewster an engineer involved in the atomic bomb project with little knowledge of the military or political situation in Japan.[85] In contrast, Navy Undersecretary Ralph Bard knew more about the political aspect of the decision to use the atomic bomb. As a member of the Interim Committee, he had initially consented to its June 1 decision to use the atomic bomb against Japan without warning. But he changed his mind. On June 27, Bard sent a recommendation to Harrison. The navy undersecretary believed that the Japanese were looking for the means to terminate the war. If they were given information about the imminent Soviet entry into the war and assurances of the preservation of the emperor, coupled with a warning about use of the atomic bomb, Japan might be persuaded to surrender. He advocated a warning two or three days before the first use of the atomic bomb.[86]

Stimson's postwar contention that "no responsible member of the government" suggested that the atomic bomb should not be used is therefore somewhat misleading. Such dissenting views were voiced by Szilard, Brewster, Bard, and others, although they were not cabinet members. Stimson, Forrestal, and Leahy were quite aware of their views and may even have agreed with them, but they also knew that Byrnes, and above all Truman, did not share them. Byrnes, like Groves, was eager to use the weapon. And Truman sided with Byrnes.

Alternatives to the use of the atomic bomb did exist. Choosing to exclude other alternatives and drop it was a conscious decision on the part of Truman and Byrnes. It would be more accurate to say that no responsible member of the government who had misgivings about such use of the bomb chose to challenge Truman's decision.

Morality of the Atomic Bombing

When the atomic bombs were dropped on Hiroshima and Nagasaki, no nation raised a word of protest. The only exception was the Japanese government, which on August 10 sent a letter of protest through the Swiss legation to the United States government. This letter declared the American use of the atomic bombs was a violation of Articles 22 and 23 of the Hague Convention Respecting the Law and Customs of War on Land, which prohibited the use of cruel weapons, such as poisonous gas. The Japanese protest declared, "in the name of the Japanese Imperial Government as well as in the name of humanity and civilization," that "the use of the atomic bombs, which surpass the indiscriminate cruelty of any other existing weapons and projectiles" was a crime against humanity, and demanded that "the further use of such inhumane weapons be immediately ceased."[87] The U.S. government did not respond to this protest. Needless to say, the Japanese officials responsible for various atrocities committed during the war were not a champion of "humanity and civilization." Nevertheless, can we dismiss the argument simply because it was raised by them?

On August 8, 1945, between the atomic bombings of Hiroshima and Nagasaki, the United States, the United Kingdom, France, and the Soviet Union signed the London Agreement to prosecute war crimes. Article 2 (b) of the Charter annexed to the London Agreement defined war crimes as "violations of the laws or customs of war," which include "murder, ill-treatment or deportation to slave labor or for any other purpose of civilian population of or in occupied territory, murder or ill-treatment of prisoners of war or persons on the seas, killing of hostages, plunder of public or private property, wanton destruction of cities, towns or villages, or devastation *not justified by military necessity* [emphasis added]." Thus "wanton destruction of cities" justified "by military necessity" was excluded from war crimes. In this way, the Allied Powers specifically excluded area bombings from war crimes.[88] In his concluding report at the Nuremberg International Tribunal, prosecutor Telford Taylor declared both German and Allied bombing legal, because "the air bombardment of cities and factories has become a recognized part of modern warfare, as practiced by all nations," thus nullifying the fourth Hague Convention of 1907, which forbade air bombardment of civilians.[89] At the International Military Tribunal for the Far East, the defense lawyers brought up the atomic bombing as a crime committed by the Americans. In his sole minority view, Indian justice Radhabonod Pal condemned the American use of the atomic bomb as a violation of international law.[90] But this opinion was not supported by the tribunal.

In 1951, Japan gained independence by accepting the San Francisco Peace Treaty. Article 19 (a) of the treaty stipulated that Japan waive all claims against the Allied Powers "arising out of the war or out of actions taken because of the existence of a state of war." By this clause, the Japanese lost all legal rights to protest against the American use of the atomic bombs on Hiroshima and Nagasaki.

As Japan was integrated into the American global strategy and Japan's defense became closely linked with its security alliance with the United States, the Japanese government stopped raising any words of protest against the atomic bombings. In fact, the letter sent by the Japanese government on August 10, 1945, remains the sole instance of official protest.

We now come to the difficult question raised in the beginning of this essay: Can the Japanese legitimately question that the atomic bombing of Hiroshima and Nagasaki was a justifiable action? Should the Japanese government's protest that the atomic bombings violated the existing international law be dismissed because the protesters, who themselves committed war crimes, have no right to accuse others of violating international law?

Japanese protest of the American decision to drop the atomic bomb should not be placed in the context of Japan's responsibility for the war, but rather in the context of lawful conduct of warfare. Needless to say, Japan must atone for initiating the war of aggression and for countless atrocities during the war. But the American atomic bombings of Hiroshima and Nagasaki should be judged independently in light of international law that existed at the time. Moreover, the Japanese *and* the rest of the world have the right to raise the question of the morality of the action.

It is worth remembering that those who were killed in Hiroshima were not only 100,000 Japanese, but also 20,000 to 30,000 Koreans, unknown numbers of Chinese, and some POWs from the United States, Australia, the Netherlands, and Britain. At least eleven American POWs were killed in the POW prison, about 1,300 feet from ground zero in Hiroshima. In Nagasaki at least sixteen Dutch prisoners of war were killed by the atomic bomb. For thirty-five years after the war's end, the U.S. government kept the deaths of the POWs in Hiroshima and Nagasaki secret. At Section 82 of the grave site of the Jefferson Barracks National Cemetery in Missouri, eight of these eleven Hiroshima victims are listed, but the site and the cause of their deaths are not mentioned.

Eric Markusen and David Kopf inquire about the relationship between strategic bombings and genocide. Helen Fein, a scholar on genocide, identifies the following five criteria, on the basis of the United Nations Genocide Convention, that spell out "necessary and sufficient conditions to impute genocide."

1. There is a sustained attack, or continuity of attacks, by the perpetrator to physically destroy group members.
2. The perpetrator is a collective or organized actor or a commander of organized actors.
3. Victims are selected because they are members of a collectivity.
4. The victims are defenseless or are killed regardless of whether they surrendered or resisted.
5. The destruction of group members is undertaken with intent to kill, and murder is sanctioned by the perpetrators.[91]

Based on these criteria, Markusen and Kopf come to the clear and unequivocal answer that strategic bombing is genocide. They cite reasons why this conclusion is important. The first and the most fundamental reason is that "government mass killing has been and continues to be a threat to the survival of millions of human beings." And yet our understanding of this threat is rudimentary and inadequate. The authors warn: "Some of the leading nations of the world continue to base their national security on what has appropriately been described as a policy of retaliatory genocide with nuclear weapons." They further state, "Psychologically normal, 'good' people can and have participated in demonic projects. Not only totalitarian regimes but also democracies have been willing to directly engage in genocidal killing, to support client states that engage in it, and to make the preparations for it."[92] If strategic bombing is genocide, the use of nuclear weapons against civilians is also a clear case of genocide.

Unlike Markusen and Kopf, however, who lump together strategic bombing and atomic bombing, I would make a clear distinction between the two by singling out atomic bombing as an extreme case of genocide, much worse than conventional strategic bombing, and a category all its own. The discussion of whether strategic bombing and atomic bombing are genocidal focuses on mass, indiscriminate killing of civilian populations. Along this same line of thinking, Michael Walzer, in his *Just and Unjust Wars*, makes the following remarks:

> If killing millions (or many thousands) of men and women was militarily necessary for their conquest and overthrow, then it was morally necessary—in order not to kill those people—to settle for something less. . . . If people have a right not to be forced to fight, they also have a right not to be forced to continue fighting beyond the point when the war might justly be concluded. Beyond that point, there can be no supreme emergences, no arguments about military necessity, no cost-accounting in human lives. To press the war further than that is to re-commit the crime of aggression. In the summer of 1945, the victorious Americans owed the Japanese people an experiment in negotiations. To use the atomic bomb, to kill and terrorize civilians, without even attempting such an experiment, was a double crime.[93]

Walzer's argument, however, is faulty. In August 1945 there was no necessity to kill many thousands of people in order to end the war. Other choices were available, but these alternatives were consciously not chosen.

There is another problem in Walzer's argument. Like the genocide scholars cited above, he considered the use of the atomic bombing immoral because it was targeted against civilians. But there is another question we should ponder. What if atomic weapons are targeted at military objects and personnel? Is this a war crime, if not genocide? I am inclined to think it is. To argue that some conventional weapons are as powerful as nuclear weapons and therefore to make nuclear weapons operational is to lower the threshold of the use of nuclear weapons. But use of nuclear weapon is properly a taboo. This taboo was broken in Hiroshima and Nagasaki. More than anything else, the immorality of the atomic bombings lies in this fact.

Norman Naimark describes a horrifying spectacle of mass rapes of German women perpetrated by the Red Army soldiers conquering Germany at the end of the war in Europe. In the midst of mayhem, in a street of Berlin, one drunken Soviet tank officer grabbed a German child and threw him into a burning building, instantly killing the boy. The accompanying officer, shocked at the scene, asked his comrade, "Why did you do that? Of what was the child guilty?" To this, the officer answered, "You just shut up, captain! Do you have children? Well, they killed mine."[94]

When Marshall cautioned about consequences of civilian casualties, Groves replied that he was thinking about the Bataan death march. After dropping the two atomic bombs on Japan, Truman declared that he had used the atomic bombs "against those who attacked us without warning at Pearl Harbor, against those who have starved and beaten and executed American prisoners of war." When an act of revenge is elevated from a drunken soldier to a state policy, and the number of victims is multiplied to 100,000, should we cease to call it a war crime?

6

STRATEGIC BOMBING OF CHONGQING BY IMPERIAL JAPANESE ARMY AND NAVAL FORCES

Tetsuo Maeda

In Tokyo, two air raid lawsuits are being heard in the Tokyo District Court. One is the Lawsuit of the Chongqing Heavy Bombings, the other is the Lawsuit of the Great Tokyo Air Raids. The former was filed by Chinese civilians against the Japanese government, the latter by Japanese civilians against their own government. In both cases, victims of air raids are addressing the Japanese government's actions and responsibilities, and demanding apologies and compensation.

Already seventy years have elapsed since the beginning of the bombing of Chongqing, a campaign conducted from 1938 till 1943, while sixty-three years have passed since the bombing of Tokyo in 1945. Nevertheless, these bombing incidents are still very much remembered and continue to evoke a wide range of arguments.

The Japanese government has never fully or officially admitted that it carried out the carpet bombings of Chongqing. In the government's compiled records of warfare, the Chongqing bombings are treated as a rightful attack employing proper tactics of war and with military objectives, and civilian casualties are dismissed as "incidental damage" acceptable in accordance with international law.

When answering the plaintiffs' demand for compensation payments, it is expected that the Japanese government will argue that the aggrieved party has no right to take legal action because the Chinese government renounced its right to compensation for war damages in the Japan-China Joint Communiqué (1972) and the Japan-China Peace Treaty (1978). (Thus far, the Japanese government has not presented arguments in the Chongqing bombings lawsuit. But its position can be anticipated by studying the government's responses in earlier court cases, including the Lawsuit of Bacteriological Warfare and the Lawsuit of Poison Gas.)

The Chongqing plaintiffs, forty Chinese civilians mostly in their late seventies, are hoping to prove the undeniable truth about the carpet bombings of the city. They are presenting evidence from the Japanese Imperial military's operation records at the Japanese Ministry of Defense War History Library, from damage reports provided by the Chinese side, and from testimony by survivors of the bombings, including the plaintiffs themselves. Regarding the question of jurisdiction, the plaintiffs are arguing that they are not restricted in their right to proceed with the lawsuit even though the Chinese government is bound by treaties that limit its right to proceed with war-damage lawsuits. The plaintiffs say the treaties are valid only between the two countries, and thus their demands that the Japanese government make an official apology and pay compensation of 10 million yen per person to the victims are cognizable.

In the other court case, the Lawsuit of the Great Tokyo Air Raids, the victims are also demanding that the Japanese government pay them compensation. In the last months of World War II—from November 1, 1944, to the early morning of August 15, 1945, when Japan surrendered—U.S. forces bombed the Tokyo area over a hundred times. The attacks were especially fierce during the air raid of March 10, 1945, when Tokyo's downtown district was burned out by incendiary napalm bombs dropped by a total of 325 B-29 bombers. The attack killed 83,793 persons, injured and displaced a million more, and destroyed 268,000 dwellings. The above numbers are from records published by the Group of Keeping Records of Tokyo Air Raids in its *Great Tokyo Air Raids War Damage* (1973) and by the Tokyo Metropolitan Government in *The Tokyo War Damage* (1953), and are widely accepted as reliable numbers.

No official monument to the tragedy has been built, and the air raid victims have received neither compensation nor apology. The Japanese government position has been that civilian victims (unlike soldiers) are not entitled to receive official assistance because they are not employed by the government. Former prime minister Junichiro Koizumi told the Diet in

2004 that "soldiers and paramilitary personnel having employment relationships with the government will receive pensions when injured or killed, but civilian war victims without such relationships with the government are not considered eligible (for pension payments)," and thus rejected official assistance for civilian victims.

Countering that statement in court, the plaintiffs argued that during the period in question, the government had declared "total war," and had, through neighborhood community associations, called for all-out mobilization and made requisitions of civilian food, clothing, and housing. They say it is obvious that civilians were systematically involved in the war, which the government started, and suffered casualties during the air raids.

They further argue that, while there is no question that U.S. forces should be challenged for the carpet bombings, which were in defiance of international law, in fact the Japanese military initiated carpet bombing years earlier in Chinese cities such as Chongqing. This is conduct for which the Japanese government should take responsibility; it must apologize for its actions, commemorate those who lost their lives, and provide official assistance to survivors.

The two court cases show that the memories of the air raids are still indelible in the minds of many people, and that these people's pain and anger are directed against the Japanese government. Why are these aged victims of war raising their voices now? For one thing, in spite of having renounced war with its so-called peace constitution issued after the defeat of war, the Japanese government has since revived its military power under the name of Self-Defense Forces. Over the last five years, based on the Japan-U.S. alliance, Japan has forward-deployed these forces to Iraq and to the Indian Ocean. Also, the tactic of carpet bombing has not yet been eradicated but continues to terrorize the global community.

Regarding the Chongqing bombing, the following statement by Japanese supporters of the victims examines the roots of the problem:

Statement by the Tokyo-based support network, "Linking Arms with the Victims of the Chongqing Heavy Bombings"

We are well into the 21st century, but in a sense the wars of the 20th century are not yet finished. Photographs and memories remain from the aerial bombings in Tokyo, Dresden, Hiroshima and Nagasaki, where a new type of war rained terror from the skies, turning crowded cities into bleak landscapes of utter destruction filled with charred, dead bodies. Indeed, the last century was the century of aerial bombings.

How did this practice of aerial bombardment begin? The method was first used in the bombing of Guernica, Spain by the Germans in April, 1937; and then from 1938–1942 in the Japanese military's carpet bombings of Chongqing, the provisional Chinese "resistance" capital. At that time and in that place, a new and barbarous war action that violated the law of war and the International Humanitarian Law began. Because this action has remained unsettled, the offences were later replayed, in wars in Korea, Vietnam and Kosovo; and still now are spreading fear among the people of Iraq. And so we could say that the "wars of the 20th century" are not over yet.

We should not forget that the first chapter in the chronicles of "war from the sky" was written by Japanese forces at Chongqing, and therefore we Japanese must face the backlash of history, and remember that before receiving damages, we inflicted damages on others.

Japan was the first to officially name aerial bombing operations as "strategic bombing" and to carry out air raids systematically and continuously.

Five years before 66 Japanese cities were attacked by the U.S. forces with incendiary bombs, Japanese forces used aerial bombing over 200 times on the people of Chongqing, raining down indiscriminate terror and killing over 20,000.

The Japanese people have neglected to acknowledge their responsibilities in history. By regarding themselves only as the victims of the attacks on Tokyo and Hiroshima, they have spent the long period since then disregarding the events that led to these attacks, such as the aerial bombings Japanese forces launched against others.

Presently, the aged survivors of the "Chongqing Heavy Bombings" have stood up against the Japanese government to ask for historical truth and justice, and for an apology and compensation through the court. On March 30, 2007, they will present the case to the Tokyo District Court. We have established "Linking Arms with the Victims of the Chongqing Heavy Bombings" to support the Chinese plaintiffs. We hereby wish to address the public, asking them to join the movement and help spread awareness.

What should be done? The only reply to this question is to recognize and remember our rendering of hardship to others, and to make apologies for these crimes. On March 27, 1997, the 60th anniversary of the day Guernica was bombed, then German President Roman Herzog apologized to the citizens of Guernica: "The victims of that brutal attack have been exposed to tremendous sufferings. We hereby swear that the horror caused by the bombings of the German Air Force will never be repeated. We wish to extend a hand of friendship and reconciliation and hope for peace for the future for the people of both nations." In 2000, on the 55th anniversary of the British air raids on Dresden, Queen Elizabeth II dispatched the Duke of Kent with an apology to the people of Dresden and a goodwill proposal to sponsor reconstruction of the city's bombed-out Frauenkirche Cathedral.

In contrast, the Japanese government has not made any apologies or even recognized the facts of the Chongqing bombings. May 2007 marks the 67th anniversary of the "May 3 and May 4" barrage, two days when Chongqing suffered the heaviest casualties of the Japanese bombings. We must not waste any more time, we must act out of respect for the survivors and for history.

Physicist and military strategist Patrick Maynard Stuart Blackett gave a classic definition of aerial bombing: "plans to defeat the enemy by destroying their capital cities completely" and "the intention to accomplish fatal damages and achieve the decisive result by using only air force." Since World War I, aerial bombings have introduced a three-dimensional, vertical siege or blockade, which succeeded medieval-style sieges of castles or cities.[1]

Aerial bombing has been described differently, depending on who was doing it and when—for example, we have "area bombing" by the British, "terror bombing" by Germans, and "strategic bombing" by Americans. The Japanese forces used the term "key area bombing."[2]

When attacking remote places in China, such as Chongqing, the Japanese military used the term "political strategic warfare bombing." This is similar to the term "strategic bombing" later adopted by American forces. It is interesting that this term was already recorded in the mandate of strategy for Japanese forces in 1940.

Comparing the power of the U.S. Air Force and the Japanese Air Divisions in the Japanese Army and Navy, the American aircraft were B-29s with four engines, whereas the Japanese used twin-engine Type 96 Land Attacking Aircraft (the Mitsubishi G3M, later nicknamed the Nell by the Allies). The typically mobilized number of aircraft was 300 for the U.S. and 100 for the Japanese, the per-plane bomb was load four tons versus about one ton, and the incendiary was napalm versus thermite. However, despite the significant difference in firepower and delivery platforms between the American and Japanese forces, according to Patrick M.S. Blackett's definition of aerial attacks there were no qualitative differences between what the Japanese and Americans did.

As is widely acknowledged, the effectiveness of aerial warfare was dramatically demonstrated by the bombing of Guernica on April 26, 1937. It was the first time in history that attacks were carried out against a city and civilians exclusively from the air, with a systematic use of incendiary weapons. Beginning one year after the attack on Guernica, in the early phase of the Japan-China War, and continuing through the U.S. entry into the Asia Pacific War some four years later, Japanese forces replayed the horrors of Guernica in Chongqing, ever enlarging the scope of the carpet bombing while developing and refining new methods and features.

The Japanese action began two years before the bombings of cities started in the European war theater. However, because it was happening in the Far East, few in the West were aware that a new kind of aerial attack was evolving.

Chongqing, a commercial city in Sichuan province, in southwestern China, was the provisional capital of Chiang Kai-shek's forces fighting the Japanese invasion. Chongqing is surrounded by a tall chain of mountains and the canyons of the Yangtze River. Chinese people proudly called the city their great rear base, as the natural fortifications made the city safe from attack by Japanese ground forces.

The Japanese forces were, however, determined to attack Chongqing. The high command thought that aerial attacks could damage the political and economic infrastructure of Chongqing and break the morale of the Chinese. This, they believed, would weaken the Chiang Kai-shek regime and lead to its surrender. The air attacks also targeted salt-production locations scattered across Sichuan province, as well as the supply routes used for relief goods arriving from the United States, Great Britain, and the Soviet Union.[3]

Japan first started to build up its aerial war power after World War I, which was late compared with the Europeans and Americans. During the war, the only air attack by Japanese forces was a small-scale bombing of the German army fortress at Qingdao, China. This was launched from a seaplane carrier. Originally, the air forces in the army and navy developed with support from France (for the Army Air Force) and from Great Britain (Navy Air Force).

After 1931, as a result of its continuing war operations in China, the Japanese air force rapidly became independent. Japanese heavy industry was able to produce and develop improved aircraft designs one after the other. Japanese pilots gained combat experience by fighting with the feeble Chinese air force and through encounters with Russian planes during airspace and border disputes. Although it was almost totally unknown outside East Asia, by the latter half of the 1930s Japan had become one of the world's most advanced air powers.

Japan introduced three new aerial warfare tactics during the Asia Pacific War, which were copied by subsequent strategists. The present aerial attack configurations of the U.S. Air Force were developed by studying Japanese tactics. The first tactic was killing by scaled-up carpet bombings, inherited from Guernica and further developed during the bombings of Chongqing. The second was war power projection from the sea, using carriers to deploy aircraft against land targets. This was proved by the lightning attack on Pearl Harbor, which sparked Japan's war with the United States. The third was suicide bombing, which the Japanese air force termed "special missions." This type of attack was initially used at the naval battle at Leyte, Philippines, and peaked at Okinawa, when planes were widely used as manned missiles. The sudden horror from the skies that took its place in wars of the twentieth century had its roots in tactics used by the Japanese forces during the Asia Pacific War. This horror boomeranged back to Japan in extreme form with the disasters of Hiroshima and Nagasaki.

The essential qualities of the Chongqing bombings are also the fundamentals of strategic bombing:

1. Bombing cities, indiscriminately targeting civilians.
2. Mechanical and *insensible* attacks characterized by "the loss of sense against killing"—in other words, ensuring that the distance between the killer and the victim is so great that they are unable to see one other.
3. The repeated use of antipersonnel weapons to bring "terror from the sky"—which led to the development of incendiary weapons.

The Japanese air force bombing of Chongqing was planned to destroy the entire city, so the attacks were repetitive and continuous. Guernica was bombed once, but the Chongqing bombings were mainly concentrated over a period of two years and four months between May 1938 and August 1941, although the bombing continued up until 1943. During this period there were a total of 218 attacks, according to an announcement from the Chinese side, using fragmentation and incendiary bombs. These killed 11,885 persons, most of them civilians. The campaign also employed bombs with delayed fuses, which brought psychological damage and long-term effects comparable to those resulting from the use of cluster bombs in the Iraq War.[4]

The raids were conducted exclusively by air, mainly by Navy Air Force bombers. Unlike the air raids on Nanjing and Shanghai, where ground forces later effected occupations, in the case of Chongqing there were only attacks from the sky—as in the bombings of Baghdad in the 1990–91 Gulf War and in the first stage of the current Iraq War. The term "strategic bombing" was used for the first time, and the object was to make the people of Chongqing weary of war and break their will to fight—much like the "shock and awe" tactics of the Iraq War. The Japanese forces had also manufactured chemical and biological bombs, although these weapons were not used on Chongqing.[5]

The essence of the Chongqing bombing was to target city dwellers, maintaining a distance of several thousand meters between the killer and the victim. Without eye contact, the attackers could behave in a mechanical manner and perform indiscriminate murder. Because the attacks continued over a long time, the bombing of Chongqing can be thought of as an "extended Guernica." Because types of bombs currently classified as weapons of mass destruction had also been prepared, the plan could be interpreted as "Hiroshima before Hiroshima."

The next question is why this kind of warfare was created. The Second Sino-Japan War started in July 1937. Owing to the waiting game played by Nationalists, who sacrificed land to gain time, and to the guerrilla war fought by the Eighth Army of the communists led by Mao Tse-tung, Japanese ground forces were stuck in a hopeless situation. They had been fighting to occupy major cities, but the Chiang Kai-shek regime fought back with a do-or-die resistance. When the cities of Nanjing and Wuhan fell, Chiang retreated to Chongqing, located upstream on the Yangtze River, and established a provisional capital of "free China" there.

Nineteen universities, thirteen newspapers, and literary persons and cultural facilities from all over China soon moved into Chongqing. Many foreign embassies also relocated there. Journalists such as Edgar Snow, Theodore H. White, Agnes Smedley, Carl Mydans, and others visited this resistance capital, often at great risk. Theodore White stayed in Chongqing through almost the entire period of the Japanese air raids. His experiences were related in contributions to *Time* magazine, and later in his memoirs, *In Search of History: A Personal Adventure.*[6]

The Japanese ground forces had pursued the Nationalist army to Wuhan, located on the Yangtze River, 780 kilometers downstream from Chongqing. The Japanese Army occupied Wuhan, but this was the limit of its advance due to the jagged mountain terrain and its feeble log bridges. The renowned poet Li Po wrote about these mountain roads, "How dangerous it must be. And how tall are the mountains. And the Shoku bridge road is more difficult than climbing up to the blue sky." The navy also faced the seething waters of the Yangtze River and its gorges. Continued Li Po, "The crying of the monkeys heard from both sides of the shores are never-ending, and with my small vessel I am passing by the mountains of difficult terrain."

The Japanese Army and Navy considered it impossible to advance troops any farther than Wuhan. The publication *Kaigun Koku-shi* 4: *Senshi Hen* (Navy Air Force History, vol. 4, War History) described the situation as follows; "Since the operations of Army and Navy [are limited], and for the early settlement of the war, the only military force in the position to positively deliver blows to the enemy is the air force. Therefore the attack operations to crush the enemy will be consigned to the air force. The majority of the operations of the ground forces will be to provide airport bases in order to expand the staging areas for the air force. Therefore, the Army and Navy Air Divisions must cooperate to fight positively to overthrow the enemy."[7]

At that time the Japanese government was bound by the statement issued by the then prime minister Fumimaro Konoe in January 1938, announcing, "Hereafter we are refusing to deal with the Nationalist Government of China." Because of this statement, the Japanese government had no room left to move—officials themselves closed the door to peace negotiations. Aiming for a breakthrough, there were political maneuvers under way to set up a puppet government in Nanjing. This plan was contingent on defeating the Chiang Kai-shek regime at Chongqing. Under these circumstances, the idea to use the air force to "destroy the city completely and to defeat the enemy" was adopted. The air strikes were designed to shatter morale and force the citizens of Chongqing to choose between sticking with Chiang or surrendering to the Japanese.

Under those circumstances, the supreme mandate, Continental Command No. 241, dated December 2, 1938, under the name of the emperor, was communicated through the chief of staff to troop commanders. The command ordered that "the chiefs in China are to concentrate on assault aircraft operations to shake and take control over the military and political center of Chongqing." The operations policy was described as "conducting war tactics by aerial fighting to crush the will of the enemy to continue fighting."

In the command's closing paragraph, it was mentioned that "all troops are allowed to use special smoke weapons (red cylinder, red bomb and green cylinder). However, it is strictly ordered to keep the usage of the [poison] gas secret, and when these weapons are used, to take care not to leave any evidence." This sentence reveals their identity as chemical weapons.[8]

The Japanese Army constructed an air force base at Wuhan, with a flying distance to Chongqing of 780 kilometers. The Agreement of Army and Navy Headquarters Concerning Air Operations mandated duties and operation tactics for commanders at the front. For the initial operation, 90 army and 50 navy bombers were mobilized. At the peak period of the attacks, the number of navy bombers reached nearly 200. If escort fighters are also counted, over 300 military planes were involved, which constituted an epoch-making aerial armada.[9]

The bombings of Chongqing commenced at the end of 1938. This was more than one year before the British and Germans would start their carpet bombings in Berlin and London, and more than six years before the Americans started similar attacks against Japanese cities. The main Japanese bomber force comprised the Navy First and Second Flying Squadron and the Army Air Platoon. The twin-engine naval bomber the Type 96 Land Attacking Aircraft was developed as a reinforcement armament to encounter the U. S. naval fleet. Although it had to take off from land and had a maximum bomb load of only 800 kilograms, it boasted an extended range of 5,000 kilometers, more than enough for the round-trip from Wuhan to Chongqing. Production of the Type 96 increased to over one hundred planes, and it became the main aircraft in the force bombing Chongqing. By this time, the new Zero combat fighter had also arrived and was escorting the bombers.

The commander of the Combined Air Fleet was Major General Takijiro Onishi, who would years later develop the kamikaze attack strategy. In charge of operational planning was Lieutenant General Narumi Inoue, who was the chief of staff of the Navy Fleet in China. Inoue motivated his officers and soldiers by telling them that the bombing of Chongqing was "equivalent to the Sea of Japan naval battle during the Russo-Japanese War."[10]

Chongqing is located on a peninsula at the confluence of the Yangtze and Jialing Rivers. The entire city sits atop a sandstone formation, with a series of sharp ridges surrounding an elevated center. In 1938, the majority of Chongqing's population lived in small bamboo and wood houses cramped together beside these ridges. The city center had a modern appearance, while the back streets reflected a more rustic and traditional way of living. Chongqing's total area at the time was about the same as the area of downtown Tokyo bombed in the great Tokyo air raids, and roughly equivalent to the total area of Hiroshima when the atomic bomb was dropped. Before it became the provisional capital of the Guomindang government, Chongqing was a city of about 300,000. In its new role, the opening of government agencies, diplomatic facilities, factories, universities, newspapers, and so on, quickly swelled the population. By the time the Japanese bombings started, more than one million people were living in Chongqing.

It is true that Chongqing was a military center, but it was not a military fortress where large numbers of troops were stationed. Also, unlike Shanghai and Nanjing, the Japanese did not bomb Chongqing in preparation for advances by the Imperial Ground Forces. Thus bombing Chongqing was clearly in violation of "the principle of military objects" in the international law of war.

The 1932 Hague Rules of Air Warfare, Article 24, Paragraph 1, states: "Aerial bombardment is legitimate only when directed at a military objective, that is to say, an object of which the destruction or injury would constitute a distinct military advantage to the belligerent." The article defines the objects of aerial bombardment as "military works; military establishments or depots; factories constituting important and well-known centers engaged in the manufacture of arms, ammunition, or distinctively military supplies; lines of communication or transportation used for military purposes" (Paragraph 2). Paragraph 3 is also relevant: "The bombardment of cities, towns, villages, dwellings, or buildings not in the immediate neighborhood of the operations of land forces is prohibited. In cases where the objectives specified in Paragraph 2 are so situated, that they cannot be bombarded without the indiscriminate bombardment of the civilian population, the aircraft must abstain from bombardment."

While the Japanese government can say that it did not ratify the Rules of Aerial Warfare and therefore are not bound by it, the government cannot remain free from an obligation to recognize and respect the rules as legitimate international law. Although the Rules of Aerial Warfare remained unratified, the Japanese representatives proposed the banning of all kinds of aerial bombing when this law was first debated.

A command paper was issued on December 25, 1938, for the first bombing of Chongqing by the Japanese Army Air Force:

> The Air Force will direct our main attack force to the bombing of the urban zone of Chongqing, and shake the Chiang regime from sky and on the ground. The attack is set for 13:00 on December 26.
>
> The main targets of our two attacking units are to be the Central Park and the Public Security Department in the area of government buildings in the urban zone of Chongqing. The secondary target is to be Chongqing Airport.[11]

By stating that the target of the bombing was the urban zone, the command paper shows that bombing was intended to shatter the morale of citizens. The aerial attacks were planned as carpet bombing from the start. The impact on civilians was not regarded as incidental damage, but rather as an end in itself. Although this act was criminal under the law of war, aerial bombing was not included among the charges set out at the Tokyo War Crimes Tribunal, simply because the winning countries, the United States and the United Kingdom, had committed the same crime.

The air raids were not hit-and-run, but rather a continuous "shock and awe" campaign of shrapnel and fire. The Chongqing operation involved control of the sky and unbroken bombing. The Japanese military termed this "day and night contiguous bombing." To the citizens of Chongqing, it was "fatigue bombing." There were two particularly infamous periods: one was an intensified attack on the urban zone on May 3 and 4, 1939, which resulted in the largest number of casualties of the campaign; the other was the longest unbroken period of bombing, from May 18 to September 4, 1940. Both these events escalated the level of human suffering during wartime to horrifying new levels.

The attacks on May 3 and 4 were the first systematic carpet bombings of Chongqing. Over these two days, seventy-two bombers rained fragmentation and incendiary bombs on the city, and a total of 4,400 people were killed. By comparison, the total number of casualties in Guernica two years earlier was 1,654. The death and destruction from the two days of bombing at Chongqing were unprecedented. Chongqing-based *Time* magazine correspondent Theodore H. White described the bombing;

> The electric power lines had been bombed out; so, too, had the trunk of Chungking's water system, which ran down the main street. There was no light but that of the fires, no water to fight the fires, and the fires were spreading up and down the alleys of old Chungking. One could hear the bamboo joints popping as the fire ate the bamboo timbers; now there was noise, women keened, men yelled, babies cried. Some sat rocking back and forth on the ground, chanting. I could hear screaming in the back alleys; several times I saw people dart out of the slope alleyways into the main street, their clothes on fire, then roll over and over again to put out the fires.[12]

White's writing, together with the pictures of photojournalist Carl Mydans published in *Time* and *Life*, had a great influence on American public opinion regarding Japan.

Han Suyin, a Chinese-Belgian who later became a well-known writer, wrote in her novel *Birdless Summer* about the night of the bombing:

> The crowd rushing through the street with both sides of the close-packed houses already burning with fire to look for somewhere they could hide themselves from the bombing. They were looking for shelters. And they entered a large (bank) building made of stone. And inside the bank there was no illumination except one small kerosene lamp with a feeble flame flickering. But surprising the outside of the building was a sea of fire! On the same night accompanied by the staff of the bank and with about 100 citizens we left the town and found shelter in the building of the branch office of the bank. We had to leave the city because there were rumors that the Japanese airplanes would continue their bombings till Chongqing city was reduced to a heap of debris.[13]

Major Toshiie Irisa, who was in command of the attacking units, also documented the attacks, in the Third Fleet Outline Report:

> The 1st Attacking Unit, composed of 27 bombers, descended at evening gloom from between the clouds and mountain tops to carry out our second bombing

of the day on the enemy's capital city at 20:30. We carried out heavy bombings on the Chongqing Air Defense Headquarters, the Chairman's Office, and the entire western side of the city, and we inflicted catastrophic damage on the enemy.[14]

Over the two days, the campaign comprised seventy-two bombers, 504 pilots and a total payload of 600 tons of fragmentation and incendiary bombs. Not one Japanese Imperial Army soldier had set foot on the soil; the attackers had released their bombs from an attitude of 3,000 meters, introducing people to the bitter taste of terror from the sky. The campaign left 4,400 dead and thousands more wounded. The death toll surpassed that of Guernica to establish a macabre new record for aerial bombing.

The other intensified bombing period, from May to September of 1940, was called the No. 101 Operation and coincided with the beginning of the German blitzkrieg. When the aerial bombings of London by the Germans and Berlin by the English began that August, Chongqing had already been subjected to intense and increasing carpet bombing for two years. In his notes from the front at the time, Squadron Chief Captain Fumio Iwatani wrote, "The Leadership of Operations have at last made up their minds to completely destroy the out-of-town districts as well. Starting from the east side, the districts have been designated as Sections A, B, C, and D, and these are being carpet-bombed section by section."[15] The results of the No. 101 Operation bombings were reported to the Naval Ministry by the chief military officer of the Shanghai Secret Military Agency as follows:

In the afternoon of June 28, a total of 120 Japanese bombers attacked Chongqing and dropped 1,000 incendiary bombs. Due to the high temperature and dry weather, the fires that the bombs started quickly spread across the city. Efforts to battle the fires were in vain as the urban area was transformed to a berserk fury, totally engulfed in flames. Many junks burned and sunk in the Yangtze and Jialing rivers, and countless dead bodies were seen floating downstream.[16]

The hellfire was unlike anything the world had seen before. A brief summary of No. 101 Operation was compiled:[17]

Total days of attacks: Navy 50 days (54 times); Army 21 days.
Number of sorties: Navy bombers 3,627; Army bombers 727; Escort fighters 201.
Total bomb load: 27,107 bombs; 2,957 tons.

Details of attacks on Chongqing city (excluding the airport):
Navy 29 days; Army 8 days.
Number of sorties: Navy 1,737; Army 286.
Total bomb load: 10,021 bombs; 1,405 tons.

Japanese casualties:
Dead in action: Navy 54; Army 35.
Missing: Navy 16; Army 6.
Self-destructed planes: Navy 8; Army 8.

Compared with the Allies' "area bombing" of Germany and the "strategic bombing" of Japan from 1943 to 1945, the No. 101 Operation was relatively small-scale. But it is important to note that while both Germany and Japan had the power to fight back, China had virtually no way or means to counter the brutal Japanese air raids on their cities. When the numbers of casualties are examined, we find an extreme disparity—Japanese casualties are very low and Chinese casualties are very high. This is the nature of the Chongqing bombings—one side systematically slaughtering the other.

But despite the best efforts of the Japanese forces, the ongoing air raids did not break the will of the Chinese people. The provisional councillors of Chongqing passed a resolution stating:

The Japanese Military Clique is relying on their brutal power and they are bombing our rear city with their air armada. Many innocent citizens have been made victims and many cultural organizations, schools, news organizations, and temples have received damages. The object of the enemy is clear. They want to crush our morale of resistance, and furthermore the Japanese forces are trying to establish a plan to reign supreme over Asia. Today we are informing the Japanese Military Clique that the plan to conquer Asia will never become a reality. The grudge they have planted in our minds with the bombings will not be erased, even after a hundred years.[18]

Although Chongqing's buildings and streets were reduced to heaps of debris, the military and civilians worked together to bore into the sandstone beneath the city to build an enormous and sturdy underground tunnel where they could take shelter. The people continued their resistance and maintained their will to fight in spite of the massive civilian casualties inflicted by the bombings.

Japanese military commanders thought that a "terror from the sky" bombing campaign would break the will of the enemy and lead them to surrender. This type of thinking proved false in the case of the Chongqing bombings, and also in other aerial bombings. We can see the futility of attempting to bomb people into submission by studying the reactions of those whose cities were bombed in World War II and later wars. During the Korean War, people in North Korea were hit with more napalm and incendiary bombs than were dropped on Japan in the Pacific War, but they still did not give up. Also during the Vietnam War, the people fought back after the massive "north bombings," which again proved that the bombing of cities does not crush the will of the people.

Eventually the "boomerang" of strategic bombing hit back at Japan with redoubled ferocity in the bombings of Japanese cities. The initial air raid was in June 1944 when the northern part of the island of Kyushu was hit by B-29 bombers, which took off from a U.S. air base near Chengdu, in the same province (Sichuan) as Chongqing, under the direction of the U.S. Air Force headquarters in Chongqing. This was one of the most hard-hitting illustrations of cause and effect in the history of war.

What can we learn from the Chongqing bombings? Let's turn once more to *In Search of History*, by Theodore White:

> More people were killed [in the first night's bombing] than ever before by bombardiers. But what was most important about the killings was their purpose of terror. Nanking and Shanghai had already been bombed; those, however, were military bombings. There was no military target within the old walls of Chungking. Yet the Japanese had chosen, deliberately, to burn it to the ground, and all the people within it, to break some spirit they could not understand, to break the resistance of the government that had taken refuge somewhere in Chungking's suburbs. I never thereafter felt any guilt when we came to bomb the Japanese; when we bombed, we bombed purposefully, to erase Japan's industry and war-making power; no American planes swooped low to machine-gun people in the streets, as had the Japanese.[19]

Through his writings, Theodore White expressed his approval of the bombings of Japanese cities by the American air force. But this way of thinking is a two-edged blade. Today, the logic of terror and revenge provides ammunition for supporters of the "declaration of war against terrorism" by U.S. president George W. Bush and also for supporters of the "jihad declaration" by al Qaeda leader Osama bin Laden. Also, both the Israeli side and the Palestine side refer to the logic of terror and revenge in attempts to validate their actions against each other. To be accurate, it is important to know who started the cycle of bloodshed. The party that has thrown the boomerang of indiscriminate bombing must cease hostilities and strive to make amends; otherwise the cycle of hatred cannot be broken.

At present, the citizens of Baghdad are in the same position as the people of Chongqing seventy years ago. They, too, must regard the bombing of Iraq by U.S. forces as "a senseless terror attack." They, too, must be thinking, "The grudge they have planted in our minds with the bombings will not be erased, even after a hundred years." The side that started the fight should call it off. Otherwise they may have to either surrender or face the consequences. Japan surrendered, and the United States withdrew from Vietnam.

Indiscriminate bombing from the sky wiped out the line between combat and noncombat areas, and made victims invisible to aggressors.

The carpet bombing of Chongqing by the Japanese air forces provided a model from which the American forces' ideology of strategic bombing was born. However, in the end, Japan was unable to continue the war and was forced to surrender. It will be the turn of the Americans to adjust the accounts of this method. The continuing escalation of acts of terror on one side and corresponding "counterterror" reactions on the other suggests the possibility of the frightening emergence in the near future of a terror attack using nuclear weapons. We do not have much time left to stop this development. Regarding the nature of weapons, the following principles can be learned from the history of war:

1. All usable weapons *will* be used someday.
2. The warring party in a disadvantageous position will try to use any weapon available to it.
3. If one party begins to use a specific weapon, the other party will respond with the same weapon, which will increase the level of mutual reactions.

It is not possible to find any cases in the history of war that contradict these principles. There are many examples, including the use of dumdum bullets, poison gas, and unlimited attacks by submarines. This leaves us the important question of how nuclear weapons could be handled so as to make them an exception. We know from past track records that there is no guarantee that any party would absolutely restrict the use of nuclear weapons. Some French strategists from the 1970s issued a worst-case scenario warning as follows: The most dangerous situation would be "nuclear terrorism," of which two possible forms can be projected. One would be terrorism of provocation (an example is the assassination of the Archduke Franz Ferdinand of Austria at Sarajevo in 1914, which sparked the outbreak of World War I); the other would be terrorism of extinction (a group considering themselves victims of political injustice and having their minds set as being a scapegoat would not hesitate to blast the earth at one stroke).[20]

War history constantly repeats itself. Examples of genuine terrorism in recent years include the 1995 Tokyo subway sarin gas attacks by Aum religious fanatics, and the 9/11 attacks of 2001, which were an extension of the Japanese military's manned-missile kamikaze suicide attacks from half a century earlier—adding innocent passengers to the "cargo." Acts of terrorism based on unknown ideals and occurring at unexpected locations continue to shake the world. As nuclear devices take their place on the extended list of weapons, we must, regrettably, realize that the three principles of weapons still apply.

Terrorism is violence based on anger escalating out of control, resulting from a hopeless power imbalance. Therefore we must expect that terrorists will use any available weapons. In November 2001, Osama bin Laden made the following comments: "If the United States dares to attack us with nuclear or chemical weapons, we declare that we will retaliate by using the same kind of weapons. In Japan [upon which atomic bombs were dropped] and other countries where the United States has killed hundreds of thousands of people, the U.S. does not regard their acts as a crime."[21]

If nothing is done, the eventual meeting of terror and nuclear weapons will be unavoidable. The Bush doctrine of trying to suppress nuclear terrorism by threats of nuclear use is fundamentally meaningless, because the deterrent effect of nuclear weapons becomes effective only when based on reasonable judgment and rational preference. Without a firm determination to step forward for reconciliation, it will not be possible to prevent the fall of the imperial United States of America or avoid worldwide acts of destruction on a massive scale.

On March 27, 1997, when the sixtieth anniversary of the bombing of Guernica was commemorated at Guernica, the cultural capital of the Basque people, German president Roman Herzog wrote a letter apologizing for the Nazi bombing and asked for reconciliation with the survivors and the bereaved families of the deceased. The letter read, "We hereby admit the criminal involvement of the German forces. We wish to extend a hand of friendship and reconciliation to the people whom are still suffering from the brutal attacks." The mayor of Guernica replied, "We were wishing and waiting for the apologies of President Herzog."[22] Through this act of contrition, the crime of the bombings of Guernica was settled, and both parties could move forward with dignity, respect, and friendship. Sadly, the Japanese government has still not made any such apologies to the citizens of Chongqing.

7

BOMBING CIVILIANS FROM THE TWENTIETH TO THE TWENTY-FIRST CENTURIES

Marilyn B. Young

SENATOR FULBRIGHT: And this [reprisal raids] was interpreted to mean if we showed the will then the North Vietnamese would surrender. I mean, being faced with such overwhelming power, they would stop. Is that really the way they were thinking?

MR. THOMPSON: "Would be brought to their knees" was the phrase that was used.

—Fulbright hearings, 1968

Airpower . . . can profoundly influence the human condition. Through selective engagement, airpower can support a recovering population; encourage one element while discouraging another; monitor, deter, transport, and connect; and assist in establishing the conditions for a safe and secure future.

—Robyn Read, USAF Colonel (ret.), 2005

World War II ended with the biggest bang then possible, administered in what was believed to be a righteous cause, the defeat of Japan. A total bombing was the logical conclusion to a total war. Then and since, to many in the armed forces, particularly the air force, anything short of the massive use of available weaponry to attain American ends is immoral. "The memory of World War II," Ron Schaffer has written, "seems to have led some air force leaders to feel that all-out annihilation war was the sole tradition of America's armed forces." The possibility of "obliterating everything in the enemy country, turning everything to ash" gave U.S. Air Force generals like Ira Eaker and Curtis LeMay, wholly secure in the air and able to attack any enemy at will, a sense of irresistible power. Limited war was an oxymoron; worse, it was the world ending in an unseemly whimper.[1] The only problem the advocates of unbridled airpower foresaw was the timorousness of a civilian leadership unwilling to use its weapons.

I shall explore in this essay the ways in which the definition of limited war fought with limited means was, in Korea and in Vietnam, slowly but certainly transformed into total war fought all out—short of nuclear weapons. Starting with Korea and undergoing sophisticated development in Vietnam, airpower was understood as a special language addressed to the enemy, and to all those who might in the future become the enemy. It was, at the same time, a language intended to reassure America's allies. And it was a language that incorporated one very crucial silence: behind all the bombs dropped was the sound of the one that *could* drop but did not . . . yet.

On June 25, 1950, North Korean tanks rolled across the 38th parallel, an echo of another blitzkrieg eleven years earlier. President Harry S. Truman's first response to the news was to prepare to wipe out all Soviet air bases in East Asia. His logic was impeccable. The North Koreans were acting as Soviet proxies, testing Western resolve as Hitler had tested it in Munich; the history of politics and warfare on the Korean peninsula prior to June 1950 was irrelevant.[2] His second response, upon learning that wiping out the bases would require time and the use of nuclear weapons, was to open all of Korea south of the 38th parallel to air force bombing. The goal was only in part to halt the North Korean advance. Of equal importance was conveying messages of resolve to Pyongyang and support to Seoul. A few days later, with the same goals in mind, Truman sent the bombers north of the 38th parallel, opening a campaign of destruction that, in ferocity and total tonnage dropped, rivaled the campaigns so recently concluded in Europe and Japan.

What was it about bombing that made it so attractive to U.S. policy makers as a mode of communication? The answer begins with a fallacy: World War II ended in a blaze of bombing, ergo, bombing ended the war. According to Earl Tilford, although airpower has never fulfilled the promises of its prophets, after World War II the "doctrine of strategic bombardment, like the doctrine of the resurrection of the body in Christianity, had to be accepted on faith."[3] Those who doubted the efficacy of strategic bombing were committed to tactical bombing.[4] Colonel Raymond Sleeper, contemplating the post–Korean War future, argued that the objective of a limited war was not the total destruction of the enemy but rather a means of waging "peace through air persuasion." His model was the supple use of airpower to punish and coerce ostensibly employed by the British Royal Air Force in various colonial expeditions.[5] Secretary of State Robert McNamara, with the experience of the Cuban missile crisis behind him, developed this idea, convinced, as H.R. McMaster has written, that "the aim of force was not to impose one's will on the enemy but to communicate with him. Gradually intensifying military action would convey American resolve and thereby convince an adversary to alter his behavior."[6]

What and how one bombed could convey different messages to the enemy: a restricted target list held the threat of an unrestricted one, conventional bombing the threat of nuclear possibilities. Moreover, as in Vietnam, bombing could be turned on and off with greater ease and less domestic impact than sending or withdrawing troops. The alert opponent would presumably get the idea and move toward an acceptable settlement. And if he did not? Well, that was the beauty of it: bombing could be intensified, target lists expanded, new airborne ordnance developed, and the lethality of extant weapons improved.

To garner domestic support for war, images of air war also made striking pictures, preferable to those of ground combat—thousands of bombs tumbling to earth, while their effects on impact were never imposed on the viewer.[7] Raining down destruction has been the prerogative of the gods since before Zeus. Combat troops were as awkward as their nickname, *grunts*, suggested. They were burdened by their heavy packs, moving arduously through steaming or frozen landscapes. Pilots were *aces*, carried into the wild blue yonder at unimaginable speed.[8] It is not surprising that President George W. Bush landed a jet on an aircraft carrier to announce the end of combat in Iraq.

Airpower embodies American technology at its most dashing. At regular intervals, the air force and allied technocrats claim that innovations in air technology herald an entirely new age of warfare. Korea and Vietnam were, so to speak, living laboratories for the development of new weapons: the 1,200-pound radio-guided Tarzon bomb (featured in Korean-era Movietone newsreels);[9] white-phosphorous-enhanced napalm; cluster bombs (CBUs) carrying up to 700 bomblets, each bomblet containing 200 to 300 tiny steel balls or fiberglass fléchettes; delayed-fuse cluster bombs; airburst cluster bombs; toxic defoliants; varieties of nerve gas; sets of six B 52s, operating at altitudes too high to be heard on the ground, capable of delivering up to thirty tons of explosives each. A usual mission consisted of six planes in formation, which together could devastate an area one half mile wide by three miles long. Older technologies were retrofitted: slow cargo planes ("Puff the Magic Dragon"[10]) equipped with rapid-fire machine guns capable of firing 6,000 rounds a minute; World War I–era Skyraiders, carrying bomb loads of 7,500 pounds and fitted with four 20-millimeter cannon that together fired over 2,000 rounds per minute.

The statistics stun; they also provide distance. They are impossible to take in, as abstract as the planning responsible for producing them. In Korea over a three-year period, U.S./UN forces flew 1,040,708 sorties and dropped 386,037 tons of bombs and 32,357 tons of napalm. If one counts all types of airborne ordnance, including rockets and machine-gun ammunition, the total tonnage comes to 698,000.[11] Throughout World War II, in all sectors, the United States dropped 2 million tons of bombs; for Indochina the total figure is 8 million tons, with an explosive power equivalent to 640 Hiroshima-size bombs. Three million tons were dropped on Laos, exceeding the total for Germany and Japan by both the U.S. and Great Britain.[12] For nine years, an average of one planeload of bombs fell on Laos every eight minutes. In addition, 150,000 acres of forest were destroyed through the chemical warfare known as defoliation. For South Vietnam, the figure is 19 million gallons of defoliant dropped on an area comprising 20 percent of South Vietnam—some 6 million acres.[13] In an even briefer period, between 1969 and 1973, 539,129 tons of bombs were dropped in Cambodia, largely by B-52s, of which 257,465 tons fell in the last six months of the war (as compared to 160,771 tons on Japan from 1942–1945).[14] The estimated toll of the dead, the majority civilian, is equally difficult to absorb: 2 to 3 million in Korea; 2 to 4 million in Vietnam.

To the policy makers, air war is abstract. They listen attentively for a response to the messages they send and discuss the possibility that many more may have to be sent. For those who deliver the messages, who actually drop the bombs, air war can be either abstract (in a high-flying B-29 or B-52, for example) or concrete. Often it is a combination. Let me offer an example that combines the abstract with the concrete. During the Korean War, one pilot confided to a reporter that napalm had become the most valued of all the weapons at his disposal. "The first couple of times I went in on a napalm strike," Federic Champlin told E.J. Kahn,

I had kind of an empty feeling. I thought afterward, Well, maybe I shouldn't
have done it. Maybe those people I set afire were innocent civilians. But you
get conditioned, especially after you've hit what looks like a civilian and the
A-frame on his back lights up like a Roman candle—a sure enough sign that
he's been carrying ammunition. Normally speaking, I have no qualms about
my job. Besides, we don't generally use napalm on people we can see. We use it
on hill positions, or buildings. And one thing about napalm is that when you've
hit a village and have seen it go up in flames, you know that you've accomplished something. Nothing makes a pilot feel worse than to work over an area
and not see that he's accomplished anything.[15]

A "hill position," a "building" (in Vietnam, "hooches," sometimes
"structures")—not people. For the man with the A-frame on his back, air
war can only be concrete. In 1950, in the month of November alone, 3,300
tons of napalm were dropped on North Korean cities and towns, including the city of Kanggye, 65 percent of which was destroyed by incendiary
bombs. In Korea, the British correspondent Reginald Thompson believed
he was seeing a "new technique of machine warfare. The slightest resistance brought down a deluge of destruction, blotting out the area. Dive
bombers, tanks and artillery blasted strong points, large or small, in town
and hamlet, while the troops waited at the roadside as spectators until the
way was cleared for them. . . ."[16]

Years later, another pilot, flying a small spotter plane to call in napalm
strikes in South Vietnam, told Jonathan Schell how he identified the enemy: "If they run away." He added: "Sometimes, when you see a field of
people, it looks like just a bunch of farmers. Now, you see, the Vietnamese
people—they're not interested in the U.S. Air Force, and they don't look
at the planes going over them. But down in that field you'll see *one guy*
whose conical hat keeps bouncing up and down. He's looking, because
he wants to know where you're going." Then, Major Billings continued,
"you make a couple of passes . . . and then, one of them makes a break for
it—it's the guy that was looking up at you—and he's your V.C. So you
look where he goes, and call in an air strike." Once, Billings remembered, he "about ran a guy to death," chasing him through the fields for
an hour before calling in planes to finish the job. Schell thought this
amounted to "sniping with bombs," and Billings agreed.[17] For Billings,
the people themselves were concrete abstractions, ideas all too literally in
the flesh.

In addition to the bombs that *were* dropped on Korea, there were those that were constantly contemplated but never used. On June 29, 1950, just four days after the war began, the possibility of using nuclear weapons in the event of Chinese intervention in the war was broached in the National Security Council. In June, as again when the subject came up in July at a State Department policy and planning staff meeting, the questions was not so much whether to use nuclear weapons but rather under what conditions they might be used: if there was overt Chinese and Soviet intervention; if their use were essential to victory; "if the bombs could be used without excessive destruction of noncombatants."[18] Talk of using the bomb increased dramatically after the Chinese entered the war in late October 1950, and President Truman's casual reference to the possibility in a press conference brought a nervous Prime Minister Clement Atlee to Washington on the next plane. A joint communiqué, however, expressed only a sincere hope that "world conditions would never call for the use of the atomic bomb."[19]

General Douglas MacArthur thought the conditions were ripe in December 1950 and requested permission to drop a total of thirty-four bombs on a variety of targets. "I would have dropped 30 or so atomic bombs . . . strung across the neck of Manchuria," he told an interviewer, and "spread behind us—from the Sea of Japan to the Yellow Sea—a belt of radioactive cobalt . . . it has an active life of between 60 and 120 years. For at least 60 years, there could have been no land invasion of Korea from the North." MacArthur's replacement, General Matthew Ridgway, requested thirty-eight atomic bombs.[20] In the event, nuclear weapons were not used; the destruction of northern and central Korea had been accomplished with conventional weapons alone.

The cease-fire that ended the Korean War followed a crescendo of bombing, which was then taken as proof that airpower was as decisive in limited wars as it had been in total war. The cities and towns of central and northern Korea had been leveled. In what Bruce Cumings has called the "final act of this barbaric air war," North Korea's main irrigation dams were destroyed in the spring of 1953, shortly after the rice had been transplanted. "The subsequent floods scooped clean 27 miles of valley below. . . . The Westerner can little conceive the awesome meaning which the loss of [rice] has for the Asian—starvation and slow death."[21] By 1952, according to a UN estimate, one out of nine men, women, and children in North Korea had been killed. In the South, 5,000,000 people had been displaced and 100,000 children were described as *unaccompanied*. "The countless ruined villages are the most terrible and universal mark of the war on the Korean landscape. To wipe out cover for North Korean vehicles and personnel, hundreds of thatch-roofed houses were burned by air-dropped jellied gasoline or artillery fire," Walter Sullivan, former *New York Times* Korea correspondent, reported in *The Nation*. J. Donald Kingsley, head of the reconstruction agency, called Korea "the most devastated land and its people the most destitute in the history of modern warfare."[22]

Freda Kirchwey, in an essay for *The Nation*, tried to explain the general indifference of the American public to the destruction:

> We were all hardened by the methods of mass-slaughter practiced first by the Germans and Japanese and then, in self-defense, adopted and developed to the pitch of perfection illustrated at Hiroshima and Nagasaki by the Western allies and, particularly, the Americans. We became accustomed to "area" bombing, "saturation" bombing, all the hideous forms of strategic air war aimed at wiping out not only military and industrial installations but whole populations. . . . A deep scar was left on the mind of Western man, and, again, particularly on the American mind, by the repression of pity and the attempt to off-load all responsibility onto the enemy.

Kirchwey thought that this repression explained the lack of protest "against the orgy of agony and destruction now in progress in Korea." Nothing the North Koreans, Chinese, or Russians had done "excuses the terrible shambles created up and down the Korean peninsula by the American-led forces, by American planes raining down napalm and fire bombs, and by heavy land and naval artillery." And now Korea, "blotted out in the name of collective security, blames the people who drop the fire bombs," which might seem unfair to the military mind but was inevitable:

> For a force which subordinates everything to the job of killing the enemy becomes an enemy itself. . . . And after a while plain horror displaces a sense of righteousness even among the defenders of righteousness, and thus the cause itself becomes hateful. This has happened in Korea. Soon, as we learn the facts, it will overtake us here in America.[23]

· · ·

"The American mind," Kirchwey was certain, "mercurial and impulsive, tough and tender, is going to react against the horrors of mechanized warfare in Korea."[24]

The air force reached different conclusions. In 1957, a collection of essays was published whose title declared its thesis: *Airpower: The Decisive Force in Korea*. The authors of one of the essays in the collection describe an air operation they considered exceptionally successful. Late in 1952, a small group of air commanders set out to demonstrate the extent to which airpower alone could "occupy" territory. Their intention was to show the North Koreans that the United States could "exert an effective form of air pressure at any time or any place, could capture and air control any desired segment of his territory for was long as the military situation warranted." The campaign began in January 1953. For five days, twenty-four hours a day, "a devastating force walked the earth over a 2-by-4 mile target area" and for six days thereafter nothing in the area moved. After 2,292 combat sorties, "Air forces bought a piece of real estate 100 miles behind enemy lines and ruled it for 11 days." But on the fourteenth day, "with typical Communist swiftness," "hordes" of "Red laborers and soldiers" began repair work; six days after the attack, a bypass was in place and rail links had been restored. The bridges attacked had been rebuilt, as had the highways and rail links. Still, the report was certain, "in the gnarled steel and wrenched earth the Communists saw the specter of a new concept in war—air envelopment."[25] One might imagine that the Americans had a lesson to learn here: that bridges could be rebuilt; that a "curtain of fire" created by such raids could cost the enemy a week's time, but not stop them. Instead, against the evidence, many in the air force concluded that had such airpower been applied earlier in the war, it would have ended earlier and on better terms.

In what turned out to be the final phase of the talks, President Eisenhower threatened to use nuclear weapons if the Chinese did not sign a cease-fire agreement. It has become part of the Eisenhower legend that this last threat broke the stalemate and, in Eisenhower's words, gave the United States "an armistice on a single battleground," though not "peace in the world."[26] In the event, as most authorities agree, the Chinese may not have even been aware of the threat, much less responded to it. Chinese acceptance of the concessions demanded at Panmunjom (all of them relating to the issue of repatriation of prisoners of war) was granted for reasons to do with Chinese, North Korean, and Soviet politics, not U.S. atomic flashing.[27] Nevertheless, in addition to the Republican Party, many senior officers in the air force were convinced of the value of such threats and the necessity, if it came to that, of acting on them.[28]

Whatever the air force learned from the Korean War, what the politicians drew from it was more specific and could be boiled down to one dictum: fight the war, but avoid Chinese intervention. Unlike Freda Kirchwey, military and civilian policy makers (and, for that matter, the majority of the American public) never, to my knowledge, questioned the morality of either the ends or the means of fighting in Korea. The difficult question that faced administrations, from Kennedy through Nixon, was tactical: how to use military force in Southeast Asia without unduly upsetting the Chinese. President Kennedy's solution was to concentrate on counterinsurgency, which, as it failed to achieve its end, devolved into a brutal ten-year bombing campaign in South Vietnam.

Although this reverses the actual chronology, I want to deal first with the air war in North Vietnam, keeping in mind that the use of airpower in the South started earlier, lasted longer, and dropped far more tonnage than in the North. The stated goal of the Vietnam War was to create and sustain, south of the 17th parallel, a stable anticommunist regime under local leadership friendly to the United States. This is what Eisenhower had accomplished in Korea. The assumption of American policy makers, even those convinced the insurgency had its roots in the south, was that the movement in South Vietnam was dependent on North Vietnam for support and direction. North Vietnamese men and matériel fueled the struggle in the South. Sever that fuel line and the South Vietnamese government would be dealing with an enfeebled guerrilla force, well within its capacity to defeat. Some military men, like General Lawton Collins, argued that "no amount of aerial bombing can prevent completely the forward movement of supplies, particularly in regions where ample manpower is available."[29] President Lyndon B. Johnson also recalled the Korean experience in conversations with his close friend Senator Richard Russell of Georgia in the late spring and early summer of June 1964. No one, Johnson declared, wanted to send combat troops to Vietnam. Yet *some* sort of military action had to be taken, lest he be considered weak. "America," an old Texas friend had warned him, "wants, by God, prestige and power"; he had no choice but to "stand up for America." Johnson's advisers strongly urged a bombing campaign against North Vietnam, one that would not risk Chinese intervention.

"Bomb the North," Russell asked, "and kill old men, women, and children?" No, no, Johnson reassured him, entering into that abstract world of
air warfare in which buildings, highways, and structures are destroyed
without killing people, just "selected targets, watch this trail they're coming down."

"We tried it in Korea," Russell protested. "We even got a lot of old B-29s
to increase the bomb load and sent 'em over there and just dropped millions and millions of bombs, day and night . . . they would knock the road
at night and in the morning, the damn people would be back travelling
over it. . . . We never could actually interdict all their lines of communication, although we had absolute control of the seas and the air, and we never
did stop them. And you ain't gonna stop these people, either."[30]

Robert McNamara, the secretary of defense Johnson had inherited
from Kennedy, was among the most passionate advocates of bombing the
North, of "communicating" with bombs,[31] and he now moved to gain approval for this course. On the day of his election victory, Lyndon Baines
Johnson convened a working group of the National Security Council to
discuss the options in Vietnam. The president was offered three options:
to maintain the current level of bombing (including the covert bombing
of Laos, which began in May 1964) in which reprisal raids against the
North would be flown in response to what the proposal called "VC spec-
taculars" in the South; to move at once to "fast/full squeeze"—a rapid and
powerful increase in bombing of the North; or to begin a program of
"progressive squeeze-and-talk," which would involve a "crescendo of additional military moves" against targets in North Vietnam and Laos combined with offers to negotiate with Hanoi. Bombing was a "bargaining
chip" to be cashed in for a settlement on U.S. terms.[32] The possibility of
using nuclear weapons was raised and rejected, although General Earle
Wheeler believed the question remained open and that "in extremis" it
should be considered.[33] The choices were structured so that only one
made sense, what Raymond Sleeper ten years earlier had named "air
persuasion."

On February 13, 1965, McNamara's Operation Rolling Thunder began.
It was the "longest sustained strategic air bombardment in history." At
lunch each Tuesday, Johnson and his advisers would select the targets,
which were then communicated to Admiral U.S. Grant Sharp, the commander in charge of Rolling Thunder. One example of McNamara's effort

to hone the messages bombing communicated was reflected in a target list that included attacking "moving targets such as convoys and troops" but not "highways, railroads or bridges with no moving traffic on them." A frustrated officer responsible for carrying out these orders pointed out the "difficulty of recognizing groups of civilians on the ground from troops. . . . I recognize this as my problem but believe that it can be better defined."[34]

It was especially a problem for the people on the ground. In the first year, 55,000 sorties were flown, and tonnage increased from 200 per week to 1,600 per week. (For a sense of perspective, there were 83,000 sorties in the South in that same year.) Over its course, Operation Rolling Thunder "hammered the north with 304,000 tactical sorties . . . and 2,380 B-52 sorties, which had dropped 643,000 tons of bombs."[35] In an ultimate expression of the abstract nature of the bombing campaign, one presidential adviser, McGeorge Bundy, made it clear that Rolling Thunder did not actually have to work to succeed. Even if the operation failed, Bundy argued, it would "at minimum damp down the charge that we did not do all that we could have done, and this charge will be important in many countries, including our own." Of equal importance, the bombing "set a higher price for the future upon all adventures of guerrilla warfare, and it should therefore somewhat increase our ability to deter such adventures."[36]

In December 1966 and again in 1967, the Pentagon paused and requested the Jason Division of the Institute for Defense Analysis to assess the effect of the bombing on North Vietnam. The report was a "categorical rejection of bombing as a tool of our policy in Southeast Asia. . . ." None of the administration's goals had been met: the flow of men and supplies south continued. Indeed, since "the beginning of the Rolling Thunder air strikes on NVN, the flow of men and materiel from NVN to SVN has greatly increased, and present evidence provides no basis for concluding that the damage inflicted on North Vietnam by the bombing program has had any significant effect on the flow." The expectation that bombing would "erode the determination of Hanoi and its people clearly overestimated the persuasive and disruptive effects of the bombing and, correspondingly, underestimated the tenacity and recuperative capabilities of the North Vietnamese." The government had ignored the "well-documented" fact that "a direct, frontal attack on a society tends to strengthen the social fabric of the nation, to increase popular support of the existing government, to improve the determination of both the leadership and the populace to fight back, to induce a variety of protective measures that reduce the society's vulnerability to future attack and to develop an increased capacity for quick repairs. . . ."[37]

Despite these reports, the bombing of an ever-expanded list of targets in North Vietnam continued; the bombing halt Johnson declared in March 1968 did not decrease the tonnage of bombs dropped on Indochina; the area south of the 19th parallel in South Vietnam, and Laos and Cambodia, now received the bombs that had been more widely distributed previously. Hanoi got McNamara's message—America's unparalleled military might—but did not listen. By the time it was Richard Nixon's turn to communicate with the Vietnamese, there was only one message left: the United States would continue to bomb until it had broken Hanoi's will.

Richard Nixon's contempt for his predecessors' approach to the war was most clearly expressed in a conversation with Republican delegates to the Miami convention before his election: "How do you bring a war to a conclusion?" he asked his attentive listeners. "I'll tell you how Korea was ended. We got in there and had this messy war on our hands. Eisenhower . . . let the word go out diplomatically to the Chinese and the North [Koreans] that we would not tolerate this continual ground war of attrition. And within a matter of months, they negotiated." The notion that the threat of nuclear bombs had brought the Chinese to heel in Korea was, as Jeffrey Kimball, the historian of Nixon's war, has observed, "part of Republican historical doctrine. . . ." Nixon not only believed it, he incorporated its principles into what he called his "madman" approach to negotiations in Vietnam. As he explained to his longtime aide Bob Haldeman during the 1968 presidential campaign: "[The North Vietnamese will] believe any threat of force that Nixon makes because it's Nixon. . . . I call it the Madman Theory, Bob. I want the North Vietnamese to believe I've reached the point where I might do *anything* to stop the war. We'll just slip the word to them that, 'for God's sake, you know Nixon is obsessed about Communism. We can't restrain him when he's angry—and he has his hand on the nuclear button'—and Ho Chi Minh himself will be in Paris in two days begging for peace."[38] Maddened by Vietnamese resistance, the president of the United States would pretend to be crazy.

Johnson's advisers had been convinced they could, as they put it, "orchestrate the violence" and through the exercise of graduated pressure bring about an acceptable end to the war. Richard Nixon brought to the negotiating table the threat of doing *anything,* which is to say *everything,* to end the war on U.S. terms. One version of the madman approach was Nixon's 1969 full-scale SAC alert, intended to frighten the Soviet Union into bringing pressure on Hanoi to make peace on U.S. terms.[39] Other possible threats included a land invasion of North Vietnam, the systematic bombing of dams and dikes, and the saturation bombing of Hanoi and Haiphong. After the war, a North Vietnamese diplomat explained to a reporter the flaw in Nixon's thinking. Both he and Kissinger believed there were good and bad threats: a good threat would be "to make a false threat that the enemy believes is a true threat." A bad threat was one that was true but disbelieved by the enemy. But there was a third category, Nguyen Co Thach observed: "for those who do not care whether the threat is true or not."[40] This possibility, an ongoing refusal to respond to the messages of force, introduces into the militarists' dichotomy an element of uncertainty they have never acknowledged.

The war in Vietnam came to an end, like the war in Korea, with a final act of devastation, one as irrelevant to the outcome of the war as the destruction of Korea's dams had been—an act, then, of pure abstraction. Ignoring the advice of his secretaries of state and defense, Nixon decided to act on one of the plans in his madman scenario: the saturation bombing of Hanoi and Haiphong. "When you bite the bullet," he told Nelson Rockefeller later, "bite it hard—go for the big play." In a reflective mood, he compared his decision with that of Kennedy during the Cuban missile crisis. "Decided," Bob Haldeman noted in his diary, "this [decision] was tougher . . . especially since it didn't have to be made." For twelve days the two cities were carpet-bombed around the clock by a combination of B-52s and fighter bombers that dropped 36,452 tons of bombs.[41] General Curtis LeMay was convinced that had bombing at this level been undertaken from the start, it would have ended in "any given two week period." The Christmas bombing joined Eisenhower's nuclear threats in the sacred canon of Republic Party war-making convictions. But the final agreement signed after the Christmas bombing was virtually identical to the one on the table before the bombing. As John Negroponte, then an aide to Kissinger, put it: "We bombed the North Vietnamese into accepting our concessions."[42] According to Jeffrey Kimball, the bombing was "aimed less at punishing Hanoi into making concessions and more at providing Saigon with incentives to cooperate." The decisive potential value of the bombing was that it would convince "hawks that [Nixon] had been tough, compelling the enemy to accept an agreement that was in reality an am-

biguous compromise" but could be sold as a "clear-cut victory for his skillful management of war and diplomacy."[43] It is possible, had Watergate not
cut his presidency short, that Nixon would have renewed saturation
bombing in the face of a Saigon government defeat in 1975. Certainly
many politicians and senior military officers, especially in the air force, remain convinced that had he done so the United States would have won the
war. In 1978, General Ira Eaker, in whose mind's eye North Vietnam had
escaped unscathed, mused: "how much better it would have been, if necessary, to destroy North Vietnam than to lose our first war."[44]

This conviction has had its coda in the doctrine of "shock and awe" embraced by the Bush administration. But what the wars in Korea and Vietnam demonstrate is that immediate massive bombing does not really
differ from gradually escalating bombing. It only raises the level at which
bombing begins. At the heart of both policies is a genuinely mad conviction: that American power is such that it must prevail in any situation in
which it has declared an interest; that the only obstacle to its triumph is the
lack of determination to use that power.

In the summer of 1950, Japanese civilians at Yokota Air Base loaded the
B-29s that had firebombed Tokyo five years earlier, for targets in North
and South Korea. Four years later, leftover cluster bombs from the Korean
War were shipped from Japanese storage facilities for use by the French
against the Vietnamese. For the entire duration of the American war
against Vietnam, military facilities in Japan and Okinawa (as well as
troops from South Korea) were vital to the U.S. effort. In turn, Japan and
Korea shifted from being targets of U.S. bombing to more profitable service as base and supplier. Recently, the United States has made an effort
to draw Vietnam into its East Asian "strategic designs, focused primarily
on keeping China contained." The current situation in Korea brings us
almost full circle (the nuclearization of Japan may complete the circle).
Ian Bremer, a senior fellow at the World Policy Institute, recently urged
that the only appropriate way for the United States to address North
Korea was to "talk tough," using the language of "the real threat of military escalation."[45] This far into the twenty-first century, America's twentieth-
century faith in the language of violence has not changed.

Coda: "Doing it Right"—Airpower from Gulf to Gulf

The military reforms that followed U.S. defeat in Vietnam are beyond the scope of this epilogue. However, it is important to note that the turning away from counterinsurgency, currently a major charge against the military by prowar pundits, was not an oversight. According to Andrew J. Bacevich, the experience of Vietnam had persuaded senior military officials that the best way to avoid another Vietnam debacle was to avoid a future war that resembled Vietnam in any way. In the wake of the precipitate withdrawal of U.S. troops from Lebanon after the bombing of the Marine barracks in October 1983, Secretary of Defense Caspar Weinberger issued a statement defining, and by defining, hoping to restrict, the terms under which the nation should go to war: forces should be committed to combat only when the vital national interests of the United States or its allies are involved; they should be committed "wholeheartedly and with the clear intention of winning"; and troops should not be sent abroad without a "reasonable assurance" of the support of U.S. public opinion and Congress. Finally, the use of force should be "considered only as a last resort."

In 1990, as the march toward Operation Desert Storm began, Colin Powell, head of the Joint Chiefs of Staff under George H.W. Bush, added to Weinberger's list. As succinctly summarized by Charles Krauthammer, the "idea [of the Powell Doctrine] was not to match Iraqi power but to entirely overwhelm it in planes, tanks, technology, manpower, and will. That would make the war short and make the victory certain." "For decades," Krauthammer went on, enthusiastically but inaccurately, "the United States had followed a policy of proportionality: restraint because of the fear of escalation. It was under this theory that Maj. Powell watched his men bleed and die purposelessly in Vietnam." Under the banner of "never again," instead of the gradual escalation of bombs and troops, both were to be deployed at full strength.

First, though, Iraq was to be "softened up" by airpower. Instead of Vietnam's old, lumbering bombs, new high-tech precision weapons would reduce both U.S. casualties and the damage done to civilians in the course of eliminating legitimate military targets. No one opposed using the new weapons, but tactical disputes remained. The architect of a new strategy, Colonel John Warden, believed the new weapons would allow the air force to target the "central nervous system" of the modern state—electrical

power, communications, transportation, and sources of energy.[46] Warden
was appalled by those air force officers who seemed to think doing Vietnam very fast was the same as not doing it at all. His opponents called for
dropping large payloads ever closer to Baghdad until Saddam Hussein
agreed to withdraw from Kuwait. They also insisted on targeting Iraqi
ground troops. Like Warden, the officers who advocated such tactics did
so in the name of "never again." Warden was adamant: "This is not your
Rolling Thunder. This is real war, and one of the things we want to emphasize right from the start is that this is not Vietnam! This is doing it
right! This is using airpower!"[47]

The general impression left by the use of high-tech air power in Gulf
War I is that it worked very well. TV viewers could virtually merge with
precision weapons as, over and over, they looked through the cross-hairs
in the nose cone of a descending missile. Viewers did not merge with what
happened when the missile landed. Indeed, the game-boy TV reporting of
the war, Paul Walker, director of the Institute for Peace and International
Security at MIT, wrote, "created an illusion of remote, bloodless, pushbut-
ton battle in which only military targets were assumed destroyed."[48] A
Global Security report on airpower in the Gulf War described it with restrained lyricism: "In the final analysis, in its swiftness, decisiveness, and
scope, the coalition's victory came from the wise and appropriate application of airpower."[49]

A terrible sense of well-being derived also from the conviction that this,
at last, was total war, as opposed to the limited, constrained, one-hand-
tied-behind-the-back experience of Vietnam. Publications from the *New
York Times* to the *Air Force Journal of Logistics* trumpeted the statistics:
Iraq had been pounded, in just a month and a half, more heavily than Germany in World War II, than Southeast Asia in ten years of war. The numbers were wrong, as anyone who did the math at the time could have
demonstrated. Edwin E. Moise, a professor at Clemson State, did do the
math and questioned the figures at the time. Afterward, when the full statistics were released, it was clear, Moise wrote, "how little had actually
been dropped—88,500 tons of aerial ordnance,"[50] less than a month's
worth of Vietnam bombing in 1968. Nor were all of the bombs smart.
Only 7 percent were at all intelligent, and of those, 40 percent missed their
targets. The 60 percent that worked did indeed destroy information networks and Saddam Hussein's command and control system. However,
Saddam's system "turned out to be more redundant and more able to re-

constitute itself than first thought," and "fiber-optic networks and computerized switching systems proved particularly tough to put out of action."[51]

Less discussed than the high-tech weapons was the reappearance of B-52 carpet bombing and the ongoing use of cluster bombs and napalm. Some areas of Iraq—the city of Basra, for example—were essentially free-fire zones. The military claimed Basra was entirely a "military town," but failed to explain where the city's 800,000 inhabitants had gone. The *Los Angeles Times* described the city under bombardment as a "hellish nighttime of fires and smoke so dense that witnesses say the sun hasn't been clearly visible for several days at a time. . . ."[52] Still, smart or dumb, as intense as first claimed or not, the sense that Gulf War I represented a total triumph for the air force remained. As President George H.W. Bush put it in May 1991, "Gulf Lesson One is the value of airpower."

President Bill Clinton and his secretary of state, Madeleine Albright, were fast studies. If airpower was good in a war, it was also good in situations that did not rise to the level of war. Albright put the question to Colin Powell directly: "What's the point in having this superb military that you're always talking about, if we can't use it?"[53] And so they used it. For a decade after the war in the Gulf ended, in the Gulf itself, in Bosnia, and again in Kosovo, the Clinton administration used air strikes, Andrew Bacevich noted, the way the Royal Navy used gunboats in the nineteenth century. As in Vietnam, the bombs and missiles were presumed to speak. President Bill Clinton was their interpreter in the fall of 1996, after Saddam Hussein had attacked the Kurdish protected zone in northern Iraq: "Our missiles sent the following message to Saddam Hussein. When you abuse your own people or threaten your neighbors you must pay a price." In December 1998, Saddam Hussein expelled UN weapons inspectors, and the U.S. Air Force, aided by the Royal Air Force, spoke again. The statistics are impressive: for four days, 600 sorties were flown against 97 targets, 330 cruise missiles were fired from aircraft carriers, and, for good measure, B-52s dropped another 90. Saddam Hussein responded by abolishing the no-fly zone and activating his antiaircraft batteries—to which Clinton responded with more bombs.[54]

And so it went for the rest of Clinton's presidency. Bacevich, after listing the names of the multiplying operations and the tonnage they delivered, called it an "inconclusive air war of attrition." There were no U.S. or UK casualties, no lost planes. At the same time, Bacevich concluded, operationally, "the results achieved were negligible." Politically, on the other hand, there were achievements: "In the eyes of American clients in the Persian Gulf . . . the persistent sparring with Saddam affirmed the continuing need for a robust U.S. military presence in the region." In Afghanistan and the Sudan, as in the Balkans, the Clinton adminis-tration "made long-range precision air strikes an emblem of American statecraft."[55]

If air strikes were now America's logo, and Lesson One was airpower, the question remained, what sort of airpower? Used how? In the years be-tween the Gulf Wars, defense intellectuals applied themselves to this sub-ject. Among these was Harlan Ullman, a senior fellow at the Center for Strategic and International Studies. Ullman and a colleague, James P. Wade, published *Shock and Awe: Achieving Rapid Dominance* in 1996 and seven years later watched as their theories were put into action over Bagh-dad. Ullman's plan, repeated throughout the "countdown" to the war, looked forward to "showering" Baghdad with more bombs in the first forty-eight or at most seventy-two hours of war than were used for the thirty-nine days of Gulf War I, so as to "take the city down." The idea of shock and awe is to gain "rapid dominance," Ullman wrote. "This ability to impose massive shock and awe . . . will so overload the perception, knowledge and understanding of [the] adversary that there will be no choice except to cease and desist or risk complete and total destruction."

In response to criticism of this frankly barbarous concept, Ullman in-sisted people had gotten it all wrong. He complained to a British inter-viewer that the phrase "has created a Doomsday approach," and he much preferred the more technical term: "effects-based operations." He insisted he did not mean "indiscriminate, terror-inducing destructiveness." On the contrary, the idea is to do "minimum damage, minimum casualties, using minimum force—even though," he conceded, "that may be a lot." Con-text, Ullman told Oliver Burkeman, was all. "The question is: how do you influence the will and perception of the enemy, to get them to behave how you want them to?" The difference between Ullman's theory and a cave-man with a very big rock was "the combination of technology and philos-ophy."[56] His philosophy was explicitly drawn from the use of nuclear weapons in Hiroshima and Nagasaki, which were, in his words, "the max-imum case of changing behavior."[57] Baghdad would be hit by 800 cruise missiles in the first two days of the war, destroying "everything that makes life in Baghdad livable. . . . You will have this simultaneous effect, rather like the nuclear weapons at Hiroshima, not taking days or weeks but in minutes."[58]

On Thursday, March 20, 2003, at 8:09 P.M., the effects-based operation began. "Wave after wave of explosions rolled down the Tigris valley. . . . The cadence, at once ordered and chaotic, continued as the evening drew towards midnight." Explosions occurred as often as every ten seconds. The bombs hit their targets with greater accuracy than in 1991, but their shrapnel was more generously distributed and their impact blew out windows, shook walls, and collapsed roofs in the surrounding neighborhood. One of the few American reporters who wrote about the bombardment of the city, Anthony Shadid, described what it was like: "Perhaps the most terrifying sensations of life in a city under siege are the sounds of the bombers. In a siege, one's hearing becomes exquisitely sensitive. Much of the time, one waits for the faint sound, the whisper that signals the plane's arrival. The entire body listens. Every muscle tightens, and one stops breathing. Time slows in the interim." Yasmine, one of his Iraqi friends, demanded, "Do those people up there have the faintest idea what is happening down here when they unload?"[59] Harlan Ullman was disappointed. There had not been enough shock, not nearly enough awe. This had been nothing more than the strategic bombing of Baghdad.

It is unnecessary to rehearse here how much of the mission that George W. Bush announced, on May 2, 2003, had been accomplished, remains to be accomplished in July 2008. What is necessary, however, is to point out that the air war in Iraq more or less disappeared from sight even as it continued (and continues) to be carried on. I cannot think of another use of airpower—other than spy planes or the openly "secret" bombing of Laos and Cambodia, performed so invisibly. The air war in Iraq sends no messages. Its purpose is to hunt and kill insurgents, and that it does with indifference to the consequences for those who live in or near the precisely targeted buildings. Relatively few reporters pay much attention to it, and, in contrast to Vietnam, the military does not regularly announce the tonnage dropped or the sorties flown.

Some reporters have put isolated figures together that offer some estimation of the extent of bombing. Ellen Knickmeyer, a reporter for the *Washington Post*, estimated that the number of air strikes had increased fivefold from January to November 2005.[60] In an article that ran on January 11, 2006, Drew Brown, reporting for the *Detroit Times*, listed such figures as U.S. Central Command Air Force (CENTAF) had released: there had been 306 close-air-support strikes in 2005, a 43 percent rise over 2004.[61] Dahr Jamail, an independent journalist, reported that carrier-based navy and marine planes dropped twenty-six tons of ordnance on Fallujah during the battle for that city in November of 2004. Most reports from the CENTAF are vague: "Air Force F-16 Fighting Falcons flew air strikes against anti-Iraqi forces near Balad. The F-16s successfully dropped a precision-guided bomb on a building used by insurgents. F-16s and a Predator also flew air strikes against anti-Iraqi forces in the vicinity of Karabilah. The Predator successfully fired a Hellfire missile against insurgent positions."[62]

After Fallujah, the air war seems to have gone entirely underground. Nick Turse, an investigative journalist, has tried to track it, with marginal success. "A secret air war is being waged in Iraq," he has written. "The U.S. military keeps information on the munitions expended in its air efforts under tight wraps, refusing to offer details on the scale of use and so minimizing the importance of air power in Iraq."[63] There was some irony, therefore, in an op-ed piece by Charles Dunlap Jr., a major general in the air force, who, in the course of insisting that defeating the insurgency in Iraq was not "all about winning hearts and mind," asked how many Americans knew that in 2007 there had been a fivefold increase in air strikes over the preceding year. The answer is, not many. Major General Rick Lynch, in a throwaway reference to airpower, remarked that during a battle on January 10 in Arab Jabour, U.S. bombers had "dropped 40,000 pounds of bombs in 10 minutes to clear an insurgent stronghold."[64]

Robyn Read, a retired air force colonel, has pondered the questions of what airpower can do in counterinsurgency warfare once the period of "'kinetic kill'" is finished:

> The answer is about finding and pursuing the path of least resistance to the political end state, caveated with a planner's full understanding that least resistance must successfully contend with collateral effects, unintended consequences, legal and moral restraints, and the well-being of the coalition's aggregate interest in the endeavor. EBO [effects-based operations] provides a functional yet flexible framework for thinking about this problem, or more correctly, this problem set.

The CIA has developed a genuinely new approach to this "problem set": targeted killings. Predator drones originally designed for surveillance have been armed with Hellfire antiarmor missiles and used to assassinate suspected terrorists both in and outside of combat zones. No one knows how many such strikes have taken place, nor how many people they have killed. However, one former official working in the program told a reporter: "We have the plans in place to do them globally." Some problems persist: "In most cases, we need the approval of the host country to do them. However, there are a few countries where the president has decided that we can whack someone without the approval or knowledge of the host government."[65]

We know most about the use of drones outside of combat areas when they go wrong, as they did in the January 2006 in an attack on the village of Damadola, Pakistan, where, it was believed, senior members of al Qaeda were attending a meeting. It remains unclear whether they were or had been in the village; what is known is that eighteen civilians, including many women and children, were killed. There was bipartisan support for the strike in the United States, though of course the deaths of innocents were regretted. As Senator Evan Bayh (D-Indiana) put it on the Wolf Blitzer show, "Now, it's a regrettable situation, but what else are we supposed to do? It's like the Wild, Wild West out there. The Pakistani border [with Afghanistan] is a real problem."[66] Andrew Bacevich, alone among the mainstream commentators I have read, thought the problem lay elsewhere: "For the United States to unleash a salvo of missiles at a Pakistani village thought to house an al-Qaeda chieftain is the equivalent of the Mexican government bombing a southern California condo complex suspected of harboring a drug kingpin."[67] Lee Strickland, who retired from the CIA in 2004, praised the deterrent power of these killings: "You give shelter to Al Qaeda figures, you may well get your village blown up. Conversely, you have to note that this can also create local animosity and instability." This is the venerable wisdom that guided the United States for fifteen years in Vietnam.

8

THE UNITED STATES AND STRATEGIC BOMBING: FROM PROPHECY TO MEMORY

Michael Sherry

"Having found the bomb we have used it," President Harry Truman said immediately after America's atomic attack on Japan in 1945. But the United States had not simply "found" the bomb—its futurists and scientists and policy makers had first imagined it and then developed it. Indeed, for most of the history of strategic bombing, prophecy and practice were closely linked.[1]

"More than any other modern weapon, the bomber was imagined before it was invented," I wrote twenty years ago.[2] How else, after all, could people know what to invent? If that truism applies to most technologies, it applies especially to this case. The imagination—prophecy—usually led the way. The technology and applications usually followed. That is no surprise, but it does run counter to the technological determinism—given marvelously succinct statement by Truman—common in popular and even scholarly understandings. Those suggest that people and institutions invent first—almost as if by accident, divine will, or the inexorable course of progress—then figure out what to do with their inventions. I suggest almost the opposite: imagining air war preceded and prompted the technological, strategic, and political developments that made bombing possible, in a process starting in the nineteenth century and gaining speed after the Wright brothers' first flight in 1903.

The relationship between prophecy and action was not, of course, rigid or unvarying. The imagination worked off of rudiments of emerging technology—the glimmer of new inventions spurred the imagination. Some technologies developed so secretly, incrementally, or accidentally that they were divorced from prophecy. Some were never used despite predictions that they would be—the case, by and large, with chemical and biological weapons, whose use in air war was widely and fearfully predicted in the 1920s and 1930s. But in the early twentieth century, a flurry of imaginative efforts held out the lure or the danger—or both—of airpower, and charted technical, strategic, and political paths for its development.

Prophecy was an international business. Many of its famous tracts were European—H.G. Wells's *The War in the Air* (1908), the Italian Giulio Douhet's *Command of the Air* (1921), and Basil Liddell Hart's *Paris, or the Future of War* (1925), for example. But by the 1920s, Americans were weighing in heavily. Already General Billy Mitchell was describing Japan's "congested" and "inflammable" cities as an "ideal target." Mitchell's famous destruction of derelict German battleships in his staged demonstration of airpower in 1921 was also an act of prophecy, for prophecy was as much performative as written. Indeed, World War I, with its bomber attacks on England, France, and Germany, was such a performance—seen by commanders and pundits during and after the war as trial runs for the day to come of decisive air war. The ghastly cost of ground combat and the grim toll from submarine warfare added urgency to the hopes for bombing's decisiveness. With World War I, prophecy and practice entered into a tight feedback loop, each shaping the other.

Prophets variously asserted that airpower had the potential to bring quick victory in war, to deter nations from even going to war, or to lead the world into catastrophic destruction. For Wells, the most prescient of the lot, war by air would tempt or force a widening array of nations to resort to it, would dissolve into "universal guerrilla warfare," and would be "at once enormously destructive and entirely indecisive," as he wrote in 1908. Others predicted air-launched chemical and biological warfare on a world-ending scale. In Stuart Chase's chilling 1929 piece for the *New Republic*, "The Two-Hour War," such warfare would mean that English civilization would come, "in something like half an hour, to a close. Finished and done," as each city "duly makes its exit from the list of habitable places on the planet. Not even a rat, not even an ant, not even a roach would survive," and in New York—"her many tall buildings crashing like glorified tenpins"—people "would hardly have time to seize their check books before being summoned to the waiting rooms of the recording angel." But most prophets—even Chase insofar as he foresaw only a "Two-Hour War"—turned those grim prospects into a virtue: a few hours or days of aerial attack on an enemy's capital, morale, key industries, or strategic linchpins would yield victory, or the mere threat of such an attack would stay the hand of a potential aggressor or deter all parties from resorting to war. Meanwhile other visionaries argued that the aerial technology developed to blast faraway cities might instead, as civil aviation, knit the world together, promoting commercial and cultural exchange that would usher in understanding and harmony among nations. That vision was nourished by feats like Charles Lindbergh's solo flight from New York to Paris in 1927, a global media event. After all, the engines that powered the bomber could also propel the airliner.[3]

What effect did prediction have? It empowered politicians, or the media and public opinion acting on them, to pour resources into development of the bomber—in America's case, the B-17, first built in the 1930s and its workhorse for bombing in Europe during World War II. Often written by military officers, prophecy was studied in war colleges, used by airpower advocates to imagine strategy, and seized on by manufacturers, who saw the bomber's development as a way to stabilize their industries in a fickle and competitive market for civilian aircraft and to promote technical progress that would spill over into civilian airplanes. At times, prophecy provided the gleam in the eye for quite specific developments. Some atomic scientists, like Leo Szilard, were influenced by Wells's prophecy of atomic warfare in his 1913 novel *The World Set Free*. Others in the 1930s browsed *Astounding Science Fiction*, a magazine that Spencer Weart calls "as close as anyone could find to a probe sunk into the back brain of American technology."[4] Prophecy allowed developers of airpower to foresee what they might then invent. True, U.S. officials did not in the 1930s publicly identify the countries that might be attacked by America's nascent fleet of bombers, whose ostensible and most salable purpose at the time was to destroy any enemy forces approaching American or hemispheric shores. But others, like Mitchell in his retirement, speculated openly about the ease of striking Japan's cities. Prophecy continued to run ahead of practice during World War II: Walt Disney imagined an orgiastic destruction of Japan by air in his 1943 animated feature *Victory Through Air Power* (based on Alexander P. De Seversky's 1942 book), well before the United

States could carry it out. Prophecy thus not only sanctioned the weapons of air war but goaded public opinion to embrace its use. It played this role also for subsidiary inventions and countermeasures: radarlike techniques were imagined before radar was invented.

How all this worked in practice varied with the politics, circumstances, and resources of the various nations involved. Prophecy was not the only factor—it hardly could be when the prophets disagreed with each other about which forms and uses of airpower were destined to prevail. Germany and France, with strong traditions and resources for ground warfare, embraced the long-range bomber less wholeheartedly than the United States or Great Britain. Japan, with its powerful navy and its distance from likely enemies, bent bomber development more to its seagoing needs. Italy lacked the resources to compete effectively, and so on. Arguably the Axis powers initiated the city bombing that came to characterize World War II—Japan in China during the 1930s, Germany by attacking Warsaw in 1939—but the British and Americans became its foremost practitioners.

The United States had the human and economic resources, the distance from potential enemies, the leadership, and the time to pursue airpower in all its dimensions—as independent strategic force, component of sea power, and weapon in ground warfare. It also had a political system that discouraged making hard choices among these options—it was easier during World War II to satisfy all the claimants to airpower than to choose any one of them, even as President Franklin Roosevelt championed strategic bombing. From FDR on down, Americans also had faith that their technological prowess, especially in long-range bombing, could minimize their costs in ground combat. Their technological fanaticism—whereby machines both unleashed and disguised the ferocity of their war making— stood in contrast to the human fanaticism they saw in their enemies, especially the Japanese. Dominant American attitudes toward the Japanese as a bestial, inferior race deserving of American revenge made the prospect of incinerating Japan's cities especially inviting, while Americans' isolation from aerial retaliation made bombing even more attractive to them. And their culture during the war—the speeches of politicians, the campaigns of government agencies, the advertisements of corporations—promised that wartime ingenuity would unleash peacetime technological abundance, the rainbow to follow the sacrifices of a generation that endured the Great Depression and World War II. As a Philco Corporation ad promised in 1944, its work "today" to help win the air war would "tomorrow" bring "greater peacetime joys, born of war research . . . television, finer radios, phonographs and refrigerators."[5]

By 1945, America stood alone in the competition to wage air war, with Britain struggling to hang on and the Soviet Union struggling, with some success, to catch up. Even before Hiroshima and Nagasaki, the United States had carried out more destruction and killed more people with its bombers than any other nation. Its death toll was amassed through its firebombing of Japanese cities (it was still "pinpoint, precision" bombing, one air force officer insisted to skeptical reporters) and through its role in the Anglo-American bombing of Germany, its satellites, and sometimes its conquered enemies.[6] All that bombing hardly won the war by itself—Allied supremacy on the seas and Allied land armies, especially the Soviets', played a vital role, albeit assisted by tactical airpower. And U.S. bombing hardly stopped Americans' death in war—more than 400,000 military personnel, including thousands in the U.S. air forces, died in or outside of combat. But America's technological and economic supremacy did help keep its losses the smallest among the major powers. And bombing did contribute to Allied victory, which was all that most U.S. commanders and leaders expected of it by 1943—once the awful realities of the war had fully set in, the more ecstatic visions of "victory through airpower" moved to the margins of high-level strategic calculation, at least until the atomic bomb became available. Although the United States lagged behind Britain and Germany in jet fighters and long-range rockets, it would soon catch up. Meanwhile it had the world's supreme bomber—the B-29—and, more important, the capacity to produce it in large numbers, to deploy it to forward bases, and to equip it with the best crews and technology. General Curtis LeMay put more than 300 B-29s over Tokyo in a single night for the great fire raid of March 9, 1945, which killed 100,000 or more in that city, and he kept up the firebombing for months. In the feedback loop between imagination and invention, work on the atomic bomb before the August 6 attack prompted prophecy among many American scientists and policy makers, who assigned a purpose to the bomb's use far beyond Japan's defeat—to instruct the world on the dangers of nuclear weapons or on the supremacy of American power. It was the first instance of what Marilyn Young calls "atomic flashing" (see page 161).

Prophecy usually served multiple functions and played to diverse audiences. It guided the development of airpower but also of opposition to it, as some of the prophets intended. Once off the desk, any given prophecy left the author's control and might be used for many argumentative purposes. The great prophesies—Wells's *The War in the Air*, Herman Kahn's *On Thermonuclear War* (1961), the doomsday films of the 1950s and 1960s, Jonathan Schell's *The Fate of the Earth* (1982)—functioned as both how-to and why-not-to manuals, as both road maps and warning signs. Some authors seemed conflicted about which they were trying to offer—the case, it seems, with Kahn.[7] Foes of strategic bombing rarely had the upper hand—the backers of bigger bombers and better missiles usually prevailed. But the point here is that they both drew from, and helped create, the same well of prophecy.

Deterrence, imagined from early in the twentieth century, defined the mushy middle ground between these camps after World War II. Since deterrence involved preventing rather than waging a future war, it became the supreme realm for prophecy—the place where the imagination could run wild. Deterrence spoke to both camps. It allowed the how-to folks to get their weapons and technologies—their B-52 bombers, intercontinental rockets, hydrogen bombs, and stealth aircraft. But deterrence also gave the why-not-to advocates hope that the weapons would not be used, and it inspired scenarios to help them argue why they should not be used. In the context of deterrence, prophecy could be explicit, as in doomsday films. It also could be indirect, as in science fiction films like *The Day the Earth Stood Still* (1951), in which aliens threaten to destroy earth if its nations do not learn to live in peace, or merely implicit, as in the film *Strategic Air Command* (1955), in which the bombers never attack because America's readiness to use them is affirmed.

Not surprisingly, given the awful toll by air inflicted during World War II and the prospect of nuclear conflict, the decades after 1945 were the great age of prophecy and alarm. Even politicians' boasts might be understood as a kind of prophecy, albeit of a near-term sort. When President Lyndon Johnson allegedly gloated, after his bombing raids on North Vietnam during the 1964 Tonkin Gulf crisis, that "I didn't just screw Ho Chi Minh, I cut his pecker off," he was also predicting the triumph of American airpower in a forthcoming U.S. war in Vietnam. Similarly in 1968, president-to-be Richard Nixon predicted that once North Vietnamese leader Ho Chi Minh knew that Nixon had "his hand on the nuclear button," Ho would be "in Paris in two days begging for peace."[8] The immense, jargon-laden, and often computer-driven studies by strategic planners and civilian think tanks were a form of prophecy largely invisible to the public, but work by Kahn and others entered the public realm. Widely read novels became widely seen star-studded movies—the case with Nevil Shute's *On the Beach* (1957; film, 1959) and Eugene Burdick and Harvey Wheeler's *Fail-Safe* (1962; film, 1964)—while the television series *The Twilight Zone* often featured grim scenarios of nuclear war and postnuclear trauma. Though set in World War II, acclaimed novels about air war such as Joseph Heller's *Catch-22* (1961) and Kurt Vonnegut's *Slaughterhouse-Five* (1969) were in both intent and reception as much admonitory about the future as reflective about the past. They were anti-war or antinuclear books, like many other novels, short stories, and polemical tracts. But there were also hundreds of other writings now largely forgotten—appearing in science fiction, popular science, technological and military publications, and religious venues—that promoted U.S. supremacy or sketched America's triumph in nuclear war or in forcing the communists not to wage it.

Stanley Kubrick's 1964 film, *Dr. Strangelove, or How I Learned to Stop Worrying and Love the Bomb*, climaxed this great age of prophecy, and perhaps also hastened its end, because Kubrick offered a wicked satire not only on the madness of nuclear war but also on the prophetic genre itself. Straight-faced prophecy could hardly survive in comparison to Kubrick's film, while it also lost out to the different concerns unleashed by America's Vietnam War and by the cultural and political upheavals of that era.

The prophetic imagination had legs, however, surging again in the 1970s, when it sometimes brazenly served the purposes of end-times Christian writers. In the decade's best-selling nonfiction book, *The Late Great Planet Earth* (1970; a movie version narrated by Orson Welles followed in 1977), author Hal Lindsey "relentlessly turned the Bible into a manual of atomic-age combat," Paul Boyer has written, and much in that vein followed for decades in end-times fiction and film.[9]

In other circles, the prophetic imagination took fictional form less often than it earlier had. Instead it emerged in scientific, policy, and polemical tracts that—amid the final, baroque phase of Soviet-American weapons competition—foresaw Soviet victory, championed American supremacy, or envisioned the ultimate cataclysm. That genre of nonfiction prophecy climaxed with Schell's chilling and much-debated prediction of how nuclear war would cause human extinction, *The Fate of the Earth*.

Yet by the 1980s the tight connection between prophecy and practice was dissipating, as was prophecy itself. Schell's 1982 book was the last great piece of American prophecy, after which little emerged, at least in the obvious, nation-grabbing form of big books and movies. Prophecy about air war was still there—in war-gaming done by Americans, for example, or in visions of aerial destruction of the West indulged in by Islamic terrorists. Surely, once airplanes slammed into the World Trade Towers, a whole new skein of imagination was unleashed. But 9/11 was hardly what had been imagined for a century—it was airplane power, not airpower. As object of dread fascination, airpower—what missiles and bombers could do to enemies or to humankind itself—moved to the sidelines of the prophetic imagination.

Americans now more often glimpsed airpower as an artifact of the past, as when, in 1976, the Confederate Air Force had staged a simulation of America's attack on Hiroshima, with *Enola Gay* pilot Paul Tibbets once again at the controls of a B-29. The story of American airpower was retold in countless video documentaries, recalled in memoirs—among the best by Americans was Samuel Hynes's *Flights of Passage* (1988)—recounted in scholarship and coffee-table books, celebrated at the National Air and Space Museum in Washington, and enshrined at the lofty Air Force Memorial, opened adjacent to Arlington Cemetery in 2006. Of course memory work regarding bombing stretched back to its very start—its history had long been the subject of officers, filmmakers, writers, and scholars. But by late in the century, airpower had become encased in a new framework of memory, though one punctuated by occasional fresh exercises in American bombing. That framework did prove surprisingly resistant to Hollywood treatment: ground and naval combat had long been riper subjects for moviemaking, and *Saving Private Ryan* (1998) proved far more successful than *Pearl Harbor* (2001), which closed with Doolittle's bombers striking Japan in 1942. The best films often came from elsewhere: the English film *Hope and Glory* (1987), about German attacks on Britain, and the animated Japanese feature *Grave of the Fireflies* (Japanese version 1988, English 1992, shown on Turner Classic Movies in 2006), about orphans in the aftermath of Japan's firebombing. And popular fiction sometimes offered complicated views: Joseph Kanon's *The Good German* (a 2001 novel and 2006 movie) offered a bleak picture indeed of Berlin in 1945 ravaged by Anglo-American bombing (and Russian shelling). But a celebratory stance dominated America's look at its airpower past.

How much the dominant framework was memory emerged in the

"museum war" that erupted in 1994 over the National Air and Space Museum's plan for an exhibit centered on the *Enola Gay*. Critics, mostly conservative pundits and politicians and groups claiming to speak for veterans, got the exhibit scrapped on the grounds that it dismissed Japan's wartime culpability, wallowed in the grisly details of atomic destruction, and ignored the redemptive purpose served by American use of the bomb. It was a war-winning device that saved millions of lives, the loudest voices insisted, despite its costs and despite much evidence that American firebombing, the Soviet Union's entry into the war, and indeed the whole course of Allied war making also accounted for victory. The *Enola Gay* episode suggested that despite countercurrents in the armed forces and in political culture, many Americans resisted a critical view of their airpower past, just as they resisted the perspectives of other peoples on that past. Perhaps such resistance was the victor's prerogative—the winners of war control its story—but it often extended to the Korean and Vietnam wars, in which the utility of American airpower was decidedly dubious and the United States met stalemate and then defeat. To be sure, near the surface of the ugly *Enola Gay* controversy lay dreams and fears about America's prospective airpower: how to remember the past stirs passions mostly fiercely when it intersects questions about how to behave in the future. Even so, it made a big difference that the touchstone of debate was the imagined past, not the imagined future.[10]

W.G. Sebald's *On the Natural History of Destruction* (2003) further highlighted the shift from prophecy to memory. His book and the lectures on which it was based attracted widespread attention in Germany and elsewhere before and after his death in 2001, not least because of his reputation as a leading writer (born in Germany in 1944, he lived in England most of his adult life). Sebald condemned the silence in Germany's literate culture and in "the consciousness of the reemergent nation" about the bombing its cities had endured during World War II, and he sketched the devastation and terror that had occurred, especially in Hamburg, though he spent as much time flogging the absence of memory as exploring what it should contain.[11] Sebald's claims and others' work to follow became embroiled in controversy over whether Germans were elevating their status as World War II's victims over their culpability as the war's mass murderers.[12] But more to the point here, both Sebald and his respondents emphatically focused only on the past. Retrospection can also serve admonitory purposes, but there is no intrinsic connection between looking backward and warning forward, and Sebald's work contained hardly a wispy hint of "never again." Insofar as it pointed to the future, it called for a healthy German consciousness about the past, not a state of alarm (or optimism) about future air war.

It is not that prophecy about war ceased, but it gravitated elsewhere, to other forms of war, above all terrorism. That shift, gaining speed for decades, was propelled further by 9/11. In prophecy about terrorism, airpower might play a role—as an instrument for delivering a terrorist bomb or a means of retaliation by nations under terrorist attack. But airpower was no longer the central focus of prophecy about war; it was simply one of many imagined weapons.

Why did prophecy about airpower diminish? Changes in the international system, in culture, and in uses of airpower were at work. The most obvious explanation is that prophecy withered after the threat of superpower conflict petered out in the late 1980s. Most of the great prophecy of the twentieth century had imagined conflict between two or more powers of similar status and might. It had pitted Britain against Germany, showed the United States incinerating Japan or the Soviet Union, or, in Wells's case, imagined "universal guerrilla warfare." The end of the Cold War, the Soviet-American agreements to limit or scrap weapons, and the dwindling likelihood of superpower conflict brought that tradition to a close, although a new fear of nuclear terrorism and "rogue" nuclear powers operated as a diffuse replacement for it. It had always been more fun, or terrifying, to imagine roughly equal powers squaring off against each other, because their prospective wars entailed enormous destruction and therefore compelled fresh efforts to figure out how to win or prevent a possible war.

In contrast, post–Cold War uses of airpower hardly excited the American imagination. Bombers attacking Baghdad, B-52s over Belgrade, Russian planes hitting Grozny, rulers bombing their own peoples—the scale of those operations (however devastating for the locals) and the fact that they involved such unequal forces did not stir Americans' apocalyptic fears and fantasies. Indeed, given the remarkably few casualties that Americans suffered in bombing Belgrade and Baghdad, these operations hardly stirred Americans at all, except as giant fireworks shows that confirmed American supremacy. Airpower, especially in U.S. hands, had returned largely to the function it often had early in the twentieth century—a weapon of imperial rule. And it was largely the possession of one nation, the United States, not contending rivals.

Yet to see the waxing and waning of fear about air war as the direct mirrors of great-power conflict oversimplifies the matter. Fear had waxed in the 1920s when great-power war, though imaginable, hardly seemed imminent, and it did so again in the late 1970s and early 1980s when, for all the rhetorical intensity of Soviet-American conflict, nuclear war was probably less imminent than it had been in the 1950s and early 1960s. Other factors also played into the shift from prophecy to memory.

That shift was characteristic of late-twentieth-century culture generally, not just of attention to air war. In the United States and elsewhere, postmodern culture seemed to prize ransacking the past more than anticipating the future, and it was accompanied by a worldwide flourishing of memorial and historical work about the dead of the century's wars. While memorialization was sometimes admonitory, especially regarding the Nazi Holocaust and the Vietnam War, its primary orientation was backward in time, and its dominant tone was elegiac, sorrowful, or dismayed rather than anticipatory or alarmist. That shift was evident in the best fiction about war, such as English novelist Pat Barker's much-praised *Regeneration* trilogy (1991, 1994, 1995), centered on ground combat during World War I. As postmodern culture shifted attention to the past, it also undercut the primacy of any single anxiety. AIDS, global warming, terrorism, genocide: many apocalyptic dangers competed for attention and representation, and just as postmodern culture resisted any master narrative, it resisted any master anxiety. The danger of air war took its place in the era's bubbling, ever-changing stew of concerns.

Change in the practice of air war also accounted for prophecy's decline. Bombing had seemingly become so refined and precise—as American air prophets once claimed it would and new champions now claimed it had— that it no longer involved the scale of destruction that once fired the imagination. Airpower had become more a sharp knife than a blunt fist—Belgrade in 1999 did not meet Berlin's fate in 1944; Baghdad in 1991 and 2003 was not Tokyo in 1945. It really was possible—if everything worked right, which it did not always— to take out the Serbs' radio tower and interior ministry while leaving adjacent structures intact. America's "shock and awe" attacks on Baghdad in 2003—the offspring of Cold War theories about "decapitating" the enemy through airpower—never struck Saddam Hussein, and they proved irrelevant or even counterproductive to the war that followed President George Bush's May 20 speech under the banner MISSION ACCOMPLISHED. But those attacks did help accomplish the

initial mission of the "Coalition of the Willing"—Saddam's overthrow—
and their destructiveness probably paled in comparison to the looting, insurgent attacks, and sectarian violence that followed for years in Iraq, in a
depressing reminder that, as in the past, air war was not always the worst
form of warfare. Decades of efforts to refine airpower made it more acceptable, or at least less controversial, and less controversy meant less call
for prophecy.

Or so it seems. Americans probably learned less about the human and
economic costs of turn-of-the-millennium bombing than they had during
World War II. U.S. bombers were used against state or nonstate forces
that lacked the will or the ability to count their dead (or publicize their
counts). No one made the exhaustive efforts to quantify such things that
many warring powers engaged in after World War II. And bombing's
costs were less visible but economically and environmentally invidious.
Furthermore, official and media filters screened out most of the evidence
of bombing's destructiveness—in 1991 and 2003, American bombing came
across on U.S. television screens more as a fascinating video game than
as a devastating onslaught. And with U.S. casualties so few, Americans
lacked a direct attachment to the costs of war—one's own losses may
prompt interest in others' suffering. And of course airpower succeeded at
less evident cost because it was used solely by one side—Milošević could
not strike back at New York, and Saddam Hussein could not hit Los Angeles, or even Tel Aviv very effectively. Any form of warfare will look
pretty good when it is not contested. Airpower's image as a more refined
weapon was primarily a function of the end of superpower conflict and the
completion of U.S. hegemony than of its technical perfection. It will look
very different if a challenge to U.S. aerial supremacy ever emerges. In that
situation, scenarios will again envision warring parties setting loose an un-
controlled escalation of aerial attacks.

As airpower became a more refined instrument of warfare, its development also became more incremental and gradual. Gone, it seems, were the
days of breakthrough technologies that transformed air war in a few
years—the first bombers of World War I; the atomic bombs and jet planes
of the 1940s; the intercontinental rockets of the 1950s. Perhaps the closest
to breakthroughs in later decades were stealth aircraft and pilotless
drones. But they changed airpower only at its margins, and the thinking behind them was quite old. In World War II, American commanders
considered using thousands of battle-weary bombers in pilotless attacks.

Technological change in airpower certainly continued at a brisk and expensive pace, and if visionaries get their way, American forces will be able some day to attack earth from space—certainly a transformative prospect. But meanwhile, breakthroughs that fire the imagination seemed on hold when U.S. B-52 bombers, first designed in the 1940s and built in the 1950s, still operated in Afghanistan in 2006, albeit gutted and retrofitted. Could one imagine the United States in 1975 still relying on World War I–era battleships? Instead of quivering at the prospect of the next big technical advance, Americans ended up worrying about planes ramming into buildings.

The connections between civilian and military aviation that once nourished prophecy also sharply diminished. Into the early jet age, the symbiosis between civilian and military aviation had been strong—technologies for one arena got adapted for the other (not, obviously, in the weapons, though prediction initially ran riot about how nuclear weapons technology would yield civilian wonders). Popular and literate imagination played off of that symbiosis, aircraft manufacturers touted their achievements in one arena as applicable to the other (the B-52 as harbinger of civilian jetliners), and promoters of new technologies showed them off to the public in order to enlist political support for them. The symbiosis had mundane dimensions as well: military and civilian aircraft often used the same airfields, for example. By the late twentieth century, the two arenas had become largely disconnected, and military aviation had disappeared from sight except for carefully staged air shows. Most warplanes developed by the Western powers operated in a rarefied technological world of their own (airliners had no use for stealth technology), and military technologies were often shrouded longer in secrecy during their development.

Perhaps aerial warfare is following a course once traversed by naval warfare. In the nineteenth and early twentieth centuries, when naval technologies leaped forward in both the civil and military arenas, prophecy about battleships and submarines as decisive weapons had flourished. It waned after World War I and more after World War II, displaced in the apocalyptic imagination and in the cutting edges of technology by airpower (except insofar as submarines could launch nuclear-tipped missiles and carriers could send forth nuke-carrying bombers). Not that naval warfare ceased to evolve or to be important—least of all for the United States, which continued to project much of its power through its navy. But its showiest breakthroughs were in the past, its uses seemed less at the center of war making, its connections to civilian travel and commerce had faded away, and its capacity to stir great hope and fear had diminished. That may also be the fate now—or perhaps only for the moment—with airpower, displaced in part by terrorism and counterterrorism as principal modes of warfare.

Where the civilian-military connection persisted was less with the planes or the weapons than in war gaming. Military and civilian war games often drew on similar computer technologies, and similar or shared versions of war games were sometimes used to recruit new service personnel. The predictive imagination continued to operate in the fantasy world of computerized war games, "where the military and sectors of the entertainment industry are collaboratively producing wargames, interactive training simulations, virtual environments, and narrative films visualizing future technologies, tactics, and scenarios." But in civilian war gaming, the primary fascination seemed to lie with how the players manipulated their miniaturized, private microworld, not with the external world in which weapons might get used. Of course that focus also increasingly characterized American war making as the computer became a major battlefield tool. Computer war gaming contained a prophetic dimension, but most of it was designed for its own consumers, not for broad public impact, and its focus on airpower was limited, for as much of it was oriented toward replaying past wars, not waging mock wars of the future. Here, too, memory was a dominant framework. Among hundreds—perhaps thousands— of computer and board war games like Stalingrad: Pivot on the Volga, those games addressing future air war were surprisingly few.[13]

A final explanation for prophecy's decline points not to American supremacy but to American vulnerability. Prophecy, whether it relished American power or warned against it, had rested on what others might do to the United States and on what the it had already done to others. After 1945, American prophecy had drawn from the deep well of World War II—on the great aerial campaigns of the war, and most of all on Hiroshima and Nagasaki. The atomic attacks of August 1945 were the linchpins of postwar prophecy, though not always acknowledged as such.

But 9/11 happened to the United States, not to others. After it, Americans could not so easily imagine a future in which their airpower would be in control. It was one thing to imagine America's destruction when it had never happened—to imagine it, for example, by transposing Hiroshima and Nagasaki on to American cities, as was often done after

World War II. It was much scarier to imagine America's destruction after it had occurred. 9/11 seemed to produce a stunned silence of the American imagination in this regard. Immediately after it, scattered fears and predictions did surface about how al Qaeda might follow up with more attacks. If it could do so much damage with four airliners, would it not try again with fourteen or forty, or this time with nuclear weapons? Yet that sort of prophecy did not seem to last long or run deep. Moreover, 9/11 itself seemed rapidly erased in imagination—especially visual evidence of it, like that of bodies falling from the World Trade Towers. Likewise, imagination about a new and worse 9/11 seemed stunted. Once the future had to be imagined in terms of *American* suffering, it was perhaps better not to imagine it at all. Oddly enough, America's destruction by air had been more thinkable—more readily imagined—when it was unthinkable. Or to give this a more benign spin: once Americans had the reality, who needed the imagination any more? Indeed, given the past century's terrible record of airpower, who needed prophecy (much less the sort that propels further developments in warfare) any more to imagine what the future could be like? The past is the prophecy.

But for those in the present, the past is also full of holes. Bombing's past resisted treatment not only in Hollywood but in other forms of culture. While reenactors busily restaged many scenes from America's military past, the costs and technologies of air war made its reenactment difficult and discouraged large-scale participation, despite the efforts of the Confederate Air Force. Slogging through the countryside in order to refight Bull Run or the Bulge was one thing; replaying the bombing of Dresden or Danang another. Subtler gaps in memory also occurred. In his 1949 essay "Here Is New York," E.B. White wrote that

> The city, for the first time in its long history, is destructible. A single flight of planes no bigger than a wedge of geese can quickly end this island fantasy, burn the towers, crumble the bridges, turn the underground passages into lethal chambers, cremate the millions.... In the mind of whatever perverted dreamer might loose the lightning, New York must hold a steady irresistible charm.[14]

As Paul K. Saint-Amour notes, White's words were often quoted after 9/11 "as proof of the essay's prescience," but doing so owed "to a certain amnesia" that "efface[d] White's referent (nuclear war) and historical context (the dawning nuclear condition)."[15] Despite all the memory work of recent decades, much is now forgotten—not only about what happened in war, but about what was once predicted for it. "The best way to forget something is to commemorate it," observes a character, referring to Britain's memorials to its World War I dead, in Alan Bennett's play and movie *The History Boys*. That may be a glib observation—state-sponsored commemoration serves many purposes, and it is only one form that memory takes. Still, memory turns out to be fickle as a guide not only to the future but to the past.

The framework of memory for understanding air war presumably will not be dominant forever. Younger generations will have less investment in recalling the awful glories of World War II or the painful failures of the Vietnam War. New forms of warfare—"postindustrial," "postmodern," "asymmetrical," and the like—have captured attention, and they, too, will become the objects of memory. All cultures have systems of remembrance, but memory was also a distinctly postmodern cultural mode, not a timeless preoccupation. Prophecy gave way to memory late in the twentieth century. What will displace memory as a framework for understanding? Historians are lousy at answering such a question, but they are right to expect that it will arise.

9

BOMBING AND THE MORALITY OF WAR

C.A.J. Coady

War is a ghastly, often insane activity, and it is the primary insight of the pacifist movement that we should get rid of it as a method of resolving disputes and dealing with international or internal wrongdoing, real or perceived. I certainly favor working to eliminate war as a political instrument, and I don't think that the hope of ending war is an entirely utopian aspiration. But any such hope faces two major difficulties. The first is that we need to provide feasible future alternatives to war for dealing with gross injustices, and the second is that we need to face squarely what is to be done to deal with such matters prior to the abolition of war.

With respect to these problems, pacifists have not always provided much in the way of solutions. My own view, in brief, is that, in response to the first, we need to turn war into something much more like policing so that egregious injustices on the international scene will be confronted, if necessary, by internationally controlled and authorized violence that is the responsibility of a trained, standing UN force. In response to the second, I think that we should capitalize on the relatively recent revival of just-war theory to emphasize the severe constraints that any resort to war must satisfy if even the most minimal moral considerations are to apply. Neither of these responses is meant to rule out much greater emphasis on nonviolent techniques for resolving political disputes, or further research on the development of such techniques and education in them.

BY MICHAEL LEUNIG

In what follows, I will be addressing the second response, and in particular the just-war principle of discrimination. This is a principle concerned with constraints upon the way in which war is waged, rather than resort to war in the first place. It is thus a principle in what is sometimes called the *jus in bello* (justice in war, or JIB, as I shall abbreviate it) rather than the *jus ad bellum* (the right to war, or JAB). This principle is particularly relevant to bombing just because the development of high explosives of which the bomb is the prime example has made for much greater lack of discrimination in the waging of war than most, possibly all, previous technologies of armed conflict. This point is particularly relevant to the issue of "collateral damage," which I will discuss later.

The Principle of Discrimination and the Nature of Terrorism

Before discussing this matter further, I should make it clear that my concern is primarily with the *morality* of various forms of bombing, not with its legality. There is a complex relation between law and ethics, but I think it is clear that law needs ethical reflection at its foundation, though it is also clear that the law, whether local or international, often lags behind moral insights. (For the purposes of this discussion, I will use the terms "ethics" and "morality" and their cognates interchangeably, though in other contexts there can be some point in distinguishing them.) It took the carnage of World War II bombings to have international law explicitly recognize the immunity of noncombatants from intentional direct attack, though this had been a principle of just-war ethical theory much earlier. In the matter of collateral damage and the associated issue of dual-purpose targets, to be discussed later, the protections afforded by Geneva and its protocols seem to me clearly morally inadequate and lagging behind the realities they are designed to address. The development of all forms of law is subject to competing pressures, most notably the interests of the powerful on the one hand and the considerations of moral reasoning on the other. International law will require compromise and concession in a way that moral principles do not, although compromise is itself a matter that should be subject to moral control.

The principle of discrimination is first of all a moral principle that has received some legal recognition. As such, it basically seeks to restrict the waging of war to properly military targets, and so its central thrust is to provide for the immunity of noncombatants. There are some other matters covered by the principle, but the immunity of noncombatants is at its heart, and so in what follows I shall treat discrimination as a principle for the immunity of noncombatants.

In its primary form, the principle prohibits intentionally killing or gravely harming noncombatants, but it does this partly because it seeks to keep them immune from the harms of war, especially death. Hence its concerns also reach even to such killing and harming that is not intentional, or, as some might say, not *directly* intentional; these are the harms of what has come to be called "collateral damage," to which I will turn later. This principle helps make a link between the condemnation of such state outrages as the deliberate bombing of civilian populations and the terrorist tactics of substate agents. Both attack illegitimate targets, and indeed I regard both as terrorism. The bias in favor of treating only substate agents as capable of terrorism seems to me just that: a political bias. I think that we should define terrorism as organized violence against noncombatants ("innocents" in a special sense) or their property for political purposes, no matter what agents employ it.

I have often argued for this elsewhere and attempted to deal with the objections raised to it. This is not the place to repeat the arguments in any detail. My argument supports what I call a tactical definition of terrorism, as opposed to a political status definition; I concentrate upon terrorism as the use of a certain sort of violent means that can be used by any agents, state or nonstate, whereas political status definitions treat terrorism as any use of violence by substate agents against the state. Tactical definitions provide an important link between terrorism and interstate or revolutionary war, even if terrorism doesn't always take place in the context of all-out conventional warfare. The brief definition provided above is a pared-down version of a more complex account that addresses such things as including in the definition the *threat* of such violence.

There are further questions to do with the precise intermediate purposes for which the violence is deployed and the place in the definition for such purposes. My preference is to exclude any reference to such purposes, even the very plausible purpose of inducing fear, because I would rather leave the determination of these matters to empirical investigation. If it were discovered that the agents of attacks upon noncombatants were interested in gaining their ultimate political ends by inspiring anger rather than fear (in order, perhaps, to provoke overreactions that would gain their group further supporters), then I doubt that we would refuse to call their deeds terrorism simply because they did not aim at producing fear. But for our present purposes this part of the definitional debate does not matter greatly.

Somewhat broader tactical definitions will still link terrorism to the just-war principle of discrimination that disallows attacks upon noncombatants as immoral. It is perhaps worth repeating what I have said in a number of places, namely that my account does not make terrorism or the bombing of noncombatants immoral by definition. You have to take the further step of accepting the just-war principle of the immunity of noncombatants to reach the moral conclusion.

There is also the further issue of whether that principle should be treated as utterly exceptionless. I favor doing so, but many philosophers, suspicious of absolute prohibitions of any sort, think that the principle, though very powerful, can be subject to exception in extreme cases. Michael Walzer is probably the best known of these, and he has argued that the principle can be disregarded in situations of what he calls supreme emergency. I think that the prohibition on attacking the innocent is so deep and the risks of allowing the regulation of war to admit exceptions to it so great that the supreme emergency exemption should be viewed with skepticism if not dismay. We cannot debate this issue further here, and I have done so elsewhere, so I shall proceed as if the prohibition is absolute. The relevant adjustments for very extreme situations can then be made by those more impressed by the supreme emergency category than I am.

How can we make a distinction between combatants and noncombatants, and why is it morally important to do so? The moral importance of the distinction is connected with the significance of the distinction between guilt and innocence, although the categories of combatant/noncombatant and guilty/innocent do not match exactly, for reasons to be discussed later. The significance of the latter distinction is illustrated in the biblical story of the destruction of Sodom and Gomorrah. In the buildup to that destruction, Abraham engages in dialogue with God aimed at mitigating the effects of the divine wrath against Sodom. In this strange and rather charming exchange (Genesis 18:23–33), some basic moral considerations about justice are adumbrated that are relevant to the moral force of the principle of discrimination and to the issue of collateral damage. Abraham boldly challenges his Lord as follows:

> Will you destroy the good with the wicked? If there be fifty just men in the city, will you then destroy the place and not spare it for the sake of the fifty just men within it? Far be it from you to do such a thing as kill the just with the wicked, treating just and unjust alike! Far be it from you! Shall not the judge of all the earth act justly?

In response, God offers to spare the city if Abraham can find fifty just men in it, and Abraham proceeds to bargain God down from fifty to forty-five to forty to thirty to twenty and finally to ten. (God quits the scene at this point before Abraham can try for five!) What is clear from this exchange is that although, *ex hypothesi*, God has a just cause, his destructive violence must be constrained by the moral necessity to discriminate between the guilty and the innocent, those who are legitimate objects of justified destruction and those who are not. This passage from Genesis vividly illustrates the centrality of a principle of discrimination within Judeo-Christian ethics, but a moment's reflection shows its significance to be much wider than the teachings of that tradition. A version of the principle of discrimination can be found, for instance, within the Chinese philosophical tradition of writing about the ethics of war.[1]

In fact, a simple example shows how deep and widespread is the moral understanding behind the principle of the JIB. Suppose you are walking peacefully home from work one night when someone jumps out of an alley and attacks you with an ax. You struggle with the assailant, call for help, but to no avail. Then you remember that you have confiscated a handgun from one of the children you teach at school, and you still have it on you. As you struggle, your hand closes on it, and you find yourself able to point it at your attacker's chest. Surely, when all else has failed, you are entitled to shoot and even kill the assailant.

Extended to collective agents, this is the basic idea of legitimate violent defense against aggression that lies at the heart of modern just-war theory and the JAB. But it also has lessons for the JIB and the principle of discrimination. Suppose that in the course of the struggle your gun was pointing not at the attacker but across the street at a small child who is staring in amazement at what is going on. You reason that you can create a diversion by shooting the child; its screams will distract the attacker and perhaps attract others to the scene who can offer you help. But surely these strategic reasonings do not entitle you to shoot the child. The child is not attacking you, nor is she complicit in the attack. The aggression that gives you the right to direct violence against those who are attacking or positively assisting the attack—not against others, even if maiming and killing others helps your cause.

The case can be extended to the collective example of the conduct of war or other forms of political violence. (Admittedly, there are some disanalogies between the individual, domestic case and the collective example but they do not affect the reach of the moral principle involved in discrimination; they affect more the basic argument for the legitimacy of self-defense in all cases.) So the immunity of noncombatants is essentially geared to the moral warrant for prosecuting war at all; it focuses on the crucial point that you can only be entitled to direct lethal violence at the agent or agents of the grievous harm that needs overcoming. You may aim only at the destruction or overpowering of "the guilty" in this sense and not "the innocent," in the sense of those who are not engaged in the relevant harm doing. There may of course be many people in the enemy nation who are guilty of various things, but unless they are agents of the wrong that entitles you take up arms, they must count as innocents for the purposes of your justified war, hence the significance of the category of noncombatant and its relevance to innocence (in war). More interestingly still, there may be many who are prosecuting the harm of an unjust war and thus are combatants (and wrongdoers, or "guilty" in this respect) who are not strictly morally guilty for what they do because they are excusably ignorant or forced to fight. Ignorance and coercion are in some circumstances conditions that absolve of full moral guilt. Nonetheless, we are entitled to treat a deluded or coerced attacker as a wrongdoer for the purposes of defensive violence where we have no such justification for directing violence at someone who is doing nothing to harm us. Combatants who are deluded or coerced have a similar status and of course many will be neither deluded nor coerced, and we are usually in no position to tell the difference between the two groups. This then shows the connections and dissimilarities between the categories of combatant/noncombatant and guilty/innocent, and illustrates the moral reasons for the principle of discrimination and the immunity of noncombatants that it protects.

There is another clarification to be made at this point, one that marks a point of departure from the current state of international law on warfare, and from some versions of just-war theory. The terms *combatant* and *noncombatant*, as I use them, are not equivalent to *soldier* and *civilian*. This can be a source of considerable confusion because the relevant UN declarations prohibit direct attacks upon civilians. But the noncombatant idea is the more fundamental, as our simple fable illustrates, for the immunity of innocence is earned by the fact that the person is not an agent of the wrongdoing.

It is understandable that *civilian* might be used as shorthand for *noncombatant*, because most, if not all, noncombatants will be civilians, yet not all civilians will be noncombatants.[2] Very many enemy civilians will indeed be noncombatants, but the overlap is not total, for there will be agents who are technically civilians who should qualify for combatant status, such as the political leadership directing the war, civilian scientists engaged in developing weaponry, and civilians training military interrogators in torture techniques.

The philosopher Jeff McMahan has cogently criticized the idea that noncombatants, understood as all civilians, are immune from direct attack.[3] McMahan presents this criticism as an objection to traditional just-war theory, but the most he shows is that there are civilians who are as responsible, or more responsible, for the wrongdoing that allows violent response as the frontline soldiers, many of whom may have been coerced to fight or be nonculpably ignorant of the injustice of their cause. I can accept this conclusion with equanimity because my use of *noncombatant* does not entail the position McMahan criticizes. If, however, we identify traditional just war thinking with the international laws relating to war, then McMahan's criticisms are relevant because the legal prohibitions refer to "civilian immunity," but I have already noted the problems with such an identification. What is true, as McMahan admits, is that pragmatically there will often be great difficulties in determining which enemy civilians are (in my sense) combatants.

This last point suggests that there may some point to the conflation made by international law of noncombatant and civilian. And further point is given to it, in the context of legal regulation rather than basic moral insight, by the consideration that it may be useful to maintain a ban on attacking civilians when that has gained a wide degree of legal acceptance and leads to some containment of the worst effects of war. The basic moral significance of the combatant/noncombatant distinction is not utilitarian. Noncombatant immunity does not principally gain its force, for instance, from its usefulness in restricting the amount of damage that may be done by warfare but from the fact that noncombatants have done nothing to deserve being attacked. Even so, if it also serves to limit the carnage of war, this provides an additional argument for it. So if treating all civilians as noncombatants limits the evils of war, then that is a point in favor of it. It may also be easier to get agreement on this broader understanding of *noncombatant* for the purposes of legislation, and if this preserves the rights of the genuinely noncombatant at the cost of undeserved immunity for political leaders and the like, this may be a cost worth paying. (As mentioned below, there are some difficulties with relying solely on such arguments from utility.)

I shall not further address the question whether this cost is worthwhile or to what degree utilitarian justifications and more intrinsic ones are mutually reinforcing. But, whatever is the best way to frame laws about the matter, we should not ignore the fact that there can be perpetrators of great wrongs, such as aggression, who are not in uniform or bearing arms themselves, though they use and provide direct, significant support to those who do. This is particularly important in the context of discussions of terrorism. In the case of Iraq, for example, it is common to cast as terrorists those insurgents who attack and kill "civilian contractors," but many of these are civilian in name only. They are contracted to support by arms the cause that the insurgents are fighting against. If that cause, of defeating an invading and occupying force, is a just one, then their violence against the contractors may be justifiable. In any case, justified or not, it is not terrorist, because it is not directed against noncombatants. Insurgents bombing a crowded market in Baghdad would be engaged in terrorism, whereas directing their violence at George Bush or Dick Cheney, each of whom is a primary agent in initiating and maintaining the war, should not count as terrorism.

Some reject the distinction between combatants and noncombatants, even as qualified above, and argue that once you decide to employ political violence in what you see as a just cause, you do whatever is necessary to win. This approach is often associated with the philosophy of utilitarianism, but it is commonly somewhat more narrow and self-interested than the calculations recommended by that philosophy, because it considers no other value than the benefits of victory to your side. It does not usually, for instance, bother to calculate the likely consequences of such policies for the future of warfare, or the effects on the future well-being of a defeated enemy. If, however, we make the big assumption that such a victory would promote the best outcomes for all affected (in Jeremy Bentham's phrase, "the greatest happiness of the greatest number"), then we do have a utilitarian perspective. In any case, whether strictly utilitarian or not, the calculating outlook that seeks only victory without concern for moral constraints was deployed to justify the Allied city bombing in World War II. It was argued privately and sometimes publicly that a deliberate attack upon civilian populations with the purpose of destroying popular and political morale would prevent a Nazi victory. Alleged efficiency in the pursuit of a good end replaced traditional morality in the conduct of war.

So some of the argument in defense of the bombing of World War II simply ignored military tradition and just-war theory, in single-minded pursuit of victory. This style of thinking had been prominent among enthusiasts for the use of air bombardment in the period between the two world wars, notably the Italian military theorist Giulio Douhet and the British author Basil Liddell Hart.[4] Both argued that the development of the airplane and its bombing capacity made it possible to leapfrog the battle lines of opposing armies and bring the war to enemy cities. Both thought that the effect on civilian morale would lead to a rapid cessation of hostilities.

Liddell Hart's concern was partly strategic but to a large degree moral. He had been shocked by the slaughter in the trenches during World War I and hoped the bombing would produce far fewer casualties. He argued in a straightforwardly utilitarian fashion that bombing enemy civilian populations would bring home to them the horrors of war and thereby create irresistible pressures to end hostilities rapidly, so saving great numbers of lives on both sides.[5] His views were influential in a number of circles but particularly important in the effect they had on Air Marshal Sir Hugh Trenchard, head of the Royal Air Force, who, along with "Bomber" Harris, was the architect of the British air campaign against German cities and civilians. Ironically, Liddell Hart later became disillusioned with this position and wrote eloquently against it, partly because he realized that the scale of devastation was greater than any he had contemplated. In 1942, Liddell Hart wrote, "It will be ironical if the defenders of civilization depend for their victory upon the most barbaric, and unskilled, way of winning a war that the modern world has seen . . . We are now counting for victory on success in the way of degrading war to a new level—as represented by indiscriminate (night) bombing and indiscriminate starvation."[6] This is, of course, a nonutilitarian objection to the bombing, but subsequent empirical studies also showed that even in terms of outcomes the city bombing was a failure, as it played a vastly smaller part in eventual Allied victory at much greater expense than had been expected by its advocates.[7]

Liddell Hart's rethinking occurred in a climate in which vocal critics of the bombing objected to it precisely because it violated the principle of discrimination (not that they used that phrase, necessarily). It is worth pointing this out because critics today are often accused of being wise after the event, and it is important to recall that many were wise at the time. Among them were the Bishop of Chichester, George Bell, who raised moral objections in the House of Lords; several other members of Parliament, such as Lord Addison, Lord Lang, and the Marquis of Salisbury in the House of Lords, as well as Rhys Davies, Reginald Sorensen, and the very persistent Richard Stokes in the House of Commons. Then there was the novelist Vera Brittain, who helped organize the Committee for the Abolition of Night Bombing and who carried the campaign against the bombing to the public in her writings. There were also many ordinary Britons who opposed the bombing, including some who had been victims of a similar German atrocity, as was the case with six residents of Coventry who wrote to the *New Statesman* in November 1943 deploring the bombing of German cities and claiming that the "general feeling" in Coventry was "the desire that no other people shall suffer as they have done."[8]

The reaction to these dissenters was nonetheless very negative, partly because people had been deceived by government falsification of the purposes of the bombing, but also because of the emotions of war. The left-wing pacifist Brittain was virtually denounced as a Nazi sympathizer and was virulently attacked in the United States, where no one had suffered city bombing.[9] It is interesting that the innocent who have suffered unjustified enemy attacks are often less disposed to inflict the same fate on others, even members of an enemy population. As noted earlier, this seems to have been true of many of the people of Coventry, and Gallup polls during the war never showed more than 50 percent of the British people favoring direct reprisal raids on Germany.[10]

Reference to vengeance is relevant to the justifications offered for the city bombings of Germany. We have noted the early Liddell Hart style of justification, which has much in common with utilitarian philosophy in that it is both consequentialist and seeks to maximize the good outcomes for all concerned, including the enemy. It argues for the benefits to everyone that civilian massacres would bring in terms of early ending to war. But there were two other common justifications, often conflated with that one, that deserve separate attention. One is vengeance and the other is a version of self-defense that treats nations as crucially important entities and gives an overwhelming significance to one's own.

That vengeance played some part in the British bombing campaign can hardly be doubted, though more instrumental motives were probably dominant. Winston Churchill sometimes employed the vengeance theme, as when he said, referring to the "air weapon": "This was the weapon with which they boasted—the Germans boasted—they would terrorize the world. And it is an example of *poetic justice* that this should be the weapon in which they should find themselves most outmatched . . . in the ensuing struggle."[11] A key thought in this response as in many others is the treatment of the enemy population as a single guilty entity. The Australian conservative politician Richard Casey, who served in Churchill's war cabinet, was present when Churchill watched a film of RAF bombing over Germany. In his diaries, he recorded Churchill having a moment of revulsion from what he had put into effect: "Are we beasts? Are we taking this too far?" Casey responded by saying that we hadn't started it, and it was them or us.[12] Here we see the idea of the retaliatory response aimed at the single guilty entity, but also the idea that the bombing was needed for the survival of that prized entity, our nation.

Taking the vengeance idea first, we should note that whatever moral value may reside in retribution, it can only relate to delivering punishment or retaliation to someone who has offended you in the first place. Hence for it to apply to the present case, it must be supposed that the whole German nation has "started all this" and thereby earned the tit-for-tat response. But this is nonsensical. "Collective guilt" is a vicious idea when applied in this fashion; groups can act together and hence be collectively guilty, but this requires a deliberate contribution by individuals to the combined effort of the whole. This is characteristically lacking when we come to the activities of nations. Even in democracies, which allow some freedom of choice and a degree of involvement by citizens in government decisions, there are always many people who vote against the governing party or show their disagreement with or lack of interest in its decisions in a variety of ways. Even those who do vote for a government may not have known its war policies or may vote for reasons unconnected with its war policies. Voting is in general a very inexact measure of responsibility. And the idea of collective responsibility or guilt is even sillier in the case of dictatorships and tyrannies like Nazi Germany, where uncoerced democratic voting played no serious part in Hitler's gaining and keeping power. In any case, there are countless babies, infants, and young children whom it would be absurd to imagine as having dealt the blow to which we are to retaliate. Holding the German nation as a whole guilty of the war would also mean holding German Jews, Gypsies, and communists to blame as well. This influential idea of national collective guilt is as immoral as it is incoherent.

Yet it not only played a part in the atrocities of Hamburg, Dresden, Tokyo, Hiroshima, and Nagasaki (not to mention London and Coventry) but it continues even today to exert an influence in the popular mind. It is often conjoined with the idea of self-defense rather than vengeance. The two concepts are different in several respects, most notably in that vengeance requires inflicting equivalent damage on the perpetrator of harm whereas self-defense merely requires preventing the perpetrator from inflicting the harm or continuing to do so. The requirements of self-defense have a powerful moral appeal, and they are not strictly utilitarian: one may be entitled to defend oneself against an attack even if the defense does more damage than the attack would do to you. So you may kill three attackers if necessary to save your life even though three deaths might outweigh one for a utilitarian and so be impermissible. Yet self-defense cannot reach beyond inflicting injury upon an attacker. It cannot permit violent actions that may promote self-preservation but are directed at those who are not bent on harming you.

Vengeance is more complex, or ambiguous. In one construal, that of legitimate retribution, it can only reach to delivering punishment to an offender, but it seeks to pay back whether the offender is currently attacking or endangering. From the point of view of self-defense, however, once the attacker has been repelled and rendered harmless, there is no further issue of punishment involved in the idea of self-defense itself. The idea of punishment may be appropriate, but it invokes different considerations, such as compensation for harm done. In another common understanding of vengeance, the payback can reach to anyone whose being harmed will damage the original offender; hence the vengefulness of feuds or vendettas reaches out to family members whether they were guilty of offending or not. In both self-defense and vengeance, of course, the poisonous effects of the idea of collective guilt can wrongly make offenders of whole nations.

A committed utilitarian defense of city bombing need not embrace the dubious notion of collective guilt. It could argue that the basic question is not innocence or guilt, or combatant or noncombatant status, but simply whether the best overall results for all concerned would be achieved by deliberate bombing of civilians. Many intellectuals and many ordinary people, not obviously depraved, are attracted to this style of thinking, and indeed to a utilitarian defense of the bombing.

A full refutation of this sort of view would require inter alia a critique of simple utilitarianism (or its cousin, moral consequentialism), and that is beyond the scope of this chapter. Two things, however, should be remarked about this move as a defense of the Allied bombing. One is that it is not at all clear that a serious utilitarian defense of it would be successful. This is because the arguments for the good consequences of the bombing were at the time far from compelling. The idea that making inroads on civilian morale would change the political will of the leaders of a totalitarian regime during war was always suspect; it was always likely that the bombing would make the survivors hate their attackers more and thus encourage support for the Nazi leadership as the only recourse they had. This sort of thing was, after all, what the British civilians themselves experienced under the German blitz. Research after the war showed that the bombing had at best only a minimal impact on achieving an Allied victory.[13]

Second, there are more complex versions of utilitarianism that would seek to give more weight to such prohibitions as the immunity of noncombatants requires. Supporters of indirect or rule utilitarianism would argue that there is no intrinsic justification for the prohibition (of the kind I have sought to sketch) but concede that the prohibition is validated by the fact that it normally produces better outcomes than would accrue if there were no such prohibition. In particular, they would argue that the horror and slaughter of war would be much reduced by honoring of the principle of noncombatant immunity. They may be right about this, and I could accept it as a further argument for the principle, though there are those who argue that violation of the principle might actually produce better results by making the duration and ferocity of wars shorter. This was what was urged by many of the early advocates of city bombing, like Liddell Hart, though he had the decency to admit his error. Nonetheless, his earlier position and others like it show the double-edged nature of utilitarian arguments.[14]

This completes my sketch of what is wrong with terrorism, understood as a violation of the principle of discrimination. It supports the moral condemnation of the campaigns of deliberate bombing of noncombatants in the variety of circumstances already discussed by other contributors to this book. I want to turn now to the rather different matter of what (if anything) is wrong with the harming and killing of noncombatants that is not intentional. This brings us into the terrain of collateral damage.

Two Forms of Collateral Damage

The basic idea of collateral damage is present in Abraham's challenge to God discussed earlier. Abraham is objecting not only to the injustice of killing the innocent, but also to the injustice of killing them as an incidental effect of killing the wicked. As he puts it: "Will you destroy the good with the wicked?" And he goes on to insist on reducing the number of innocent that are collaterally killed, an insistence with which God apparently agrees, as the total is reduced from fifty to ten before God quits the scene. This exchange thus points to the significance of proportionality in discussing the context in which collateral damage may be acceptable.

The idea of collateral damage encompasses two quite different things. One is that of damage to property and life that is caused accidentally. The other is that of destruction or injury or death that is not accidental but is nonetheless unintended. This latter category has puzzled many people, including philosophers, because it means that an agent can know that his primary action will almost certainly have a particular consequence but can still go ahead with the action not intending that consequence. Some philosophers, such as Jeremy Bentham, and some legal systems, hold that the agent must intend the known consequences of his or her action. Even here, it is noteworthy that Bentham acknowledges some need for a distinction by talking of "oblique intention" where those he opposes want to talk of "foreseen but unintended consequences." There is an extensive literature on this topic that we cannot explore here, and it encompasses such issues as the validity of the doctrine of "double effect," the scope and significance of "negative responsibility," and the relative importance of the character of an act and an agent compared to good or bad outcomes. There is at the very least a certain plausibility in the idea that there is sometimes both point and moral relevance to the belief that certain outcomes can be foreseen but not intended. For example, I may believe with practical certainty that if I refuse a gangster's command to murder a colleague, the gangster will murder that colleague and two other people who stand in his way, but it would surely be very strange to describe me as intending, by my refusal, the deaths of all three. Here there is the will of another involved in the outcome and perhaps that is enough even to vitiate the idea that the deaths are "a consequence" of my action of refusal. But this is at least disputable, and, in any case, there are other examples that do not involve the mediation of another's will. For example, suppose I am on an archery shooting range and I realize that one of the archers has suddenly turned her weapon in my direction and is about to shoot an arrow. Perhaps she has had a nervous breakdown or has somehow become confused about targets. I leap aside in the full knowledge that the person close behind me will be hit and probably killed. Surely I did not intend by my self-preserving action to inflict injury and death on that person, even though I could reasonably foresee that outcome? Or consider my plight as a surgeon in a war zone who must choose who among the wounded to aid with scarce lifesaving drugs. In choosing to save Brown and Smith with the foreseeable consequence that Black, Jones, and Gray will die, it makes sense to describe me as intending to save Brown and Smith with the foreseen but unintended consequence that the latter three die, rather than as intending to save Brown and Smith but thereby intending to kill Black, Jones, and Gray. Certainly, the case is markedly different on the side of my character and purposes from the case where I, the surgeon, have a deep grudge against Black, Jones, and Gray and deliberately inject them with poison before going on to save the other two.

These comments make a plausible case for the category of "foreseen but unintended" and its moral relevance, but we need not assume unequivocal success in defense of the category. The point is principally to explain the initial appeal of the category and thereby to make comparative sense of the way it might be relied upon in discussions of the morality of collateral damage. As we shall see, this initial plausibility can be stretched and even eroded.

Let us call the form of collateral damage that requires the idea of foreseen but unintended damage "incidental damage" to contrast with the other form of "accidental damage." In what follows, I shall concentrate on incidental damage, but it is worth noting that the plea of "accident" or "mistake" does not necessarily avoid blame, since much accidental damage in war should have been foreseen and avoided. It is clear that a good deal of accidental killing of enemy civilians in war exhibits a culpable lack of concern for their lives and safety. As we shall see later, the insights behind the principle of discrimination prohibit various actions, such as negligent and reckless behavior that show disrespect or "depraved indifference" for the immunity of noncombatants. Even if we accept that the bombing of the Al-Jazeera bureau in Kabul in 2001 and the later bombing of the building housing Al-Jazeera staff in Baghdad, with the deaths of one of their most prominent journalists, were mistakes, there remains a question whether due care was taken to avoid the mistakes. Murder is a dreadful thing, but we cannot congratulate ourselves on avoiding it if we are casual about manslaughter and negligent homicide.

Incidental Damage and the Doctrine of Double Effect

This brings us to the category of incidental damage, in which agents proceed with an attack intending to damage a legitimate target but reasonably believing that their attack will kill innocent bystanders or neighbors (and/

or damage their property). The attackers tend to justify their actions by resort to the doctrine of double effect (DDE) or some related maxim. The DDE holds that the foreseen but unintended consequences of an action are morally acceptable when certain conditions are fulfilled. It does not hold that incidental damage is acceptable merely because it is incidental to intent. The usual conditions are:

1. The action at issue must not itself be morally bad, nor should any intended effect of it be morally bad.
2. The anticipated bad effect must be genuinely unintended and not merely secondarily intended (e.g., intended as a means to a further end).
3. The harm involved in the unintended outcome is not disproportionate to the benefit aimed at in the act.[15]

The first of these conditions simply specifies that the moral utility of the DDE arises only when what is intended by the agent (the outcome that has the unintended but foreseen bad consequence) is a benefit that is either morally neutral or morally good. The second condition is aimed at precluding what Elizabeth Anscombe once called "double-think about double effect." People faced with the difficult choices about what tactics to use in war efforts will often adopt a simple utilitarian or consequentialist stance. But where they don't adopt such a stance, there is a strong temptation to stretch the DDE in order to gain maximum tactical advantage in the deployment of violence. So it may be argued that the real intention in attacking a day care center is to win the war, not to kill the children and their caretakers. Admittedly, this is an extreme in sophistry since it blatantly ignores the fact that having an ultimate purpose for some action does not exclude having an intermediate purpose that requires fulfillment in order to achieve the ultimate objective. Generally speaking, someone who intends an end also intends the means chosen to that end.

The DDE and the restrictive conditions mentioned have been subject to sustained philosophical discussion and criticism. It will not be possible to canvass this often very complex debate here, but I will briefly note some of the issues it has raised.[16] One is the idea that intention is not as important a feature of the moral assessment of acts as the DDE requires, especially when the foreseen but unintentional outcomes of a given act are equivalent in terms of damage to those that a parallel intentional acts would have

caused. How can it matter morally that a hundred children are killed intentionally in one scenario and unintentionally (but with foresight) in another? A proper response to this criticism would have to vindicate the
significance of intentional action within a broad picture of morality and its
point, a picture broad enough to lessen the impact of this criticism's stress
upon the supposed equivalence of outcomes. A second objection concen-
trates on the proportionality requirement and argues either that the requirement is too obscure or that it will always be treated as too subordinate
to military necessity.

A third problem concerns the difficulties in individuating actions and
their attendant intentions, e.g., when does it become implausible to claim
that you intended to use your bomb only to destroy a military target when
that destruction very closely involves the destruction of noncombatants?
Consider, for example, the Israeli army's use of a one-ton bomb to blow up
a block of flats in order to kill one Hamas leader, Sheikh Salah Mustafa
Shehada, with the result that eight children (one of whom was two
months old) were killed in the bombing. It is hard to see how the action of
killing the Hamas leader could be so disentangled from the deaths of the
children as to claim with any plausibility that the bombers intended to kill
only him. This looks like a case of what Anscombe called "double-think
about double effect."

I have some sympathy for the role its proponents want DDE to play,
even though I realize that it is not free from difficulties. I think, for instance, that the notion of means that the doctrine employs needs more attention, and that the DDE is much more plausible when the foreseen
effect is *risk* to noncombatants rather than certain death, but this is not the
place to engage further in extensive debate about the doctrine. It is, however, worth remarking that unless we employ the DDE, or some other
principle that serves a similar purpose, then the possibility of waging a
modern war that sufficiently respects the immunity of noncombatants is
vastly reduced. There will be many situations in which noncombatant
deaths and injuries can be foreseen as a result of attacking important military objectives, and without something like the DDE, these attacks will
be ruled out by the immunity of noncombatants. (Of course it might be
possible to rule out some of them on utilitarian grounds without having
regard for the category of the foreseen but unintended.) This consequence
has been taken by at least one critic as a powerful argument for pacifism.[17]

Hence, theorists like Michael Walzer, who do not want to go down this path, make extensive use of the DDE.

Further Complexities

Quite apart from the explicit conditions for the application of the DDE, there is another aspect of the doctrine that needs attention. This is the requirement that we should not embark upon actions involving collateral damage, and hence should not resort to the DDE, unless we have first explored other feasible ways of achieving the good end that do not involve the harmful side effects or involve fewer or less grave such effects. And this holds even where the alternatives involve somewhat more costs to the agent. Elsewhere, I have called this a precondition for the application of the DDE since it responds to the restrictive spirit that underpins the DDE even where its form seems permissive.

In the case of war or political violence more generally, the protection of the innocent remains a primary value of the *jus in bello* and hence dictates that incidental injury or killing of the innocent is to be entirely avoided where possible.[18] The degree of risk to one's own troops or one's cause that is involved in avoiding collateral damage certainly needs to be factored into the understanding of "where possible," but some risks need to be taken where the lives of innocent people are at stake. The point needs stressing because it can guard against too ready a resort to collateral damage and too easy an attitude to the exculpatory power of the DDE. Without regard for the precondition, innocent casualties can be too lightly discounted by the idea of proportionality where the military goal is important.

The point I am making here by talking of a precondition is a longstanding part of the just-war tradition, as the following comment by Vitoria indicates: "It is never lawful to kill innocent people, even accidentally and unintentionally, except when it advances a just war *which cannot be won in any other way*" (emphasis added).[19] Vitoria is saying that the killing of the innocent in war can be licit only when it is done either accidentally or unintentionally (i.e., foreseen but not intended), but even then it is licit only where there is no alternative to it.

There are other ways in which the idea of collateral damage can be abused in either its accidental or incidental forms. One is the expansion of the permissible scope of the category of collateral damage by expansion of the scope of legitimate military targets. This is the strategy of targeting "dual-purpose" facilities, a practice that has become increasingly familiar in recent U.S. military practice, though it has a more ancient lineage. The war against Serbia over Kosovo provides many examples, as does the invasion of Iraq by the "Coalition of the Willing." The destruction of significant energy resources and communications facilities in Iraq has had a massively deleterious effect upon the civilian population, especially in Baghdad. The civilians were largely innocent of any crime that might have justified the military invasion; indeed, their well-being was supposed to be a primary reason for invading. So the value of noncombatant life and the infrastructure that supports it should weigh more heavily than it frequently does. This is not to say that there is never a case for attacking a facility that serves both military and nonmilitary purposes, but the mere existence of a dual purpose is not itself enough to legitimate an attack and thereby count the damage to noncombatants as permissible "incidental" injury. The destruction of water supplies by bombing and the noncombatant deaths from thirst and disease that ensue cannot be justified by the mere fact that enemy soldiers use the same water supplies as enemy civilians. Casual attitudes to the destruction of power supplies, oil reserves, bridges, communications networks, and media facilities need more careful scrutiny lest they really display a disregard for the rights and protections that should be accorded noncombatants.

Such scrutiny is particularly important given the latitude that current international law allows for attacks upon dual-purpose targets. The law is currently too permissive in this respect, since it rules out dual-purpose targets only where the objects proposed for destruction cause incidental damage (in my sense) that "may be expected to leave the civilian population with such inadequate food or water as to cause its starvation or force its movement."[20] It may be difficult to determine proportionality in certain circumstances, but it clearly encompasses more harms than these. Malnourishment, disease, homelessness, and a range of other serious deprivations are simply ignored, while the balancing of the military advantage against these or other harms to noncombatants is passed over.[21] Only a dubious bias in favor of "military necessity" over a moral concern for the protection of the innocent could support the permission to bomb when the target has *some* value for the enemy's military purposes but also has considerable civilian value such that its destruction will bring very significant harm to many noncombatants even if it falls short of starving them or making them refugees.

When the respect for noncombatant immunity is rejected or ignored as a moral constraint on fighting, it will be natural to target not only civilians and their property but the infrastructure that directly supports their lives or more indirectly gives those lives meaning. Hence the dam-busting raids of World War II were a natural accompaniment to the area bombing of German cities. But once it is accepted that restraint must be exercised in the targeting of civilian populations, attacks upon infrastructure become immediately more problematic. We have discussed the bombing of German cities with particular reference to the British campaign of directly targeting noncombatants and their homes. The American bombing campaigns over Germany in World War II, however, are worth attention precisely on this issue of infrastructure, because their campaign against the cities was supposed to be directed less at killing civilians and making them homeless and much more at the everyday infrastructure of German life. The American authorities professed a commitment to precision bombing with their Norden bombsight, and disavowed a policy of area bombing of noncombatants (though they were happy to resort to such a policy against the Japanese). In fact, their practice often enough seems not to have been all that different from the British, but in any case, the professed policy of destroying infrastructure is either dual-purpose targeting, which raises the moral problems mentioned above, or even worse, it is an attack on solely or very predominantly civilian assets that is primarily intended to destroy the morale of noncombatants by making their lives an extreme misery. As such it stands condemned by the principle of discrimination.

The problems in this area have given rise to conflict between Allied air commands in Iraq, and earlier in the war against Serbia. These center on different interpretations of civilian immunity in the rules of engagement of the different air forces. Much secrecy surrounds rules of engagement because of fears that the enemy might exploit knowledge of what they are. But in Iraq, it has been reported that tension developed between Australian and U.S. air commands quite early in the war because of "fundamental differences between U.S.-dominated headquarters and Australian pilots over what constituted a valid military target."[22] These differences seemed to relate to the question of how much certainty about the status of the target was required before bombing proceeded. The Australian approach was that a target was not to be bombed if there was any uncertainty about its being a legitimate military target, whereas the American approach was that designated targets were to be bombed unless it was certain that they were *not* legitimate military objectives. Clearly the onus of proof exhibited in the two approaches is widely divergent, and the outcomes for noncombatants are likely to be spectacularly different. There were also tensions about the use of cluster bombs, which Americans use but Australian policy forbids.

A related issue concerns the legitimacy of attacking "innocent shields." This is a thorny problem because both insurgents and states either deliberately seek ways to mingle their military assets with civilians as a way of protecting the assets, or simply locate them in this way in the normal course of events. In its simplest form, the problem arises when a soldier takes innocent persons hostage and uses them as a cover to escape or continue an attack. In more complex scenarios, the enemy may put some of its most dangerous weapons in among civilian populations.

Without dealing in full detail with the morality of this problem, we can cite some basic principles that should govern the response.[23] One is that killing innocent people in order to get to the guilty should normally be out of the question. When the killing or injuring can be sensibly subsumed as incidental in the way explored above, it may sometimes and reluctantly be permissible. A second principle is that where the innocents are going to die anyway at the hands of the enemy, killing them in order to destroy the enemy and prevent further illegitimate killing by that enemy may be permissible. A good example would have been the legitimacy of intercepting and destroying the hijacked planes of September 11, 2001, before they hit the New York twin towers. The innocent passengers were doomed anyway, and it could certainly be assumed that if they knew their fate, they would agree to perishing under attack and thereby preventing the terrorist success. (Efforts might be made to treat their deaths as incidental and covered by the DDE, but I am skeptical of the plausibility of this move.) A third principle is that those who create innocent shields are indeed greatly to blame (and the practice is condemned in international law), but the fact that the enemy have a share of the responsibility for the ultimate deaths and injuries to civilians does nothing to remove the issue of responsibility from those who face the problem of attacking the shields.

Earlier I mentioned cluster bombs. Both cluster bombs and antipersonnel mines clearly raise problems under the discrimination principle. In many respects, they share objectionable features with so-called weapons of mass destruction (WMD). The primary objection to such weapons is that they fail to discriminate between combatants and noncombatants. If we disregard possible radiation effects, then a nuclear bomb could legitimately be used against an isolated wholly military target in a desert or at sea, but that is not what deterrent policies are really based upon. Similarly, one can imagine scenarios for the legitimate use of cluster bombs and other antipersonnel weapons, but many actual uses of them either deliberately or negligently encompass the death and injury of noncombatants. They also share with conventional mines some future-facing moral problems to do with discrimination. With conventional mines, the problem is less the damage they cause to noncombatants at the time than the devastation to civilian populations that they continue to cause after the conflict has ended, which is also an issue with cluster bombs.

Conclusion

Whether we are dealing with war or terrorism, much discussion of collateral damage has, understandably, focused upon the *killing* of noncombatants. But there are many other kinds of harm, damage, and suffering that do not result in immediate death. When attacks on civilian infrastructure are aimed at destroying civilian morale, they stand condemned under the principle of discrimination, but even when viewed from a dual-purpose perspective, there must be doubts about many such attacks. The dual-purpose strategy tends to see the infrastructural features of an enemy population as connected with short-term military gains and short-term civilian discomforts, but the moral gaze needs to be broader than that because, especially in modern societies, the infrastructures are increasingly crucial to well-being, survival, and even sometimes to life itself. Something like this point can be extended to the problems raised by direct or incidental damage to the natural and human environment of the enemy's country. The value of forests, rivers, architectural and artistic creations, and the like can be viewed both as valuable in themselves and as part of the significant life of the enemy's civilian population, or indeed as part of the broader human heritage (hence the outrage at the Taliban's destruction of ancient Buddhist statues). Sometimes, of course, there is nothing incidental at all about such attacks, for the cultural and natural environment are often enough deliberately targeted as a sort of ethnic cleansing, but where the destruction is accidental or incidental, it still bears the burden of moral accountability in the ways sketched above.

Whatever the problems with DDE, there are moral attitudes behind the different approaches to collateral damage as reflected in the application of the DDE that are themselves of clear significance in the prosecution of war. These fall into (at least) four camps.

1. Sadistic contempt for noncombatants' lives and well-being, leading to the intentional killing of them.
2. Instrumental disdain for them, leading again to the intentional killing of them.
3. Indifference to their lives and well-being, leading to a casual attitude to collateral damage.
4. Concern for their lives and well-being, leading to attempts to avoid or limit the collateral damage.

It is the moral superiority of number 4 over 1, 2, and 3 that gives significance to the attempt to find principles that allow for the legitimacy of some foreseen but unintentional killing or harming of noncombatants. The difficulty in finding a satisfactory formula and the agonies of making concrete judgments that lead to the incidental deaths of children and other noncombatants are among the reasons for not resorting to war, revolution, or insurgency in the first place. But assuming that wars and other resorts to political violence can sometimes be justified, we need to allow for the feasible prosecution of a just war, or one believed to be just, while giving a high moral priority to protecting the lives of noncombatants. Disallowing intentional targeting of them is a crucial step forward. But we cannot rest content with that while collateral damage reaches levels that flout the value enshrined in attitude number 4. Bringing collateral damage firmly under the controlling restraints of morality, reason, and adequate law is an urgent task facing anyone concerned to make the idea of a just war more than a cynical item of political rhetoric.

10

AERIAL BOMBARDMENT OF CIVILIANS: THE CURRENT INTERNATIONAL LEGAL FRAMEWORK

Timothy L.H. McCormack and Helen Durham

Introduction

International laws relating to targeting are highly complex and highly controversial. These laws are at the heart of international humanitarian law (IHL), the area of law that regulates the conduct of armed hostilities. Questions relating to who and what can be targeted, when they can be targeted, and how they can be targeted are fundamental to the notion that legal obligations must not be abandoned in times of extreme conflict. The basic rules governing the law of targeting can appear straightforward and linear in their written form—the target must be a military objective, weapons and tactics used must be lawful, the attack must comply with the principle of proportionality, and the attacker must have taken a range of precautions to minimize civilian damage. However, the application of the rules in the heated context of battle is not as simple as a brief articulation of the rules might suggest.

This chapter aims to introduce the reader to the international legal framework surrounding the law of targeting as it relates to civilian damage. It is not intended as a critique of this area of law. Rather it will provide details of the particular rules of IHL and focus upon recent specific bombing incidents to illustrate the applicable rules and the challenges involved in their application. Before doing so, it is important to locate the rules of targeting within the broader context of IHL, an area of international law concurrently aspirational and pragmatic. Gaining an under-

BY MICHAEL LEUNIG

standing of the basic aims and limitations of IHL will provide the reader with a deeper appreciation of the complicated legal regime regulating targeting and highlight the development of the law in this area since the horrific events of Hiroshima and Nagasaki.

Over the last decade, IHL has experienced a breathtaking renaissance as a direct consequence of the spectacular developments in international criminal law and the creation of multilateral structures and processes to prosecute violations of IHL. There is a general understanding, not limited to the echelons of the elite, that those accused of atrocities should be held responsible. Daily the international media report on matters such as the trial and execution of Saddam Hussein; the death before judgement of Slobodan Milošević; the referral of ex-Liberian president Charles Taylor to the Special Court for Sierra Leone; and the saga of the Augusto Pinochet case. The creation of the two ad hoc international criminal tribunals for the former Yugoslavia (ICTY)[1] and for Rwanda (ICTR),[2] the coming into force of the International Criminal Court (ICC),[3] and a plethora of hybrid tribunals in Iraq, Kosovo, Cambodia, Sierra Leone, and Timor Leste all demonstrate growing international acceptance that impunity is no longer guaranteed for those who breach international law.

Within this context there are increasing expectations that the law of targeting will be applied rigorously and that those responsible for violations of it are likely now to face justice. With the range of new international prosecution mechanisms, the political decision of the Allies during the post–World War II trials not to prosecute Germans or Japanese for aerial bombardment of civilians due to their own use of this tactic could be seen as a thing of the past. The ICC has been established specifically to avoid the accusation of "victor's justice," which is rightly leveled at the Nuremberg and Tokyo trials. However considering the complexity of the legal framework in this area and the very fragmented nature of the activity itself (diffusion of responsibilities between those who identify the target and those who actually "push the button"), the expectation of significant prosecutions for breaches relating to targeting may be unrealistic—at least in any systematic and comprehensive sense. Indeed, in over ten years the ICTY and ICTR have developed very little jurisprudence on the laws relating to the aerial bombing of civilians, and pending cases do not suggest a dramatic change.[4] However, targeting decisions *are* subject to greater scrutiny than ever before. Immediate and widespread access to pictures of the devastating consequences of aerial bombing—dead civilians and destroyed homes and other civilian infrastructure—fuel the international condemnation and accompanying clamor for individual criminal accountability. In all major aerial bombing campaigns—the 1991 Gulf War, NATO's intervention in Kosovo, the invasion of Iraq in 2003, and Israel's recent action in southern Lebanon—there has been intense criticism of certain selected targets as well as of the amount of ordnance deployed. A rigorous critique from civil society on these matters will inevitably have an impact upon the development of IHL. A detailed understanding of the legal framework consolidates the potential for change and ensures that any debate embarked upon has technical as well as ethical relevance.

The Historical Development of International Humanitarian Law

The experience of war has been shared by every human generation. However, from earliest times, evidence also abounds that those involved in such violence have understood the importance of moderation during conflict, for strategic as well as humane purposes.[5] Ancient writings, for example those of Chinese warrior Sun Tzu in the sixth century B.C., advocated a number of humanitarian limitations, from the methods used on battlefields to the treatment of prisoners and civilians. Similar examples can be found in ancient Greece, South Asia, and medieval Europe. These recorded restrictions on the conduct of hostilities often stem from effective use of force rather than from morally binding codes.[6] Striking a balance between principles of humanity and military necessity is the underlying philosophical tension that continues to characterize the codification of IHL today.

The applicable legal regime varies according to the characterization of the type of armed conflict. Restrictions on international conflict are more comprehensive than those relating to internal armed conflict. This is a product both of the historical context within which much of the law was drafted and of states' reluctance to have limitations placed on them in their treatment of their own people. As in all areas of international law, sovereignty plays a central part in IHL developments. However, unlike some legal norms in international human rights law, there are no elements of IHL that can be "suspended" by a state.[7]

IHL does not determine the legality of the use of force. This is governed by a distinct area of international law—*jus ad bellum*, mainly codified in the UN Charter. IHL, on the other hand, tries to remain free from controversy, and its provisions apply to all sides of an armed conflict, irrespective of the merits of the resort to force or the reasons for the conflict. Thus IHL, or the law of war (*jus in bello*), aims to protect all war victims. It is of crucial importance to the integrity and respect of IHL that *jus ad bellum* remain distinct from *jus in bello*.

Attempts to "humanize" armed conflict have at times been met with a range of criticisms. Certain scholars have argued that IHL merely legitimizes rather than restrains violence.[8] Many of these criticisms highlight the tension between the pragmatic, limited aims of IHL and the expectations placed upon it. Terms such as "military necessity" and "collateral damage" indicate the depth of involvement armed forces have in the drafting and implementation of IHL rules. Whilst IHL is a restrictive area of international law in that it limits who can be attacked and how, it is also an unusually permissive legal regime. It allows combatants to wage war, granting immunity to acts such as the killing of other combatants who are not deemed protected persons. IHL also allows detaining prisoners of war, people who may not have committed crimes, and holding them until the end of hostilities. Any ethical or moral analysis of IHL must embrace its function as reducing rather than eradicating suffering during times of armed conflict.

Sources of International Humanitarian Legal Obligation

The sources of IHL include treaty law and customary international law. Increasingly, the jurisprudence arising from international criminal trials, such as those from the ICTY and ICTR, is cited as authoritative interpretation and application of IHL rules.

Much of the focus of IHL today can be found in the Four Geneva Conventions of 1949[9] and their Additional Protocols of 1977.[10] However, it is also important to acknowledge the ongoing relevance of a broader range of treaties, including the Hague Conventions of 1899 and their successors of 1907. The lesser-known Hague Conventions established a number of the fundamental principles, in particular about targeting, which are reflected (and in some instances directly replicated) in the more modern codifications.[11] There are also numerous other treaties within the IHL framework dealing with issues such as the protection of cultural property,[12] which are of relevance to the matter at hand.

The most prolific new area of IHL treaty law regulates specific weapons.[13] In recent years, the international community has created new treaties, dealing with weapons such as antipersonnel land mines[14] and blinding laser weapons.[15] It has also witnessed the culmination of long-standing negotiations on biological and chemical weapons.[16] Another area of dramatic change in the last decade has been the development of international enforcement mechanisms, reflecting concerns about the paucity of domestic prosecutions in this area of international law.

General Principles of International Humanitarian Law

Much of the substance of IHL reflects an attempt to strike a balance between military objectives and humanity. The rules are a product of negotiation and compromise. These compromises allow states to rest assured that their militaries have adequate room to maneuver to protect themselves while, it is hoped, curbing excesses that do nothing to advance national interests. The inevitable consequence of the multilateral treaty-making process is a lack of definitional precision and the inclusion of "margins of appreciation" in favor of military commanders. The resultant elasticity in the obligations and prohibitions applicable to targeting is exploited by militaries eager to achieve their objectives—hence the condemnation that follows aerial bombing campaigns.

The first obligation in targeting is *distinction*. It requires the military to attack only military objectives and prohibits attacks on civilians and civilian objects. As an eminent writer in this field puts it, distinction is the "very heart and soul of the law of war."[17]

To make distinction effective, we must define "military objective." This involves two considerations: whether the objects by their very nature, location, purpose, or use make an effective contribution to the military action and whether their destruction, capture, or neutralization offers a definite military advantage.

However, even after the decision is made that this threshold test for a military objective has been passed, the legal obligations continue. The rule on *proportionality* must also be considered. Proportionality requires that there be an acceptable relationship between the anticipated military advantage and the expected incidental harm to civilians and their property. Other regulations are also relevant, such as prohibition on attacks on cultural property.

The process of making a legitimate targeting decision is well illustrated by Australian Defence Force (ADF) Air Force Wing Commander Ian Henderson's proposed targeting process. Henderson has identified six separate steps:

1. Locating and observing the potential target and its surrounding area,
2. Assessing whether the target is a valid military objective and that it is otherwise unprotected from attack by IHL,
3. Taking all feasible precautions to minimize collateral damage,
4. Assessing whether any expected collateral damage is proportional to the anticipated military advantage,
5. Taking care to release or fire the weapon so as to hit the target precisely, and
6. Canceling or suspending the attack if it becomes apparent that any of these assessments is no longer valid.[18]

The Rule on Distinction and the Prohibition of Attacks on Civilians

No legal justification can ever be made for making the civilian population the target of a military attack. It is a basic rule of IHL that the parties to a conflict must protect civilians and civilian objects in an armed conflict. Parties are legally obliged to distinguish at all times between civilians and combatants, and between civilian objects and military objectives. Any willful attack on civilians is a war crime. Even an attack that is not directed specifically against civilians but has as its primary purpose the terrorizing of the population is itself a war crime.

This fundamental rule and its associated prohibitions are incorporated in Articles 48 and 51(2) of the 1977 Protocol I Additional to the Geneva Conventions of 1949 and are also accepted as forming customary international law rules applicable to all belligerents, whether or not they are have signed Additional Protocol I. The Rome Statute affirms the criminal status of such attacks in international armed conflict in Article 8(2)(b)(i) and (ii) and in noninternational armed conflict in Article 8(2)(e)(i).

A willful attack on the civilian population requires a blatant targeting of civilian property in circumstances where there is no military objective. The massacre by U.S. Army forces of more than 500 unarmed civilians in the Vietnamese hamlet of My Lai in 1968 tragically endures as a glaring example of this particular category of war crime. That particular incident was not, of course, a case of aerial bombardment but it does serve to illustrate the type of attack covered by the prohibition.

The Prohibition on Indiscriminate Attacks

IHL allows attacks on military objectives but prohibits any attack that fails to discriminate between military and civilian targets. The prohibition on indiscriminate attacks is incorporated in Article 51(4) of Additional Protocol I but, like the prohibition on willful attacks against the civilian population, is also an accepted rule of customary international law. An indiscriminate attack is also a war crime.

Use of weapons of mass annihilation is not the only factor that makes an attack indiscriminate. The Trial Chamber of the ICTY in the Blaškić case decided that the Croatian shelling of the Bosnian Muslim villages of Vitez and Stari Vitez on July 18, 1993, were indiscriminate attacks. The forces under the command of General Tihomir Blaškić had used handmade mortars, knowing that these weapons had minimal accuracy (the chamber actually described them as "blind weapons"). Given that most of the victims were civilians and most of the damage was done to civilian objects, the chamber decided that the use of handmade mortars in the circumstances constituted the war crime of indiscriminate attack.[19]

The Definition of a Legitimate Military Objective

The legal definition of a military objective is critical to the application of both the prohibition on indiscriminate attacks and the rule of proportionality. So much of the controversy surrounding the selection of targets, the choice of weapon type, and the amount of ordnance deployed in attacks emanates from contrasting views of this definition. Article 52(2) of Additional Protocol I incorporates a twofold test for determining whether or not a desired target constitutes a military objective, as follows:

> Attacks shall be strictly limited to military objectives. In so far as objects are concerned, military objectives are limited to those objects which by their nature, location, purpose or use make an effective contribution to military action and whose total or partial destruction, capture or neutralization, in the circumstances prevailing at the time, offers a definite military advantage.

Key states not party to Additional Protocol I (notably the United States, Israel, the Russian Federation, and China) generally accept the definition of a military objective in Article 52(2) of Additional Protocol I as reflective of customary international law and binding upon them.[20] On the basis of this definition, military planners must first be satisfied that the desired target makes an effective contribution to the military action of the opposing side and then determine that an attack on the objective will offer a definite military advantage.[21]

In relation to the first element of the test, clearly the military personnel, ships, aircraft, vehicles, equipment, airfields, buildings, bases, ammunition supplies, etc., of the opposing side all contribute to military action and can be legitimately targeted. But it is also the case that many other objects with much less obvious connection to the armed forces may also make an effective contribution to the military action of the opposing side. This first element of the treaty test has a very low threshold. The military commander need only be satisfied that the desired target by its nature, its location, its purpose, or its use makes an effective contribution to military action. Many "dual-use" objects, including bridges, roadways, railway tracks, manufacturing plants, power generation and transmission plants, radio and television broadcasting facilities, etc., may well be deemed to be making an effective contribution to the military action of the opposing side. Even objects that are normally used exclusively for civilian purposes can become military objectives by virtue of use by the opposing military. Additional Protocol I alludes to the possibility that some civilian objects can become legitimate military objectives by virtue of their appropriation for military purposes. Article 52(3), for example, states: "In case of doubt whether an object which is normally dedicated to civilian purposes, such as a place of worship, a house or other dwelling or a school, is being used to make an effective contribution to military action, it shall be presumed not to be so used."

This presumption applies only "in case of doubt." When no doubt exists that the opposing military has established a barracks, a military headquarters, a sniper's nest, or any other military activity within an otherwise exclusively civilian object, the immunity of that object from military attack is forfeited. Military use transforms it into a military objective. Additional Protocol I prohibits the use of human shields[22] and the deliberate location of military objectives within or near densely populated areas.

The second element of the test to determine legitimate military objectives is often overlooked. It obligates military commanders to determine that the attack on the desired target will offer a definite military advantage. Alexandra Boivin cites an example from the first Gulf War in which coalition forces chose not to attack Iraqi fighter planes that had been positioned adjacent to the ancient ziggurat at Ur. The decision not to attack was based in part upon the protected status of the ziggurat (historic cultural property is immune from attack) unlawfully used to shield the aircraft but also in part because of the questionable military utility of an attack. The aircraft were a significant distance from an airstrip and so an attack on them would be unlikely to produce a definite military advantage.[23]

Widespread agreement on the definition of a military objective does not guarantee consistency of practice, however. During the coalition aerial bombardment of Iraq in 2003, for example, the Australian minster for defence as well as the chief of the defence force both publicly praised Royal Australian Air Force pilots who had terminated bombing missions because they had been unable to visually confirm the identity of their allocated targets. The minister claimed that Australia's approach to targeting is more conservative than that of the United States. However, even if this more conservative approach to compliance with international legal obligations is to be preferred, the legal test for a military objective allows a substantial degree of latitude to those militaries that adopt a broader targeting approach. This elasticity explains why the prosecution of the war crime of disproportionate civilian damage is so rare. States have only been willing to agree to be bound by a legal test that incorporates a level of flexibility they find acceptable.

Furthermore, the identification of an object as a military objective is only one element of a targeting decision. In some cases even an attack on a seemingly legitimate military objective can be fettered through the broader application of other elements of IHL. For example, Article 53 of Additional Protocol I protects objects of cultural property and places of worship. Thus even if such an object is making an effective contribution to military action (illegal in itself), it is "otherwise protected from attack" by IHL. Likewise, Article 54 protects objects indispensable to the survival of the civilian population. These articles and other legal principles, such as proportionality, add qualifications after the assessment of whether the object is "making effective contribution to military action."

The Rule on Proportionality

It is accepted as a matter of law that in directing attacks at legitimate military objectives, some incidental loss of civilian life and/or damage to civilian property may occur. In an attempt to limit such suffering, international humanitarian law prohibits "[A]n attack which may be expected to cause incidental loss of civilian life, injury to civilians, damage to civilian objects or a combination thereof, which would be excessive in relation to the concrete and direct military advantage anticipated."

This proportionality rule is codified in Article 51(5)(b) of Additional Protocol I, and repeated in Article 57(2). The rule is also recognized as a norm of customary international law and, as such, is included in the ICRC Customary Law Study.[24] The prohibition, with the additional requirement that the incidental loss be "clearly" excessive, is also included in the Rome Statute such that any attack that violates the rule constitutes a war crime.

If an attack is directed at military objectives with no expected loss of civilian life or damage to civilian property, this proportionality rule is not applicable. That does not mean, however, that a military commander is entitled to use unlimited force. The basic rule, that a party's right to choose methods or means of warfare is not unlimited, applies in all situations.

The articulation of the rule on proportionality in a number of legal instruments clearly expresses an obligation of military commanders to conduct a proportionality assessment when planning an attack. There is an additional requirement to cancel or suspend an attack if circumstances change after the attack was planned and it becomes apparent that the rule will be breached.[25]

The formulation of the proportionality rule incorporates a margin of appreciation in favor of military commanders. The law stipulates that commanders are not to be judged on the basis of an ex post facto assessment of the *actual* loss of civilian life and/or damage to civilian property weighed against the *actual* military advantage gained from the attack. Instead, the test to be applied is the *expected* loss of civilian life and/or damage to civilian property weighed against the *anticipated* military advantage. Military commanders have to reach their decisions on the basis of information that is available to them at the time of the attack,[26] so their decisions cannot subsequently be judged on the basis of information that comes to light after the attack has occurred.

The Al Firdus Bunker case in Iraq illustrates the importance of the correct test for the rule of proportionality. The Al Firdus Bunker was identified by U.S. forces as a legitimate military objective during the 1991 Gulf War. The United States claimed that the bunker was camouflaged, its perimeters were protected by barbed wire, and access points were guarded by armed sentries. On the basis of information collected by planners, the military commander made an assessment that the bunker was a legitimate military objective and, on application of the rule on proportionality, determined that the incidental damage to civilians would not be excessive in relation to the military advantage gained. The objective was bombed. It was subsequently and tragically discovered that, along with its military function, civilians had been using this bunker as sleeping quarters at night, and 300 civilians were killed by the attack.[27]

U.S. authorities determined that there had been no violation of international humanitarian law because the information available at the time had allowed the military commander to make a reasonable assessment that the target was a legitimate military objective and that the expected loss of civilian life and/or damage to civilian property was not disproportionate to the expected military advantage. The lawfulness of the decision cannot be judged upon the actual loss of civilian lives.

Having discussed the basic principles involved in the international legal framework applicable to targeting—the concept of distinction, the definition of a military objective, and the rule on proportionality—we will now examine a number of case studies allowing a practical examination of these principles in action and the inherent difficulties in their application.

Implementation of the Principles of International Humanitarian Law

The legality of the threat or use of nuclear weapons

In 1996 the International Court of Justice delivered an important Advisory Opinion on the legality of the threat or use of nuclear weapons. That decision addresses broader concerns as well as targeting issues.[28] Indeed, the mayor of Hiroshima Takashi Hiraoka and a vast number of representatives from civil society had involvement in the final case. Over 3 million declarations of public conscience against the use of nuclear weapons were submitted to the ICJ by Japanese citizens. Mr. Hiraoka's testimony before the court stressed the human agency involved in the matter under deliberation:

> History is written by the victors. Thus the heinous massacre that was Hiroshima has been handed down to us as a perfectly justified act of war. As a result, for 50 years we have never directly confronted the full implications of this horrifying act for the future of the human race. . . . I would like to ask you, the judges, to visit Hiroshima and Nagasaki to verify for yourselves the actual result of the bombing to deepen your understanding of it.[29]

The Advisory Opinion on the Legality of the Threat or Use of Nuclear Weapons, delivered by the International Court of Justice, was somewhat disappointing if not entirely unexpected.[30] It clearly demonstrates the challenges involved in identifying and separating out legal aspects of complex and sensitive political issues. The case before the ICJ centered on a question raised by the General Assembly of the United Nations. The question was very much the product of significant civil society agitation, including medical professions in the World Health Organisation (WHO) and numerous legal groups. The ICJ was asked for an Advisory Opinion to determine "Is the threat or use of nuclear weapons in any circumstances permitted under international law?"

In short, the answer provided by the ICJ was ambiguous to the extent that the court could not "conclude definitively" that in all cases the threat or use of nuclear weapons is illegal. In its 1996 decision, the majority of the court determined that, despite the lack of a specific prohibition on the threat or use of nuclear weapons in conventional or in customary international law, the general principles of customary international law, particularly the principles of IHL, would apply to any threat or use of nuclear weapons. Although the court was able to conclude that the use of nuclear weapons "seems scarcely reconcilable with respect for" the principles of IHL, it felt compelled to reach a qualified conclusion because it did not have "sufficient elements to enable it to conclude with certainty that the use of nuclear weapons would necessarily be at variance with the principles and rules of law applicable in any circumstance."

As noted previously, international law has traditionally distinguished between the law regulating the legitimate resort to force (the *jus ad bellum*) and the law regulating the actual deployment of force (the *jus in bello*). Any legitimate exercise of force must be consistent with both sets of principles. The opinion, however, confuses the *jus ad bellum* with the *jus in bello*, since the majority of the court declared a nonfinding (*non liquet*), while nevertheless determining that the possibility of a legitimate use of nuclear weapons in an "extreme circumstance of self-defence, in which the very survival of a State would be at stake," could not be ruled out.

Ironically, both sides to the case declared different elements of the decision a victory. For those arguing the total prohibition of the use of such weapons, the court did acknowledge the uniquely devastating characteristics of nuclear weapons. It also observed that any threat or use of them was regulated by the international law, in particular IHL. The court reiterated the long-standing principle that the "right of belligerents to adopt means of injuring the enemy is not unlimited" and stated that the key limitations relevant to the present case were the well-known principle of distinction and the prohibition on the infliction of unnecessary suffering.

The perceived failure of the court to *apply* the principles of IHL to the threat or use of nuclear weapons led to a number of judges dissenting from the majority opinion. Judge Rosalyn Higgins recognized as self-evident that any use of nuclear weapons against a civilian target was clearly illegal. Judges Christopher Weeramantry and Abdul G. Koroma both argued that the uniquely devastating characteristics of nuclear weapons would inevitably render any use of such weapons inconsistent with the general principles of international humanitarian law and that the court's own reasoning ought to have led it "inexorably" to this conclusion. Judge Mohammed Shahabuddeen suggested that a conclusion of illegality in all circumstances was open to the court on the evidence before it and that its nonfinding was inappropriate.

Justifying breaches of IHL as a "means to greater ends" ("the very survival of a State") echoes arguments advanced by the Allies after the atomic bombing of Hiroshima and Nagasaki. On the basis of that logic and given that neither the survival of the United States nor that of any other Allied state was at stake, the Japanese government, had it possessed a weapons capability at the time, would have had a stronger legal case for an atomic attack on Washington, D.C., Los Angeles, or New York City. In the authors' opinion, just-war justifications of significant breaches of IHL are deeply inconsistent with the fundamental principles of the law of war and erode all attempts to create a normative legal framework to regulate the conduct of hostilities.

Bombardment of London, 1940

An interesting example of the interface between international law, politics, and the practical realities of warfare is a case study of the bombing of London during World War II. The use of aerial bombing by Germany and Britain during 1940 is a clear demonstration of the importance of the application of legal restraint during times of armed conflict and the dangerous implications of unintended civilian deaths that result in the escalation of revenge attacks.

The first part of World War II did not witness the bombing offensives that had been predicted during the period of war preparation. Both Germany and Great Britain had voluntarily refrained from unrestricted warfare following an appeal by the president of United States in a speech at the outbreak of hostilities.[31] Furthermore, despite the political rhetoric of the time, neither side had adequate technical capacities or training for a sustained and effective bombing campaign. Both sides were also desirous of not being seen as the first to initiate unrestricted air warfare. As Richard Overy writes, "For Hitler as for the Allies it was the very fact that the effect of air war was an unknown quality that discouraged adventurism in using aircraft."[32]

However, in August 1940, the German air force was ordered to destroy the British air force by attacking their flying units, their ground installations, and their supply organizations. At first civilians were not purposely killed, and the focus was upon legitimate military targets. Hitler's strategy at the time was to directly invade Britain, and he wanted to ensure that the Royal Air Force (RAF) could not be effective in the south of England during such an invasion. However, this strategy was not successful. The German air force (Luftwaffe) was defeated by early warning radar and the technical superiority of the RAF Spitfire aircraft. Hitler postponed the invasion indefinitely. Meanwhile Britain had been responding by bombing Germany at night, and although industrial targets were intended as the object of attack, limited technical capacities and difficulties with night vision led to an increasing lack of discrimination. In September 1940, after a heavy raid on Berlin, Hitler delivered a speech referring to the harm suffered by Germans during British bombing raids and announced that London would be made the object of German attacks in reprisal. Beginning September 7, London sustained dramatic and aggressive air raids for over a fortnight. The Luftwaffe was ordered to carry out night bombing against industry, trade, and administration. The German air force also experienced technical and tactical problems, and darkness made precision attacks difficult. The Blitz became less and less discriminate, as Hitler announced, "When they declare that they will increase their attacks on our cities, then we will raze their cities to the ground. We will stop the handiwork of these night air pirates, so help us God!"[33]

From a legal point of view, this example raises a number of compelling issues. Some commentators have claimed that actions by the Germans were justified as belligerent reprisals against the British attacks. There are also issues relating to the applicability of international legal regulation in existence at this time. While neither the 1949 Geneva Conventions nor the Additional Protocols had yet been drafted, there were in existence principles and rules central to the modern codification of IHL, such as the distinction between military objectives and nonmilitary objects. The Declaration of St. Petersburg of 1868 states that "the only legitimate object which States should endeavour to accomplish during war is to weaken the military forces of the enemy." Article 27 of the 1907 Hague Conventions on Land Warfare is clear:

> In sieges and bombardments all necessary steps should be taken to spare as far as possible buildings dedicated to religion, art, science or charitable purposes, historic monuments, hospitals and places where the sick and wounded are collected, provided they are not being used at the time for military purposes.

Furthermore, provisions requiring distinction in naval bombardment were clear, with a prohibition against bombardment of undefended ports, towns, villages, and dwellings.[34] Thus it could not be denied that there were principles governing air warfare during World War II.

The British air raids preceding the bombardment of London were incompatible with the law as it stood. While the orders were to attack military objectives, these missions were undertaken at night, and the accuracy of targeting was very low, resulting in civilian casualties and destruction of civilian infrastructure. During initial aerial bombardment by Germany, there were military objectives located in London, such as antiaircraft batteries. Had those legitimate military objectives been located away from residential areas, their bombing would have been entirely legal. However, the indiscriminate bombing of London, its large civilian population intermingled with legitimate military objectives, ensured unacceptably high civilian casualties. Despite elements of the attack that genuinely did target military objectives, overall as a single operation the bombardment of London was prima facie unlawful.

Furthermore, it appears to eminent jurists in this field that the bombardment of London cannot be seen to be justified as a reprisal—a practice that was subsequently outlawed by the Geneva Conventions and their Protocols.[35] The aerial bombings were disproportionate to the initial events and had the aim (articulated by German leaders and authorities in speeches and papers) of breaking the morale of the British people, not avenging breaches of IHL.

This case study also highlights the difficulty in imposing a legal analytical framework upon historical events, as well as the complexity of drafting international regulations relating to aerial bombing that balance humane considerations with the practical flexibility required by the military. As Frits Kalshoven writes:

> The problem is not so much the absence of all information: it is rather that for a really exact appraisal of operations . . . it will be necessary to quantify all such varied and hard-to-weigh factors as the precise extent of the damage to military, industrial and other objects, the number and seriousness of casualties among combatants and non-combatants and so on . . . One thing seems certain: that the standard cannot be a rigid one, as the belligerents themselves could never be expected nor required to apply it durante bello; indeed, to ascertain the facts with the degree of accuracy required for such an appraisal would be an absolute impracticability for them.[36]

The NATO Bombing Campaign Against Serbia

Two more recent examples highlight the problems that arise in the application of IHL and the potential prosecution of breaches of the targeting laws. The first incident is the NATO attack on a civilian passenger train at the Grdelica Gorge in the former Yugoslavia, which was criticized as violating the IHL rules of distinction, the prohibition on indiscriminate attacks, and the rule on proportionality. The second incident involves the NATO attack on the RTS (Serbian Radio and TV Station) in Belgrade, after which three questions were asked in order to determine if there had been a violation of IHL. Was the selected target a legitimate military objective? If so, then was the attack proportionate? And were all feasible precautions taken to protect the civilian employees known to be working inside the station?

The prosecutor of the ICTY established an ad hoc review committee to assess whether there was a sufficient basis to investigate allegations of breaches of IHL during NATO's Operation Allied Force in the Federal Republic of Yugoslavia (FRY). The members of this committee have remained anonymous; however, the findings and report have been made public. The committee's conclusion that the prosecutor should not institute proceedings against persons responsible for the NATO bombing campaign against Yugoslavia has been controversial. Legal commentators as well as Amnesty International and Human Rights Watch have expressed concerns over the conclusions of this committee. Professor Michael Bothe writes: "The report is an interesting document in that it well reflects the current problems concerning the interpretation of the rules relating to the protection of the civilian population, in particular the protection of the environment, the definition of military targets and the practical application of the proportionality principle."[37]

The committee reviewed several specific incidents, including the two selected for analysis here, concluding there was no need to prosecute. It cited a number of reasons, including the claim that investigations were unlikely to result in the acquisition of sufficient evidence to substantiate the laying of charges. Questions arose about the committee's legal interpretations of IHL and also about the sources it used in the examination process. As one author noted,

> The Review Committee stated that it relied heavily on NATO press statements, documents which may be considered as not being entirely reliable in the context of a war, where (as is often the case) the belligerent needs the strong support of national and international public opinion.[38]

On the other hand, another commentator concluded:

The NATO bombing campaign against the Former Republic of Yugoslavia was not remotely similar to the strategic bombing campaigns of the Second World War. Civilian casualties were relatively limited. Some casualties are inevitable in any conflict where fighting, including bombing, occurs in areas where civilians are present.[39]

The Attack on the Civilian Passenger Train at the Grdelica Gorge, 1999

On April 12, 1999, NATO launched two laser-guided bombs at the railway bridge over the Grdelica Gorge and Juzna Morava River in eastern Serbia. At the time of the attack, a five-carriage passenger train, traveling from Belgrade to Ristovac on the Macedonian border, was crossing the bridge. This train was struck by both bombs. At least ten civilians were killed, and at least another fifteen were injured. The passenger train was not the intended target; the designated target was the railway bridge, which was believed to be part of a resupply route being used for Serb forces in Kosovo.

It was only after launching the first bomb that the pilot sighted the movement of the train on the bridge at the last instant before impact. It was too late. The bomb cut the second passenger coach in half. However, the bridge was still intact, so the controller targeted a second aim point, at the opposite end of the bridge from where the train had come. In the meantime, however, the train had rolled forward, and consequently parts of the train were also hit by the second bomb.

Why did NATO consider the bridge a legitimate military target? It was believed to be part of an "integrated supply network in Serbia."[40] A NATO official maintained that the destruction of the passenger train was not intended: "One of our electro-optically guided bombs homed in on a railroad bridge just when a passenger train raced to the aim point. We never wanted to destroy that train or kill its occupants. We did want to destroy the bridge and we regret this accident."[41]

NATO officials explained that the pilot launched the missile from an aircraft some miles away, too far for visual identification of the target. He stared intently at the aim point and locked in the automatic guidance system. It was only at the very last instant that he caught a flash of movement on the screen, which was the train coming in. At that point it was too late to dump the bomb. NATO expressed regret.

Officials also tried to explain why a second bomb had been launched after the passenger train had been hit by the first. They said the mission was to take out the bridge, and once the pilot realized that he had not destroyed it, he took aim at the other end of it, the end toward which the train was moving, even though it must have been obvious that, if the bridge collapsed, the train would plunge into the gorge.

Amnesty International and Human Rights Watch both accused NATO forces of violating the rules of distinction and proportionality. Amnesty International concluded that NATO failed to distinguish between civilian and military objects, thus violating the basic IHL rule of distinction. Amnesty International said that the pilot must have been instructed to destroy the bridge regardless of the cost in civilian casualties and that this constituted a violation of the rule of proportionality. They alleged that NATO failed to take sufficient precautionary measures to ensure that there was no civilian traffic in the vicinity of the bridge before launching the first attack, suggesting that the attacking aircraft, or another aircraft, could and should have flown over the area to ensure that no trains were approaching the bridge. The pilot then could have waited until the train had crossed the bridge before launching the attack.

The ICTY review committee concluded that the bridge was a legitimate military objective and agreed that the passenger train was not deliberately targeted. After reviewing footage of the first bomb attack, the committee noted that "the train can be seen moving towards the bridge only as the bomb is in flight . . . at a point where the bomb is within a few seconds of impact." Therefore it *is* possible that the pilot failed to recognize the arrival of the train until the first bomb was in flight. The committee concluded that information in relation to the attack with the first bomb did not provide a sufficient basis to initiate a criminal investigation.

The members were divided on the second attack as to whether the person controlling the bomb was reckless. Nevertheless, the committee concluded that the second attack also should not be investigated.

The Attack on the RTS (Serbian Radio and TV Station) in Belgrade, 1999

The second example concerns Radio Televisija Srbije (RTS), a state-owned broadcasting corporation in the center of Belgrade. On April 23, 1999, NATO aircraft intentionally bombed the central studio of RTS. The attack resulted in a blacked-out news broadcast and disabled RTS broadcasting for three hours; it killed ten to seventeen people and injured many more.[42]

The bombing of RTS was part of a larger attack aimed at disrupting the Serbian command, control, and communications network. On the same night, radio relay buildings and towers were hit, along with electrical power transformer stations.

NATO officials acknowledged that the FRY communications system was a dual-use target, routinely used for both military and civilian purposes. They said the attack on RTS headquarters was conducted to "disrupt the national command network" and "degrade the Federal Republic of Yugoslavia's propaganda apparatus"—because the RTS facilities were being used to support the activities of FRY military and special police forces.

NATO officials further justified the attack on the RTS headquarters on the basis of its use as a propaganda organ. NATO believed that Yugoslav broadcast facilities were "used entirely to incite hatred and propaganda" and alleged that the Yugoslav government had put all private TV and radio stations in Serbia under military control.[43] NATO strikes against broadcast facilities were part of the campaign to "dismantle the FRY propaganda machinery." NATO's aim was to "directly strike at the very nerve center of Milošević's regime [at] those assets which were used to plan and direct and to create the political environment of intolerance in Yugoslavia." In an interview with *The Times*, British prime minister Tony Blair was reported as saying that "the media is the apparatus that keeps [Milošević] in power and we are entirely justified as NATO allies in damaging and taking on those targets."

NATO's bombing campaign on the RTS facilities raised concern among civil society groups and other actors in the international community. They raised two primary legal issues in relation to this attack: Was this target a legitimate military objective? If so, then was the attack proportionate in relation to the military advantage anticipated?

As noted previously in this chapter, in order for the RTS broadcasting station to be a military objective within the definition outlined above, its "nature, location, purpose or use must have made an effective contribution to military action," and its "total or partial destruction must offer a definite military advantage."

In its report, Amnesty International objected that, while disruption of government propaganda may contribute to undermining the morale of the population and the armed forces, it does not justify an attack on a civilian facility: "[Attacking a civilian facility] on such grounds stretches the meaning of 'effective contribution to military action' and 'definite military advantage' beyond the acceptable bounds of interpretation."[44] The group concluded that, according to the requirements of article 52(2) of Additional Protocol I, the RTS headquarters could not be considered a military objective. Therefore, in conducting this attack, NATO had violated the prohibition on attacking civilian objectives and had therefore committed a war crime.[45] As its report put it, "NATO deliberately attacked a civilian object, killing 16 civilians, for the purpose of disrupting Serbian television broadcasts in the middle of the night for approximately three hours. It is hard to see how this can be consistent with the rule of proportionality."[46]

Amnesty International suggested that, in conducting the proportionality assessment, NATO must have clearly anticipated that some of the 120 civilians[47] in the RTS building would be killed. They further suggested that NATO was aware that any attack on the RTS studio would interrupt broadcasting for only a brief period,[48] therefore making the expected harm to civilians excessive in relation to the military advantage anticipated.

In its final report to the prosecutor, the ICTY review committee noted that if the attack on RTS had been justified solely on the grounds of its use as a propaganda apparatus, then the legality of the attack may well be questioned. However, the committee decided that destroying part of the propaganda machinery was a secondary objective. The primary goal was considered to be disabling the Serbian military command and control system, and thus "destroying the nerve system and apparatus that keeps Milošević in power."

Assuming that the RTS building was a legitimate military objective, the committee concluded that "the civilian casualties were unfortunately high but do not appear to be clearly disproportionate."[49] Considering whether the attack had been disproportionate in relation to the military advantage gained, the committee recognized that focus should not exclusively be placed upon a specific incident:

> With regards to these goals, the strategic target of these attacks was the Yugoslav command and control network. The attack on the RTS building must therefore be seen as forming part of an integrated attack against numerous objects, including transmission towers and control buildings of the Yugoslav radio relay network which were "essential to Milošević's ability to direct

and control the repressive activities of his army and special police forces in Kosovo."

Upon ratification of Additional Protocol I, many states made declarations of interpretation to the effect that "the military advantage anticipated from an attack is intended to refer to the advantage anticipated from the attack considered as a whole and not only from isolated or particular parts of the attack."[50] The NATO attacks on the RTS building were part of a larger campaign targeting the Yugoslav command and control network. Therefore, when assessing proportionality, regard should be had to the military advantage gained from the attack as a whole[51] and not only the attack on the RTS facilities in central Belgrade.

The committee acknowledged that evidence relating to whether effective warning of the attack had been given was contradictory. Commenting on Amnesty International's allegation that NATO did not give warning because it would have endangered pilots, the committee acknowledged that casualties among civilians working at RTS may have been heightened because of NATO's failure to provide clear and effective advance warning.[52] On the other hand, they suggested that because Western journalists were aware of the impending attack, it is likely that Yugoslav officials were also aware of it and could have evacuated the building.[53] The committee acknowledged that this would not divest NATO of its IHL obligation to provide effective warning but that responsibility may not solely fall upon NATO under such circumstances.

These two case studies of civilian deaths illustrate many of the issues raised in this chapter. Though both planning and review were sometimes flawed, these examples show that application of the targeting principles is a complex task.

Conclusion

As well as existing concerns relating to the law of targeting and the protection of civilians and their property, there are a number of newly developing issues that will need to be addressed in the near future. One is the fact that advanced technology on one side is creating an unprecedented asymmetry on the battlefield, in particular in the area of targeting. As Michael Schmitt writes, "Today, a low-tech force facing an adversary armed with state of the art weaponry has difficulty simply surviving, let alone confronting its opponent. . . . Asymmetry in precision compels the disadvantaged side to respond asymmetrically."[54]

Greater effort is required to identify, comprehend, and effectively respond to the root causes of asymmetrical warfare. Some root causes such as environmental despoliation or economic exploitation are more readily explicable and, consequently, more amenable to resolution than are other root causes, such as religious fanaticism or ethnic hatred. International law must be part of a multidisciplinary effort to deal with causes rather than symptoms. However, irrespective of the root causes, the increasing reality of asymmetrical warfare poses serious challenges to the integrity of IHL as a legal regime.

Increasingly, forces with weaker technological capabilities are inverting a number of established IHL principles, such as exploiting the protections granted to civilians and civilian objects. Not wearing uniforms and hiding among the civilian population while involved in combat increases the risk of mistaken attack upon those who should be traditionally protected. Discarding a uniform is not illegal under IHL, but wearing civilian clothes to feign protected status with the intention of gaining proximity to the opposition is perfidious, a serious international crime and a tactic often used by suicide bombers. These factors also raise the need for further debate and clarification of the phrase "taking direct part in hostilities" in Article 51.3 of Additional Protocol I, which determines when the protective status accorded to civilians no longer applies. A related issue requiring further consideration is the growing tendency of technologically inferior forces to use human shields and to locate military objectives close to civilians in the hope of avoiding attack. The implications of such a strategy for the rule of proportionality are particularly challenging.

Other areas of continual debate include the definition of the term "military objective"—an obvious foundational principle of targeting. Some interpret the wording and concepts broadly, and some take a more limited approach. For example, the United States takes a wide view on the definition and includes economic targets that indirectly but effectively support and sustain the enemy's war fighting capability, such as oil industries that support a nation's economy. Others argue that the objects to be attacked must have a very close and direct connection with the conduct of hostilities. This tension is further fleshed out in the dialogue relating to dual-use objects. Even with a legal understanding of the obligations, commanders can have difficulty in identifying the degree of military advantage to be obtained in complex circumstances. As Marco Sassoli states, "In practice it may be extremely difficult to determine the importance of military use and of the military advantage in destroying the object, in particular if the military has priority access to all remaining infrastructure."[55]

There is also pervasive disagreement about the legality of targeting the morale of the enemy population. Targeting civilians who are not directly participating in hostilities purely for the purpose of undercutting morale is illegal, as mentioned in the section on the bombardment of London. However, some commentators argue that the issue of an attack's effect on civilian morale is irrelevant as a matter of law once a target has been identified as making an effective contribution to military action: "The fact that the attacker hopes the strike will weaken civilian morale (even intends that result) does not detract from the target's status as a military objective."[56]

International law plays an important role in influencing the behavior of nations, their militaries, and even irregular armed forces.[57] However, it is also merely the reflection of what states are willing to agree upon. IHL is a clear example of constant tension between military requirements and the protection of civilians. The process of negotiating this balance in a multilateral forum often results in achieving only the lowest common denominator. Legal norms about targeting need to be palatable to the military so that there is an impetus to follow them during the heat of battle. However, to have legitimacy, such international laws also need to reflect the beliefs and desires of "we the peoples." On a number of weapons-related topics, such as the use of antipersonnel land mines, the voices of civil society have had a direct impact on the development of the law.[58] As has been written:

> In democratic systems, the values pursued by the military and those of society at large cannot be far apart. The military's value system has to conform to that of the civil society, not vice versa. Dialogue between civil society and the military is essential, and it then has to be reflected in military decision making.[59]

For any dialogue to be useful, it must be based on an appreciation of the subject matter on both sides. This chapter has unpacked the law relating to the targeting of civilians as it stands today, provided a number of examples to reflect upon, and highlighted some of the issues needing further reflection. Finding the ideal balance of military flexibility and humanitarian concerns is not a simple task. However, the dialogue involved in this quest is greatly advanced when there is a better understanding of the legal limitations applicable to modern warfare.

NOTES

1. British "Humane Bombing" in Iraq during the Interwar Era *by Yuki Tanaka*

1. Lee Kennett, *A History of Strategic Bombing* (New York: Scribner's, 1982), pp. 1–6.

2. Tami Davis Biddle, *Rhetoric and Reality in Air Warfare: The Evolution of British and American Ideas About Strategic Bombing, 1914–1945* (Princeton, NJ: Princeton University Press, 2002), pp. 12–13.

3. Bill Gunston, *History of Military Aviation* (London: Chancellor Press, 2000), p. 11; Biddle, *Rhetoric and Reality*, p. 13.

4. Andrew Hyde, *The First Blitz: The German Air Campaign Against Britain 1917–1918* (Barnsley, UK: Leo Cooper, 2002), pp. 7–24.

5. International Committee of the Red Cross (ICRC) Web page, "International Humanitarian Law—Treaties and Documents: Hague Declaration on Projectiles from Balloons," http:www.icrc.org/ihl.nsf/INTRO/160?OpenDocument; Kennett, *History of Strategic Bombing*, p. 10.

6. Biddle, *Rhetoric and Reality*, pp. 12–13.

7. ICRC Web site, "International Humanitarian Law"; Kennett, *History of Strategic Bombing*, p. 10.

8. Kennett, *History of Strategic Bombing*, pp. 13–15.

9. Ibid., pp. 20–23.

10. Ibid., pp. 24–37; Biddle, *Rhetoric and Reality*, pp. 29–35.

11. Ralph Baker, *A Brief History of the Royal Flying Corps in World War I* (London: Robinson, 1995), pp. 468–82.

12. Giulio Douhet, *Command of the Air*, Japanese translation by Katukimi Sei (Tokyo: Fuyo Shobo, 2002), pp. 35–42.

13. Biddle, *Rhetoric and Reality*, pp. 39–40.

14. Ibid., p.48.

15. Ibid., pp. 57–67.

16. David E. Omissi, *Air Power and Colonial Control: The Royal Force 1919–1939* (Manchester: Manchester University Press, 1990), pp. 10–11.

17. Ibid., pp. 11–12.

18. Ibid., pp. 13–16; John Robert Ferris, *The Evolution of British Strategic Policy, 1919–26* (London: Macmillan Press, 1989), pp. 73–75.

19. British National Archives Document (hereafter BNAD), Air 20/8895, "Z Unit Somaliland No. 8, Military Standing and Operation Orders, Corresponding between C.O.Z. and C.O.S.F.F"; Air 5/1315, photos in the file entitled "R.A.F. Somaliland Expedition 1920: Medical Arrangements, Reports and Photographs."

20. Omissi, *Air Power*, pp. 15–16.

21. BNAD, Air 20/590, "Somaliland Air Operations, 1919–1920 Report."

22. Charles Tripp, *A History of Iraq* (Cambridge: Cambridge University Press, 2001), chap. 2, "The British Mandate," pp. 30–76.

23. Omissi, *Air Power*, pp. 20–22; Ferris, *Evolution*, pp. 67–69.

24. Omissi, *Air Power*, pp. 22–23.

25. Ibid., pp. 24–27; Ferris, *Evolution*, pp. 68–69.

26. BNAD, Air 20/10207, "Copy Ref. No. AIR/535, Air Headquarters, British Forces in Iraq."

27. Ibid.

28. BNAD, Air 5/344, Secret: Air Staff Memorandum No. 18, "Report on Operations against Beni Huchaim Tribes, Iraq, November to December, 1923."

29. BNAD, Air 5/1287, "General Resume and Daily Summary of Operations Carried Out by the Royal Air Force, Iraq, During September 1923."

30. BNAD, Air 5/338, "Extract from 6A of File 479733/24."

31. BNAD, Air 5/338, Secret: Air Staff Memorandum No. 16., 1924, "Statement by Air Marshal Sir J.M. Salmond, K.C.B., C.M.G., C.V.O., D.S.O., of His Views upon the Principles Governing the Use of Air Power in Iraq."

32. British National Archives Image Library, photos in file Air 8/72.

33. BNAD, Air 5/1287, "General Resume and Daily Summary of Operations Carried Out by the Royal Air Force, Iraq, during September 1923."

34. Omissi, *Air Power*, p. 160.

35. Ibid.

36. BNAD, Air 5/344, "Air Ministry File No. S23217, Letter from A.O.C. Iraq, December 12, 1923."

37. Lionel Charlton, *Charlton* (London: Faber & Faber, 1931), p. 271.

38. Ibid., pp. 277–78.

39. Ibid., pp. 284–85.

40. BNAD, Air 5/338, *Note on the Method of Employment of the Air Arm in Iraq*.

41. Ibid.

42. Ibid.

43. BNAD, Air 5/338, Secret: Air Staff Memorandum No. 16, 1924, "Statement by Air Marshal Sir J.M. Salmond, K.C.B., C.M.G., C.V.O., D.S.O., of His Views upon the Principles Governing the Use of Air Power in Iraq."

44. BNAD, Air 5/344, Secret: Air Staff Memorandum No.18, "Report on Operations Against Beni Huchaim Tribes, Iraq, November to December, 1923."

45. Ibid.

46. See, for example, BNAD, Air 5/1253, "Extract from Letter, Air Officer Commanding, Middle East Area, to Secretary, Air Ministry, October 11, 1920, with reference to 'War Diaries' of Royal Air Force in Mesopotamia."

47. BNAD, Air 5/338, Air Staff Memorandum No. 16.

48. Ibid.

49. Ibid.

50. Ibid., Air Ministry File No. 30, "A Secretary C.A.S."

51. Omissi, *Air Power*, p. 156.

52. For details of the bombing of Ethiopia by Italian forces in 1935–36, see Angelo Del Bocca and Giorgio Rohat, *I gas di Mussolini: Il fascismo e la Guerra d'Etiopia* (Rome: Editori Riuniti, 1996); Nicholas Rankin, *Telegram from Guernica* (London: Faber and Faber, 2003), chap. 1 and 2.

2. The Bombing Campaigns in World War II: The European Theater
by Ronald Schaffer

1. Ronald Schaffer, *Wings of Judgment: American Bombing in World War II* (New York: Oxford University Press, 1985), pp. 20–22; Tami Davis Biddle, *Rhetoric and Reality in Air Warfare: The Evolution of British and American Ideas About Strategic Bombing, 1914–1945* (Princeton, NJ: Princeton University Press), pp. 37–40, 69–73.

2. Richard J. Overy, *The Air War, 1939–1945* (London: Europa Publications, 1980), pp. 24–25.

3. Williamson Murray, *Luftwaffe* (Baltimore: Nautical & Aviation Pub. Co. of America, 1985), pp. 10–12, 15, 17–18; Overy, *Air War*, p. 35.

4. Richard Muller, *The German Air War in Russia* (Baltimore: Nautical & Aviation Pub. Co. of America, 1992), pp. 18–23, discusses the difficult early evolution of coordinated air-ground attacks by the German air force.

5. Murray, *Luftwaffe*, pp. 31–32; Frederick Taylor, *Dresden, Tuesday, February 13, 1945* (New York: HarperCollins, 2004), p. 77.

6. Murray, *Luftwaffe*, p. 40.

7. Overy, *Air War*, pp. 34–35; Murray, *Luftwaffe*, pp. 48–49, 54, 58–60.

8. Taylor, *Dresden*, pp. 102–6.

9. Ibid., pp. 107–8.

10. Murray, *Luftwaffe*, pp. 78, 84, 87, 90; Harrison E. Salisbury, *The 900 Days: The Siege of Leningrad* (New York: Harper & Row, 1969), pp. 291, 298, 516; Alexander Werth, *Russia at War* (New York: E.P. Dutton, 1964), pp. 306, 450, 453, 458; Muller, *German Air War*, pp. 50–53.

11. Biddle, *Rhetoric and Reality*, pp. 183–84.

12. Ibid., p. 196; Taylor, *Dresden*, pp. 116–17.

13. Biddle, *Rhetoric and Reality*, p. 197; Taylor, *Dresden*, pp. 118–19.

14. Biddle, *Rhetoric and Reality*, p. 199; Taylor, *Dresden*, p. 123.

15. Schaffer, *Wings*, chap. 2.

16. Martin Middlebrook, *The Battle of Hamburg: Allied Bomber Forces Against a German City in 1943* (New York: Scribner's, 1981), pp. 95, 194–96, 328.

17. Schaffer, *Wings*, pp. 65–66; Murray, *Luftwaffe*, pp. 168–69, 212–13.

18. For German aircraft and pilot losses in the first half of 1944, see Murray, *Luftwaffe*, pp. 227–28.

19. Schaffer, *Wings*, pp. 40–42.

20. For an analysis of the Balkan bombing campaigns, see Schaffer, *Wings*, pp. 54–59.

21. The Russians didn't have to, because the RAF and AAF were doing all the urban area bombing necessary. See Muller, *German Air War*, p. 42.

22. Ibid., pp. 54–59; even the highly publicized Soviet bombing of Helsinki in November 1939 appears to have contravened orders. Carl Van Dyke, *The Soviet Invasion of Finland 1939–40* (London: F. Cass, 1997), pp. 56, 93n, 96.

23. Schaffer, *Wings*, p. 68.

24. Ibid., pp. 82–84.

25. Taylor, *Dresden*, pp. 188–89; Schaffer, *Wings*, p. 97.

26. For instance, Dresdener Bank, headquartered in that city, helped finance the construction of the Auschwitz death camp, sold the possessions of Jews admitted to those camps, and lent the SS 47 million reichsmarks. *New York Times*, Feb. 18, 2006.

27. Taylor, *Dresden*, pp. 148–65; Klemperer quotation, p. 198.

28. Ibid., p. 448.

29. Ibid., pp. 183, 376.

30. Ibid., pp. 43–48.

31. Schaffer, *Wings*, pp. 86–92; Anderson quotation, p. 95.

32. Arnold quoted in Schaffer, *Wings*, 61.

33. Biddle, *Rhetoric and Reality*, pp. 1–9. See also Schaffer, *Wings*, chap. 9.

3. The Bombing War in Germany, 2005–1940: Back to the Future?
by Robert G. Moeller

1. This paper was originally delivered at the meetings of the American Historical Association in January 2005. Jane Caplan offered very useful criticisms and encouraged me to submit the paper to *History Workshop Journal*, where a substantially shorter version appeared in spring 2006. Thanks also for the suggestions of Lynn Mally, Gilad Margalit, Bill Niven, Molly Nolan, and Nicholas Stargardt, and of Charles Quilter, who pushed me toward crucial bibliography. I owe a particular debt of gratitude to Marilyn Young, who has lived with me through a couple of years of virtual exchanges about mass death, bombs, and World War II, and who always helps me to say what I mean.

2. Jörg Friedrich, *The Fire: The Bombing of Germany 1940–1945*, trans. Allison Brown (New York: Columbia University Press, 2006).

3. Jörg Friedrich, *Der Brand: Deutschland im Bombenkrieg 1940–1945* (Berlin: Propyläen Verlag, 2002). Page references in the text are to this edition. See Mary Nolan, "Germans as Victims During the Second World War," *Central European History* 38, no. 1 (2005): 7–40; and Ralf Blank, review of *Der Brand: Deutschland im Bombenkrieg*, by Jörg Friedrich, "Eine kritische Auseinandersetzung," *Militärgeschichtliche Zeitschrift* 63, no. 1 (2004): 175–86.

4. http://www.historicum.net/themen/bombenkrieg.

5. Sönke Neitzel, "'Wer Wind sät, wird Sturm ernten': Der Luftkrieg in westdeutschen Fernseh-dokumentationen," historicum.net, Dec. 8, 2003, http://www.bombenkrieg.historicum-archive.net/themen/fernsehen.html (accessed Oct. 28, 2004); also *Feuersturm: Der Bombenkrieg gegen Deutschland*, Spiegel TV history, DVD edition (see also http://www.spiegel.de/sptv/special/0,1518,237418,00.html (accessed Dec. 9, 2004).

6. W.G. Sebald, *On the Natural History of Destruction*, trans. Anthea Bell (New York: Random House, 2003), pp. 4, 10.

7. Rudy Koshar, *From Monuments to Traces: Artifacts of German Memory 1970–1990* (Berkeley: University of California Press, 2000).

8. See, e.g., Dennis E. Showalter, "Plans, Weapons, Doctrines: The Strategic Cultures of Interwar Europe," in *The Shadows of Total War: Europe, East Asia, and the United States, 1919–1939*, ed. Roger Chickering and Stig Förster (Cambridge: Cambridge University Press, 2003), p. 60; Michael S. Sherry, *The Rise of American Air Power: The Creation of Armageddon* (New Haven: Yale University Press, 1987), pp. 12–21; Richard J. Overy, "Air Power in the Second World War: Historical Themes and Theories," in *The Conduct of the Air War in the Second World War: An International Comparison*, ed. Horst Boog (New York: Berg, 1992), pp. 7–29; Richard J. Overy, *The Air War, 1939–1945* (London: Europa Publications, 1980); and Horst Boog, "The Anglo-American Strategic Air War over Europe and German Air Defense," in *Germany and the Second World War*, vol. 6 of *The Global War*, ed. Militärgeschichtliches Forschungsamt, trans. Ewald Osers, John Brownjohn, Patricia Crampton, and Louise Willmot (Oxford: Clarendon Press, 2001), pp. 469–621.

9. Geoff Simons, *Iraq: From Sumer to Saddam* (Houdmills, UK: Macmillan, 1994), pp. 180–81.

10. Conrad C. Crane, *Bombs, Cities, and Civilians: American Airpower Strategy in World War II* (Lawrence: University Press of Kansas, 1993), p. 24.

11. Overy, "Air Power," pp. 7–29.

12. See Overy, *Air War*, pp. 102–3; Sherry, *Rise of American Air Power*, pp. 76–77; Horst Boog, "The Luftwaffe and Indiscriminate Bombing up to 1942," in Boog, *Conduct of the Air War*, pp. 373–404; and James S. Corum, *The Luftwaffe: Creating the Operational Air War, 1918–1940* (Lawrence: University Press of Kansas, 1997).

13. Boog, "Anglo-American Strategic Air War," p. 561.

14. "United States Strategic Bombing Survey Summary Report (European War), Washington, D.C., Sept. 30, 1945," in *The United States Strategic Bombing Survey*, vol. 1, ed. David MacIsaac (New York: Garland, 1976); also available at http://www.ibiblio.org/hyperwar/AAF/USSBS/ETO-Summary.html (accessed Dec. 20, 2005); see also Wesley Frank Craven and James Lea Cate, *The Army Air Forces in World War II*, vol. 1, *Plans and Early Operations, January 1939 to August 1942*, vol. 2, *Europe: Torch to Pointblank, August 1942 to December 1943*, and vol. 3, *Europe: Argument to V-E Day, January 1944 to May 1945* (Chicago: University of Chicago Press, 1949–51, repr. 1983).

15. On American policy, see Sherry, *Rise of American Air Power*, 156; also Ronald Schaffer, *Wings of Judgment: American Bombing in World War II* (New York: Oxford University Press, 1985); Thomas Childers, "'*Facilis descensus averni est*': The Allied Bombing of Germany and the Issue of German Suffering," *Central European History* 38, no. 1 (2005): 75–105; and Tami Davis Biddle, *Rhetoric and Reality in Air Warfare: The Evolution of British and American Ideas About Strategic Bombing, 1914–1945* (Princeton, NJ: Princeton University Press, 2002).

16. Charles Webster and Noble Frankland, *The Strategic Air Offensive Against Germany 1949–1945*, vol. 3, *Victory* (London: Her Majesty's Stationery Office, 1961), pp. 184, 197–98; and Biddle, *Rhetoric and Reality*, p. 287.

17. Karola Fings, "Sklaven für die 'Heimatfront': Kriegsgesellschaft und Konzentrationslager," in *Die deutsche Kriegsgesellschaft 1939 bis 1945*, ed. Jörg Echternkamp, part 1 (Munich: Deutsche Verlags-Anstalt), p. 256; and Thomas W. Neumann, "Der Bombenkrieg: Zur ungeschriebenen Geschichte einer kollektiven Verletzung," in *Nachkrieg in Deutschland*, ed. Klaus Naumann (Hamburg: Hamburger Edition, 2001), p. 324.

18. Gerhard Kock, *"Der Führer sorgt für unsere Kinder ...": Die Kinderlandverschickung im Zweiten*

Weltkrieg (Paderborn: Ferdinand Schöningh, 1997), p. 143; also Michael Krause, *Flucht vor dem Bombenkrieg: "Umquatierungen" im Zweiten Weltkrieg und die Wiedereingliederung der Evakuierten in Deutschland, 1943–1963* (Düsseldorf: Droste, 1997).

19. Fredrick Taylor, *Dresden: Tuesday, February 13, 1945* (New York: HarperCollins, 2004), pp. 443–48.

20. Ralf Blank, "Kriegsalltag und Luftkrieg an der 'Heimatfront,'" in Echternkamp, *Die Deutsche Kriegsgesellschaft*, part 1, pp. 357–461. Quotation from Speer, p. 430. Quotation from Hitler in Boog, "Strategischer Luftkrieg in Europa," pp. 335–36. See also Earl L. Beck, *Under the Bombs: The German Home Front 1942–1945* (Lexington: University of Kentucky Press, 1986); and Jörg Echternkamp, "Im Kampf an der inneren und äusseren Front: Grundzüge der deutschen Gesellschaft im Zweiten Weltkrieg," in Echternkamp, *Die deutsche Kriegsgesellschaft*, part 1, pp. 1–92. Quotation from DHM Lemo, Aufzeichnungen aus dem Tagebuch von Karl Deutmann aus Adlershof bei Berlin, 3. February 1945, "Berlin in Bombensturm," http://www.dhm.de/lemo/forum/kollektives_gedaechtnis/008/index.html (accessed Dec. 28, 2005).

21. Beck, *Under the Bombs*, p. 46.

22. Krause, *Flucht vor dem Bombenkrieg*, pp. 160–61.

23. Alice Förster and Birgit Beck, "Post-Traumatic Stress Disorder and World War II: Can a Psychiatric Concept Help Us Understand Postwar Society?" in *Life After Death: Approaches to a Cultural and Social History of Europe During the 1940s and 1950s*, ed. Richard Bessel and Dirk Schumann (Cambridge: Cambridge University Press, 2003), pp. 28–29.

24. Ian Kershaw, *The "Hitler Myth": Image and Reality in the Third Reich* (Oxford: Oxford University Press, 1987), pp. 202, 205–6, 207.

25. Statistical estimates—which vary greatly—are summarized in Blank, "Kriegsalltag und Luftkrieg," pp. 459–60. See also Olaf Groehler, "The Strategic Air War and its Impact on the German Civilian Population," in Boog, *Conduct of the Air War*, pp. 291–92.

26. Friedrich concludes that it had no effect. See *Der Brand*, p. 115. Among those who credit the bombing war with contributing significantly to Allied victory are Richard Overy, *Why the Allies Won* (London: Jonathan Cape, 1995); and Biddle, *Rhetoric and Reality*, pp. 271–86.

27. Eric Langenbacher, "The Allies in World War II: The Anglo-American Bombardment of German Cities," in *Genocide, War Crimes and the West*, ed. Adam Jones (London: Zed Books, 2004), pp. 116–33.

28. Stephen A. Garrett, *Ethics and Airpower in World War II: The British Bombing of German Cities* (New York: St. Martin's Press, 1993); also Biddle, *Rhetoric and Reality*, p. 260.

29. Page references in the text are to Friedrich, *Der Brand*.

30. John W. Dower, *War Without Mercy: Race and Power in the Pacific War* (New York: Pantheon Books, 1986), pp. 55, 79.

31. Sherry, *Rise of American Air Power*, pp. 162, 261; Robin Neillands, *The Bomber War: Arthur Harris and the Allied Bomber Offensive, 1939–1945* (London: John Murray, 2001), p. 158; and Biddle, *Rhetoric and Reality*, pp. 214–61.

32. Bernard Wasserstein, *Britain and the Jews of Europe 1939–1945* (Oxford: Clarendon Press, 1979), 306–7.

33. See, e.g., Lothar Kettenacker, "Churchill's Dilemma," in *Ein Volk von Opfern? Die neue Debatte um den Bombenkrieg 1940–45*, ed. Lothar Kettenacker (Berlin: Rowohlt, 2003), pp. 48–55.

34. Blank, "Kriegsalltag und Luftkrieg," p. 437; and, in general, Jeffrey Herf, "'Der Krieg und die Juden': Nationalsozialistische Propaganda im Zweiten Weltkrieg," in Echternkamp, *Die deutsche Kriegsgesellschaft*, part 2, pp. 159–202.

35. See Nicholas Stargardt "Victims of Bombing and Retaliation," *German Historical Institute London Bulletin* 26 (2004): 57–70.

36. Ralf Blank in *Sehepunkte* 2 (2002), no. 12, http://www.sehepunkte.de/2002/12/2675.html (accessed Oct. 27, 2004).

37. Neumann, "Der Bombenkrieg," pp. 319–42.

38. "Extract from the Report by the Police President of Hamburg on the Raids on Hamburg in July and August 1943, dated 1st December 1943," in Webster and Frankland, *The Strategic Air Offensive Against Germany*, vol. 4, *Annexes and Appendices*, p. 314.

39. Jörg Friedrich, *Brandstätten: Der Anblick des Bombenkriegs* (Berlin: Propyläen, 2003).

40. "Terror from the Sky," *Exberliner*, no. 20, Oct. 2004.

41. Jeffrey Herf, *Divided Memory: The Nazi Past in the Two Germanys* (Cambridge, MA: Harvard University Press, 1997).

42. Achatz von Müller, "Volk der Täter, Volk der Opfer," *Die Zeit*, no. 44 (2003); also Klaus Naumann, "Agenda 1945: Das Jahr des Kriegsendes im aktuellen Geschichtsdiskurs," in *Kriegsende 1945: Verbrechen, Katastrophen, Befreiungen in nationaler und internationaler Perspektive*, ed. Bernd-A. Rusinek (Göttingen: Wallstein Verlag, 2004), pp. 237–53.

43. "Terror from the Sky."

44. Helmut Dubiel, *Niemand ist frei von der Geschichte: Die nationalsozialistische Herrschaft in den Debatten des Deutschen Bundestages* (Munich: Carl Hanser Verlag, 1999); also Robert G. Moeller, "Germans as Victims? Thoughts on a Post–Cold War History of World War II's Legacies," *History & Memory* 17, no. 1–2 (2005): 147–94; and, in general, Robert G. Moeller, *War Stories: The Search for a Usable Past in the Federal Republic of Germany* (Berkeley: University of California Press, 2001).

45. See, e.g., Peter Schneider, "Deutsche als Opfer? Über ein Tabu der Nachkriegsgeneration," in Kettenacker, *Ein Volk von Opfern?* pp. 159–65; and Nolan, "Germans as Victims," pp. 23–24.

46. Bill Niven, *Facing the Nazi Past: United Germany and the Legacy of the Third Reich* (London: Routledge, 2002), p. 215.

47. Douglas Peifer, H-NET book review of *Der Brand*, Nov. 4, 2003, http://h-net.msu.edu/cgi-bin/logbrowse.pl?trx=vx&list=h-german&month=0311&week=a&msg=5/R3pMxMMKXMXQSNhvwxbw&user=&pw= (accessed Dec. 8, 2004).

48. Norbert Frei, "Gefühlte Geschichte: Die Erinnerungsschlacht um den 60 Jahrestag des Kriegsendes 1945 hat begonnen. Deutschland steht vor einer Wende im Umgang mit seiner Vergangenheit," *Die Zeit*, 44/2004 (accessed online at http://www.zeit.de/, Oct. 23, 2004).

49. "Von guten Massakern und bösen Massakern," *Spiegel Online*, 2003, http://www.spiegel.de/sptv/special/0,1518,237918,00.html (accessed June 2, 2005).

50. This tendency is previewed in a 1984 work by Friedrich in which he compares the carbon monoxide poisoning of victims at Treblinka with the deaths of "a large part of the victims of the bombing war" by the same means. See Jörg Friedrich, *Die kalte Amnestie: NS-Täter in der Bundesrepublik* (Frankfurt am Main: Fischer Taschenbuch Verlag, 1984), p. 17.

51. Gilad Margalit, "Der Luftangriff auf Dresden: Seine Bedeutung für die Erinnerungerspolitik der DDR und für die Herauskristallisierung einer historischen Kriegserinnerung im Westen," in *Narrative der Shoah: Repräsentationen der Vergangenheit in Historiographie, Kunst und Politik*, ed. Susanne Düwell and Matthias Schmidt (Paderborn: Ferdinand Schöningh, 2002), pp. 189–208.

52. Jens Jäger, "Fotografie—Erinnerung—Identität: Die Trümmeraufnahmen aus deutschen Städten 1945," in *Kriegsende 1945 in Deutschland*, ed. Jörg Hillmann and John Zimmermann (Munich: R. Oldenbourg, 2002), pp. 287–300, quotation, p. 292; and Eva Vieth, "Die letzte 'Volksgemeinschaft': Das Kriegsende in den Bildern einer deutschen Illustrierten," *Kriegseude*, pp. 265–85.

53. Elizabeth Heineman, "The Hour of the Woman: Memories of Germany's 'Crisis Years' and West German National Identity," *American Historical Review* 101, no. 2 (1996): 354–95.

54. "Ansprache des Bundestagspräsidenten Dr. Ehlers anlässlich der Enthüllung des Ehrenmals für die Hamburger Luftgefallenen am 15 August 1952 auf dem Ohlsdorfer Friedhof," in *Dokumente Deutscher Kriegsschäden: Evakuierte, Kriegssachgeschädigte, Währungsgeschädigte, Die geschichtliche und rechtliche Entwicklung*, vol. 1, ed. Bundesminister für Vertriebene, Flüchtlinge und Kriegsgeschädigte (Düsseldorf: Triltsch-Druck, 1958), p. 63.

55. Margalit, "Der Luftangriff auf Dresden," p. 205.

56. Michael Hughes, *Shouldering the Burdens of Defeat: West Germany and the Reconstruction of Social Justice* (Chapel Hill: University of North Carolina Press, 1999).

57. Silke Wenk, "Bunkerarchäologien: Zur Einführung," in *Erinnerungsorte aus Beton: Bunker in Städten und Landschaften*, ed. Silke Wenk (Berlin: Christoph Links Verlag, 2001), p. 18.

58. Gregory F. Schroeder, "Ties of Urban *Heimat*: West German Cities and Their Wartime Evacuees in the 1950s," *German Studies Review*, 27, no. 2 (2004): 325–40.

59. See also Volker Hage, ed., *Hamburg 1943: Literarische Zeugnisse zum Feuersturm* (Frankfurt am Main: Fischer Taschenbuch Verlag, 2003); and Alexander Kluge, "Der Luftangriff auf Halberstadt am 8 April 1945," in *Chronik der Gefühle*, vol. 2, *Lebensläufe*, by Alexander Kluge (Frankfurt am Main: Suhrkamp Verlag, 2000), pp. 27–82.

60. The German phrase is "Wer wind sät, wird Sturm ernten." Neitzel, "'Wer Wind sät.'"

61. See http://www.frauenkirche-dresden.org/ (accessed Oct. 23, 2004).

62. Klaus Naumann, *Der Krieg als Text: Das Jahr 1945 im kulturellen Gedächtnis der Presse* (Hamburg: Hamburger Edition, 1998), pp. 33–71.

63. Michel Foucault, *The History of Sexuality*, vol. 1, *An Introduction*, trans. Robert Hurley (New York: Vintage Books, 1990), pp. 8–9. My thanks to Ulrike Strasser, who suggested that I look to Foucault for guidance on this point.

64. Boog, "Strategischer Luftkrieg in Europa," pp. 24, 81.

65. The allusion is to Matthaeus Rader's *Bavaria Sancta*, an early-seventeenth-century guide to Bavaria's saints and sacred sites. See Trevor Johnson, "Holy Dinasts and Sacred Soil: Politics and Sanctity in Matthaeus Rader's *Bavaria Sancta* (1615–1628)," in *Europa sacra: Raccolte agiografie e identià politiche in Europa fra Medioevo ed Età moderna*, ed. Sofia Boesch Gajano and Raimondo Michetti (Rome: Carocci Editore, 2002), pp. 83–100. My thanks to Ulrike Strasser for telling me about this article.

66. Here and at many other points, Friedrich provides no references. Thus, it is impossible to determine whether he is weaving these strands together, drawing on local histories of the postwar period, or uncritically reproducing popular memories of the war and postwar years.

67. Beck, *Under the Bombs*, p. 87; and Joseph Goebbels, "Das Leben geht weiter," *Das Reich*, Apr. 16, 1944, translated as "Life Goes On" by Randall Bytwerk, available at http://www.calvin.edu/academic/cas/gpa/goeb52.htm (accessed Dec. 18, 2005).

68. See Echternkamp, "Im Kampf an der inneren und äusseren Front," p. 69. On the postwar discussion, see in particular Frank Biess, *Homecomings: Returning POWs and the Legacies of Defeat in Postwar Germany* (Princeton, NJ: Princeton University Press, 2006).

69. For the full text, see http://ods-dds-ny.un.org/doc/RESOLUTION/GEN/NR0/033/47/IMG/NR003347.pdf?OpenElement (accessed Oct. 27, 2004).

70. Andreas Hillgruber, *Zweierlei Untergang: Die Zerschlagung des Deutschen Reiches und das Ende des europäischen Judentums* (Berlin: Corso bei Siedler, 1986), pp. 24–25.

71. Sonya O. Rose, *Which People's War? National Identity and Citizenship in Britain 1939–1945* (Oxford: Oxford University Press, 2003), p. 285.

72. Nolan, "Germans as Victims," pp. 32–37.

73. Mark Roseman, *A Past in Hiding: Memory and Survival in Nazi Germany* (New York: Picador, 2002), p. 272.

74. Victor Klemperer, *I Will Bear Witness: A Diary of the Nazi Years 1942–1945*, trans. Martin Chalmers (New York: Random House, 1999), pp. 406–15.

75. Blank, "Kriegsalltag und Luftkrieg," pp. 417, 426, 428–29; Friedrich, *Der Brand*, 441.

76. Karen Hagemann, "'Jede Kraft wird gebraucht': Militäreinsatz von Frauen im Ersten und Zweiten Weltkrieg," in *Erster Weltkrieg/Zweiter Weltkrieg: Ein Vergleich—Krieg, Kriegserlebnis, Kriegserfahrung in Deutschland*, ed. Bruno Thoss and Hans-Erich Volkmann (Paderborn: Ferdinand Schöningh, 2002), pp. 96, 100.

77. Gudrun Schwarz, "'During Total War, We Girls Want to Be Where We Can Really Accomplish Something': What Women Do in Wartime," in *Crimes of War: Guilt and Denial in the Twentieth Century*, ed. Omer Bartov, Atina Grossmann, and Mary Nolan (New York: The New Press, 2002), p. 121.

78. *The United States Strategic Bombing Survey*, vol. 1, *The Effects of Strategic Bombing on German Morale*, March–July, 1945 (Washington, DC: U.S. Government Printing Office, 1947), p. 18; also quoted in Michael Burleigh, *The Third Reich: A New History* (London: Macmillan, 2000), pp. 762, 765; and *The United States Strategic Bombing Survey*, vol. 4, p. 18, quoted in Jörg Echternkamp, "Im Kampf an der inneren und äusseren Front," p. 15.

79. Blank, "Kriegsalltag und Luftkrieg," pp. 388–90.

80. Friedrich, *Der Brand*, p. 435.

81. For figures on military deaths, see Rüdiger Overmans, *Deutsche militärische Verluste im Zweiten Weltkrieg* (Munich: R. Oldenbourg, 1999), pp. 283, 299.

82. See the comments of Stargardt, "Victims of Bombing."

83. Quoted in Neillands, *Bomber War*, p. 359.

84. Blank, "Kriegsalltag und Luftkrieg," pp. 397–98, 418, 423, 426–27; Fings, "Sklaven für die 'Heimatfront,'" pp. 197–204, 209–10, 231–43, 256–57; and Mark Spoerer, "Die soziale Differenzierung der ausländischen Zivilarbeiter, Kriegsgefangenen und Häftlinge im Deutschen Reich," in Echternkamp, *Die deutsche Kriegsgesellschaft*, part 2, pp. 532–33.

85. Ulrich Herbert, *A History of Foreign Labor in Germany, 1880–1980: Seasonal Workers/Forced Laborers/*

Guest Workers, trans. William Templer (Ann Arbor: University of Michigan Press, 1990), pp. 155, 183. For Friedrich's death toll, *Der Brand*, p. 327.

86. http://www.poets.org/viewmedia.php/prmMID/15309 (accessed June 23, 2008). From *The Complete Poems* by Randall Jarrell (New York: Farrar, Straus & Giroux, 1969, 1996). Thanks to Marilyn Young, who reminded me of Jarrell's poem.

87. Crane, *Bombs, Cities, and Civilians*, pp. 49–50; Overy, *Why the Allies Won*, p. 117.

88. *United States Strategic Bombing Survey Summary Report (European War)*. In the official British history of the air war, Webster and Frankland give the figure of 55,888 killed and another 9,162 wounded. See Webster and Frankland, *The Strategic Air Offensive Against Germany 1939–1945*, vol. 3, *Victory*, pp. 286–87. Overy gives the figure of 140,000 American and British airmen, *Why the Allies Won*, p. 128. Neilland's figures are 26,000 American deaths (to which he adds 18,000 wounded and 20,000 POWs) and 55,564 British. Neillands, *Bomber War*, 379. Childers comes to a total of 140,000, Childers, "Facilis descensus averni est," p. 105. And Blank cites figures of 55,500 British and takes his figures for Americans from Neillands. Blank, "Kriegsalltag und Luftkrieg," p. 460. And for Friedrich's figures, see *Der Brand*, p. 63. Elsewhere, he quotes a figure of 73,741 members of British Bomber Command "lost through death, wounds, and imprisonment," *Der Brand*, p. 45. In a 1984 work, he claims that 25,000 British pilots died in the air war over Germany, though it is not clear where he gets this figure. See Friedrich, *Die kalte Amnestie*, p. 20.

89. Gerhard L. Weinberg, *A World at Arms: A Global History of World War II* (Cambridge: Cambridge University Press, 1994), p. 894.

90. Sherry, *Rise of American Air Power*, p. 206.

91. See also Stargardt, "Victims of Bombing."

92. Charles Maier, "Forum: WWII Bombing: Comments on Friedrich, *Der Brandt* [*sic*]," H-Net Discussion Networks, Nov. 12, 2003, http://h-net.msu.edu/cgi-bin/logbrowse.pl?trx=vx&list=h-german& month=0311&week=b&msg=QjgRJtFFmWFNkLcIg29cyg&user=&pw= (accessed Dec. 8, 2004).

93. Harold Marcuse, *Legacies of Dachau: The Uses and Abuses of a Concentration Camp, 1933–2001* (Cambridge: Cambridge University Press, 2001).

94. Sigmund Freud, "Mourning and Melancholia," in *The Standard Edition of the Complete Psychological Works of Sigmund Freud*, trans. James Strachey, vol. 14 (1914–1916), pp. 238–60, quotation from p. 240; Alexander and Margarete Mitscherlich, *The Inability to Mourn*, trans. Beverley R. Placzek (New York: Grove Press, 1975).

95. Erwin Panofsky, *Meaning in the Visual Arts: Papers in and on Art History* (Garden City, NY: Doubleday Anchor Books, 1955), pp. 321–22.

96. Raymond Klibansky, Erwin Panofsky, and Fritz Saxl, *Saturn and Melancholy: Studies in the History of Natural Philosophy, Religion, and Art* (London: Thomas Nelson and Sons, 1964).

97. Jonathan Petropoulos, *Art as Politics in the Third Reich* (Chapel Hill: University of North Carolina Press, 1996), pp. 11, 101, 268.

98. Gertrud Bing, "Fritz Saxl (1890–1948): A Memoir," in *Fritz Saxl, 1890–1948: A Volume of Memorial Essays from His Friends in England*, ed. D.J. Gordon (London: Thomas Nelson and Sons, 1957), pp. 1–46. My thanks to George and Linda Bauer for helping me better to understand Dürer and Saxl.

99. Friedrich, *Brandstätten*, pp. 227–27. http://www.museen.nuernberg.de/english/duerer_e/index_ duerer_e.html (accessed Oct. 23, 2004).

100. Horst Boog, "Harris: A German View," in *Despatch on War Operations, 23rd February, 1942, to*

8th May, 1945, by Arthur T. Harris (London: Frank Cass & Co., 1995), xxxvii, 101; and Boog, "Ein Kolos-
salgemälde des Schreckens," in Kettenacker, *Ein Volk von Opfern?* pp. 131–36.

    102. "Von guten Massakern and bösen Massakern."

    103. "Terror from the Sky."

4. A Forgotten Holocaust: U.S. Bombing Strategy, the Destruction of Japanese Cities, and the American Way of War from the Pacific War to Iraq *by Mark Selden*

The author thanks Noam Chomsky, Bruce Cumings, John Dower, Laura Hein, Gavan McCormack, and
the participants in the bombing workshop, particularly Michael Sherry, for critical comments, sources, and
suggestions. The term *holocaust* used in the title draws on its original meaning. The *Oxford English Dictio-
nary* provides this definition: "Complete consumption by fire; complete destruction, especially of a large
number of persons; a great slaughter or massacre."

    1. Estimates vary, especially in the Pacific theater. See, for example, John Ellis, *World War II—A Sta-
tistical Survey* (New York: Facts on File, 1993); John W. Dower, *War Without Mercy: Race and Power in the
Pacific War* (New York: Pantheon, 1986), pp. 294–300; and Roger Chickering, Stig Forster, and Bernd
Greiner, eds., *A World at Total War: Global Conflict and the Politics of Destruction, 1937–1945* (Cambridge:
Cambridge University Press, 2005), p. 3. Chickering and Forster estimate military deaths at 15 million and
civilian deaths at more than 45 million; Wikipedia offers a wide-ranging discussion of numbers and sources.

    2. Lee Kennett, *A History of Strategic Bombing* (New York: Scribner's, 1982), pp. 9–38; Sven
Lindqvist, *A History of Bombing,* trans. Linda Haverty Rugg (New York: The New Press, 2000), pp. 31–42.

    3. "General Report of the Commission of Jurists at the Hague," *American Journal of International
Law* 17 (Oct. 1923), Suppl. pp. 250–51.

    4. A valuable synthesis of the literature on war and the noncombatant is Sahr Conway-Lanz, *Collat-
eral Damage: Americans, Noncombatant Immunity, and Atrocity After World War II* (London: Routledge,
2006). A.C. Grayling, *Among the Dead Cities: The History and Moral Legacy of the WWII Bombing of Civilians in Germany and Japan* (New York: Walker & Co., 2006), subjects the British and American choice of
area bombing in World War II in Germany and Japan to rigorous scrutiny from the perspectives of morality, international law, and effectiveness. The terms area bombing, strategic bombing, and indiscriminate
bombing refer to the wholesale destruction of large areas of cities, frequently with the annihilation of the
civilian population. By contrast, tactical bombing is directed to discrete military and/or military-industrial
targets, such as military bases and airfields, bridges, and munitions factories. In practice, given technical
limitations, bombs directed at military targets frequently exacted heavy civilian tolls. I address the issues of
state terrorism and the targeting of civilians by Japan and the United States in *War and State Terrorism: The
United States, Japan and the Asia Pacific in the Long Twentieth Century,* ed. Mark Selden and Alvin So (Lanham, MD: Rowman & Littlefield, 2004).

    5. A small number of works have drawn attention to U.S. war atrocities, typically centering on the
torture, killing, and desecration of captured Japanese soldiers. These include Peter Schrijvers, *The GI War
Against Japan: American Soldiers in Asia and the Pacific During World War II* (New York: New York Univer-
sity Press, 2002); and Dower, *War Without Mercy. The Wartime Journals of Charles Lindbergh* (New York:
Harcourt Brace Jovanovich, 1970), is seminal in disclosing atrocities committed against Japanese POWs.
Two recent works closely assess the bombing of noncombatants and the ravaging of nature and society as a

result of strategic bombing that has been ignored in much of the literature. A.C. Grayling, *Among the Dead Cities*, provides a thoroughgoing assessment of U.S. and British strategic bombing (including atomic bombing) through the lenses of ethics and international law. Grayling's premise is that Allied bombing, which "deliberately targeted German and Japanese civilian populations" and "claimed the lives of 800,000 civilian women, children and men," "is nowhere near equivalent in scale of moral atrocity to the Holocaust of European Jewry, or the death and destruction all over the world for which Nazi and Japanese aggression was collectively responsible," a figure that he places at 25 million dead. He nevertheless concludes that the U.S. and British killing of noncombatants "did in fact involve the commission of wrongs" on a very large scale. See pp. 5–6, 276–77. Michael Bess, in *Choices Under Fire: Moral Dimensions of World War II* (New York: Knopf, 2006), pp. 88–110, in a chapter on "Bombing Civilian Populations," after reviewing both strategic and ethical issues, concludes, "There can be no excuse, in the end, for the practices of large-scale area bombing and firebombing of cities; these were atrocities, pure and simple. They were atrocities because the Anglo-Americans could definitely have won the war without resorting to them." It is necessary, in my view, to go further, to inquire whether these would have constituted atrocities in circumstances in which the bombing, presumably including atomic bombing, were necessary for securing U.S. victory.

6. Grayling, *Among the Dead Cities*, pp. 90–91. Grayling goes on to note the different experiences of survivors of the two types of bombing, particularly as a result of radiation symptoms from the atomic bomb.

7. Conway-Lanz, *Collateral Damage*, provides a useful overview of international efforts to protect noncombatants throughout history and particularly since World War II. See also Timothy L.H. McCormack and Helen Durham, "Aerial Bombardment of Civilians: The Current International Legal Framework," in this volume.

8. The question of universality has been the centerpiece of Noam Chomsky's critique of the conduct of the powers, above all the United States, from his earliest political writings to the present. See, for example, the introduction to *American Power and the New Mandarins* (New York: Pantheon, 1966), pp. 4–5; *Hegemony or Survival: America's Quest for Global Dominance* (New York: Metropolitan Books, 2003), pp. 2–13, 20–23; *Failed States: The Abuse of Power and the Assault on Democracy* (New York: Metropolitan Books, 2006), pp. 3–4 and passim. The Taylor quote is from his *Nuremberg and Vietnam: An American Tragedy*, cited in Chomsky, *Failed States*, p. 83. John Dower offers trenchant comments on the scales of justice in *Embracing Defeat: Japan in the Wake of World War II* (New York: Norton/The New Press, 1999), pp. 451–74. See also Richard H. Minear, *Victors' Justice: The Tokyo War Crimes Trial* (Princeton, NJ: Princeton University Press, 1971).

9. Quoted in Lindqvist, *History of Bombing*, p. 81. The U.S. debate over the bombing of cities is detailed in Michael Sherry, *The Rise of American Air Power: The Creation of Armageddon* (New Haven: Yale University Press, 1987), pp. 23–28, 57–59; and in Ronald Schaffer, *Wings of Judgment: American Bombing in World War II* (New York: Oxford University Press, 1985), pp. 20–30, 108–9. General Billy Mitchell's contradictory message, which became air force doctrine in 1926, was that air attack "was a method of imposing will by terrorizing the whole population . . . while conserving life and property to the greatest extent." Quoted in Sherry, p. 30. See also Conway-Lanz, *Collateral Damage*, p. 10.

10. Tami Davis Biddle, "Air Power," in *The Laws of War: Constraints on Warfare in the Western World*, ed. Michael Howard, George J. Andreopoulos, and Mark R. Shulman (New Haven: Yale University Press, 1994), pp. 151–52; and Gordon Wright, *The Ordeal of Total War, 1939–1945* (New York: Harper & Row, 1968), p. 26.

11. On the Casablanca Conference and bombing, see Charles B. Macdonald, *World War II: The War Against Germany and Italy* (Army Historical Series, Office of the Chief of Military History), chap. 22. Grayling traces the British and German shift from tactical to strategic bombing in the early years of the war in *Among the Dead Cities*, pp. 31–76.

12. Max Hastings, *Bomber Command: The Myth and Reality of the Strategic Bombing Offensive* (New York: Dial Press, 1979), p. 139.

13. Sherry, *Air Power*, p. 260. The top brass, from George Marshall to air force chief Henry Arnold to Dwight Eisenhower, had all earlier given tacit approval for area bombing, yet no orders from on high spelled out a new bombing strategy.

14. Interview quoted in Richard Rhodes, *The Making of the Atomic Bomb* (New York: Simon & Schuster, 1986), p. 593.

15. Schaffer, *Wings of Judgment*, p. 97; see also Sherry, *Air Power*, pp. 260–63. Grayling makes a compelling case for the failure of area bombing of Germany to achieve its objective of breaking morale and causing heavy destruction of military-related industries, thereby forcing surrender, *Among the Dead Cities*, pp. 106–7. Robert Pape made a similar argument for Japan, stressing other factors, including naval blockade, threat of invasion, and the Soviet entry into the war as having far greater significance than the fire bombing. *Bombing to Win: Air Power and Coercion in War* (Ithaca: Cornell University Press, 1996).

16. The most eloquent criticism was the writing of Vera Brittain. Grayling, *Among the Dead Cities*, pp. 180–86. In the midst of the Dresden debate, on March 28, 1945, Churchill issued a minute questioning the area-bombing strategy and raising the question whether tactical bombing of key objectives was not more effective. The minute was withdrawn following air force protests. Charles Webster and Noble Frankland, *The Strategic Air Offensive Against Germany, 1939–45* (London: Her Majesty's Stationery Office, 1961), p. 112.

17. E. Bartlett Kerr, *Flames over Tokyo* (New York: Donald I. Fine, 1991), p. 145.

18. Tsuneishi Keiichi, "Unit 731 and the Japanese Imperial Army's Biological Warfare Program," in *Sekai senso hanzai jiten* (Encyclopedia of World War Crimes), ed. Hata Ikuhiko and Sase Masanori (Tokyo: Bungei Shunju, 2002), trans. John Junkerman, *Japan Focus*, Nov. 20, 2005, japanfocus.org/products/details/2194.

19. Kerr, *Flames over Tokyo*, pp. 31–32, 41–44, 52, 71–74. For the October 1944 recommendations of the Committee of Operations Analysts of the Air Force for area bombing, see pp. 83–88.

20. Michael Sherry, "The United States and Strategic Bombing: From Prophecy to Memory," forthcoming; Cary Karacas, "Imagining Air Raids on Tokyo, 1930–1945," paper presented at the Association for Asian Studies annual meeting, Boston, Mar. 23, 2007, pp. 2–5.

21. Sherry, *Air Power*, pp. 272–73, 404–5.

22. Cf. Stewart Udall's discussion of responsibility for the U.S. shift to area bombing, centering on President Roosevelt, Secretary of War Henry Stimson, and Air Force Secretary Robert Lovett, and the difficulty of documenting responsibility for the policy shift. Sherry and Schaffer provide the most exhaustive study of the shift in U.S. bombing policy.

23. United States Strategic Bombing Survey, *Summary Report (Pacific War)* (Washington, DC: U.S. Government Printing Office, 1946), vol. 1, p. 16.

24. Kerr, *Flames over Tokyo*, pp. 102–3, 108–14, 134–38.

252   NOTES TO PAGES 83-87

25. Rhodes, *Atomic Bomb*, pp. 596–97; Wesley Frank Craven and James Lea Gate, *The Army Air Forces in World War II*, vol. 5, *The Pacific: Matterhorn to Nagasaki June 1944 to August 1945* (Chicago: University of Chicago Press, 1953; repr. 1983, Office of Air Force History), pp. 609–13; Kerr, *Flames over Tokyo*, pp. 146–50. Karacas, "Imagining Air Raids," p. 27. In Japan in spring and summer 1945, as in virtually all subsequent bombing campaigns conducted over the next six decades, the United States ruled the sky with virtually no enemy capacity to destroy its bombers.

26. "Tokyo Under Bombardment, 1941–1945," Bethanie Institute Bulletin No. 5, translation in General Headquarters Far East Command, Military Intelligence Section, *War in Asia and the Pacific*, vol. 12, *Defense of the Homeland and End of the War*, ed. Donald Detwiler and Charles Burdick (New York: Garland, 1980); see also Karacas on the imaginative link between the Tokyo earthquake and the bombing in the Unna Juzo novel.

27. Sherry, *Air Power*, p. 276. A detailed photographic record—including images of scores of the dead, some burnt to a crisp and distorted beyond recognition, others apparently serene in death, and of acres of the city flattened as if by an immense tornado—is found in Ishikawa Koyo, *Tokyo daikushu no zenkiroku* (Complete Record of the Great Tokyo Air Attack) (Tokyo, 1992); *Tokyo kushu o kiroku suru kai ed., Tokyo daikushu no kiroku* (Record of the Great Tokyo Air Attack) (Tokyo: Sanseido, 1982); and *Dokyumento: Tokyo daikushu* (Document: The Great Tokyo Air Attack) (Tokyo: Yukeisha, 1968).

28. The survey's killed-to-injured ratio of better than two to one was far higher than most estimates for the atomic bombing of Hiroshima and Nagasaki, where killed and wounded were approximately equal. If accurate, it is indicative of the immense difficulty in escaping for those near the center of the Tokyo firestorm on that windswept night. The survey's ratio has, however, been challenged by Japanese researchers, who found much higher kill ratios at Hiroshima and Nagasaki, particularly when one includes those who died of bomb injuries months and years later. In my view, the SBS estimates both exaggerate the killed-to-injured ratio and understate the numbers killed in the Tokyo raid. The Committee for the Compilation of Materials on Damage Caused by the Atomic Bombs in Hiroshima and Nagasaki, *Hiroshima and Nagasaki: The Physical, Medical and Social Effects of the Atomic Bombing* (New York: Basic Books, 1988), pp. 420–21; cf. U.S. Strategic Bombing Survey, *Field Report Covering Air Raid Protection and Allied Subjects Tokyo* (n.p., 1946), pp. 3, 79. The U.S. Strategic Bombing Survey, *Study of Effects of Air Attack on Urban Complex Tokyo-Kawasaki-Yokohama* (n.p., 1947), p. 8, observes that Japanese police estimates of 93,076 killed and 72,840 injured in Tokyo air raids make no mention of the numbers of people missing. Surely, too, many classified as injured died subsequently of their wounds. In contrast to the monitoring of atomic bomb deaths over the subsequent six decades, the Tokyo casualty figures at best record deaths and injuries within days of the bombing.

29. Karacas, "Imagining Air Raids," p. 22.

30. *Dokyumento: Tokyo daikushu*, pp. 168–73.

31. John W. Dower, "Sensational Rumors, Seditious Graffiti, and the Nightmares of the Thought Police," in *Japan in War and Peace* (New York: The New Press, 1993), p. 117. United States Strategic Bombing Survey, *Summary Report*, vol. 1, pp. 16–20.

32. Conway-Lanz, *Collateral Damage*, p. 1.

33. Kerr, *Flames over Tokyo*, pp. 337–38.

34. Two excellent complementary accounts of important dimensions of the geopolitics and political economy of the contemporary U.S. empire are Chalmers Johnson, *The Sorrows of Empire: Militarism, Se-*

crecy, and the End of the Republic (New York: Metropolitan Books, 2004), and Michael T. Klare, *Blood and Oil* (New York: Metropolitan Books, 2004).

35. The numbers killed, specifically the numbers of noncombatants killed, in the Korean, Vietnam, and Iraq wars were greater, but each of those wars extended over many years.

36. Mark Selden, "American Nationalism and Asian Wars" (in progress).

37. Cf. John Dower's nuanced historical perspective on war and racism in American thought and practice in *War Without Mercy: Race and Power in the Pacific War* (New York: Pantheon, 1986). In *Year 501: The Conquest Continues* (Boston: South End Press, 1993) and many other works, Noam Chomsky emphasizes the continuities in Western ideologies that undergird practices leading to the annihilation of entire populations in the course of colonial and expansionist wars over half a millennium and more.

38. Geoffrey Best, *War and Law Since 1945* (Oxford: Clarendon Press, 1994), pp. 180–81.

39. See, for example, Robert Jay Lifton and Greg Mitchell, *Hiroshima in America: Fifty Years of Denial* (New York: Grossett/Putnam, 1995), parts 2–4; and Conway-Lanz, *Collateral Damage*, pp. 13–16.

40. Bombing would also be extended from cities to the countryside, as in the Agent Orange defoliation attacks that destroyed the forest cover and poisoned residents of sprayed areas of Vietnam.

41. I have explored issues of Japan's China war and the Chinese resistance in *China in Revolution: The Yenan Way Revisited* (Armonk, NY: M.E. Sharpe, 1995), and in Edward Friedman, Paul G. Pickowicz, and Mark Selden, *Chinese Village, Socialist State* (New Haven: Yale University Press, 1991). An insightful discussion of Japanese war crimes in the Pacific, locating the issues within a comparative context of atrocities committed by the United States, Germany, and other powers, is Yuki Tanaka's *Hidden Horrors: Japanese Crimes in World War II* (Boulder, CO: Westview Press, 1996). Takashi Yoshida, *The Making of the "Rape of Nanking": History and Memory in Japan, China and the United States* (Oxford: Oxford University Press, 2006), examines the understanding of the Nanjing Massacre in each country. Daqing Yang surveys the contentious Chinese and Japanese literature on the Rape of Nanjing in "A Sino-Japanese Controversy: The Nanjing Atrocity as History," *Sino-Japanese Studies*, Nov. 1990, pp. 14–35. For additional studies of Japanese war atrocities and the search for justice for victims, see articles by Utsumi Aiko, William Underwood, Yoshiko Nozaki, Gavan McCormack, Tessa Morris-Suzuki, Yuki Tanaka, Mark Selden and others at *Japan Focus*, http://japanfocus.org.

42. R.J.R. Bosworth, *Explaining Auschwitz and Hiroshima: History Writing and the Second World War 1945–1990* (London: Routledge, 1993). Wide discrepancies remain with respect to World War II casualties and deaths, notably in Asia. Cf. John Dower's compilation and discussion of the basic data, *War Without Mercy*, pp. 295–300, and "Race, Language and War in Two Cultures," in *Japan in War and Peace*, p. 257.

43. Dower, *Embracing Defeat*, pp. 443–47; Conway-Lanz, *Collateral Damage*, pp. 16–17.

44. Mark Selden, "Nationalism, Historical Memory and Contemporary Conflicts in the Asia Pacific: The Yasukuni Phenomenon, Japan, and the United States," http://japanfocus.org/products/details/2004; Takahashi Tetsuya, "The National Politics of the Yasukuni Shrine," pp. 155–80; and Caroline Rose, "The Battle for Hearts and Minds. Patriotic Education in Japan in the 1990s and Beyond," pp. 131–54, in Naoko Shimazu, ed., *Nationalisms in Japan* (London: Routledge, 2006).

45. Quoted in Noam Chomsky, "War on Terror," Amnesty International Lecture, Trinity College, Jan. 18, 2006.

46. Conway-Lanz, *Collateral Damage*, pp. 18–19. Conway-Lanz traces major U.S. debates since 1945

centered on noncombatant deaths to show that the question of intention, not the scale of civilian deaths caused by American actions, repeatedly trumped counterarguments in policy debates.

47. General Curtis LeMay, oral history, 1966, quoted in Bruce Cumings, "Korea: Forgotten Nuclear Threats," www.nautilus.org/fora/security/0503A_Cumings.html, January 11, 2005.

48. See Marilyn Young, "Bombing Civilians from the Twentieth to the Twenty-first Centuries," this volume, p. 157.

49. Bruce Cumings, *Origins of the Korean War* (Princeton, NJ: Princeton University Press, 1990), vol. 2, p. 755.

50. Seymour M. Hersh, *Chemical and Biological Warfare: America's Hidden Arsenal* (New York: Anchor Books, 1969), p. 18.

51. Ibid., pp. 28–32. See also Ronald B. Frankum Jr., *Like Rolling Thunder. The Air War in Vietnam, 1964–1975* (Lanham, MD: Rowman & Littlefield, 2005), pp. 88–92.

52. Hersh, *Chemical and Biological Warfare*, pp. 131–33. Hersh notes that the $60 million worth of defoliants and herbicides in the 1967 Pentagon budget would have been sufficient to defoliate 3.6 million acres if all were used optimally.

53. Ibid., pp. 134, 156–57. Canadian Dr. Alje Vennema described the symptoms of gas victims at Quang Ngai hospital where he worked in 1967, including two children and one adult who died.

54. Elizabeth Becker, "Kissinger Tapes Describe Crises, War and Stark Photos of Abuse," *New York Times*, May 27, 2004.

55. "Bombs Over Cambodia: New Light on US Indiscriminate Bombing," *Walrus*, Dec. 7, 2006.

56. Michael Sherry, "The United States and Strategic Bombing: From Prophecy to Memory," forthcoming.

57. Seymour Hersh, "Up in the Air: Where Is the Iraq War Headed Next?" *New Yorker*, Dec. 5, 2005; Dahr Jamail, "Living Under the Bombs," TomDispatch, Feb. 2, 2005; Michael Schwartz, "A Formula for Slaughter: The American Rules of Engagement from the Air," TomDispatch.com, Jan. 14, 2005.

58. Gilbert Burnham, Riyadh Lafta, Shannon Doocy, and Les Roberts, "Mortality After the 2003 Invasion of Iraq: A Cross-Sectional Cluster Sample Survey," *Lancet* 368, no. 9545 (Oct. 21, 2006), pp. 1421–28.

59. Anthony Arnove, "Four Years Later . . . and Counting: Billboarding the Iraqi Disaster," TomDispatch.com, Mar. 18, 2007; Seymour Hersh, "The Redirection: Is the Administration's New Policy Benefiting Our Enemies in the War on Terrorism?" *New Yorker*, Mar. 3, 2007; Michael Schwartz, "Baghdad Surges into Hell: First Results from the President's Offensive," TomDispatch.com, Feb. 12, 2007.

5. Were the Atomic Bombings of Hiroshima and Nagasaki Justified?
by Tsuyoshi Hasegawa

I would like to thank Gar Alperovitz, Barton Bernstein, Patrick McCray, and Marilyn Young for comments on the original version. I would also like to thank the participants of the conference "Terror from the Sky," held December 2006 in San Francisco: Yuki Tanaka, Mark Selden, Robert G. Moeller, Ron Schaffer, Michael Sherry, and Helen Durham.

1. Lewis Mumford, "The Morals of Extermination," *Atlantic* 204, Oct. 1959, p. 39, quoted in Eric Markusen and David Korpf, *The Holocaust and Strategic Bombing: Genocide and Total War in the Twentieth Century* (Boulder, CO: Westview Press, 1995), p. 244.

2. "Germans Mark Bombing of Dresden," BBC News, Feb. 13, 2005, http://news.bbc.co.uk/2/hi/europe/4261263.stm (accessed Sept. 3, 2008).

3. For the complexity of Japan's historical memory of the atomic bombings and its culpability of war, see John W. Dower, *Embracing Defeat: Japan in the Wake of World War II* (New York: Norton/The New Press, 1999); Tsuyoshi Hasegawa and Kazuhiko Togo, eds., *East Asia's Haunted Present: Historical Memories and the Resurgence of Nationalism* (Westwood, CT: Praeger Security International, 2008).

4. *Asahi Shimbun*, July 1, 2, 3, 4, and 5, 2008; Hasegawa Tsuyoshi, "Migi karano genbaku hihan ga motarasu nichibei domei no kiki," *Chuokoron*, Sept. 2007.

5. See Tsuyoshi Hasegawa, *Racing the Enemy: Stalin, Truman, and the Surrender of Japan* (Cambridge, MA: Belknap Press of Harvard University Press, 2005) [hereafter *Racing*]; and *Anto: Sutarin, Toruman to Nihonkofuku* (The Deadly Struggles: Stalin, Truman and the Surrender of Japan) (Tokyo: Chuokoronshinsha, 2006) [hereafter *Anto*]. Although my approach to place the war's ending in the international context is generally praised, there are debates about my two fundamental assumptions: whether or not a "race" between Truman and Stalin really existed, and whether or not Truman and the American administration believed that the atomic bombings on Hiroshima and Nagasaki were powerful enough to result in Japan's immediate surrender. On these debates, see H-Diplo Roundtables, vol. 7, no. 2 (2006), http://www.h-net.org/~diplo/roundtables; Tsuyoshi Hasegawa, ed., *The End of the Pacific War: Reappraisals* (Stanford, CA: Stanford University Press, 2006); Wilson D. Miscamble, *From Roosevelt to Truman: Potsdam, Hiroshima and the Cold War* (Cambridge: Cambridge University Press, 2007); and Michael D. Gordin, *Five Days in August: How World War II Became a Nuclear War* (Princeton, NJ: Princeton University Press, 2007). I responded to my critics in the H-Diplo Roundtables.

6. See chaps. 2 and 3 in *Racing* and *Anto*. For original sources, see *Racing* and *Anto*.

7. See chaps. 2 and 3 in *Racing* and *Anto*.

8. *Racing*, pp. 102–5; *Anto*, pp. 168–72.

9. It is important to note that Soviet renunciation of the Neutrality Pact was immediately relayed to the United States government. See Document 212 in Ministerstvo inostrannykh del, *Sovetsko-Amerikanskie otnosheniia vo vremia Velikoi Otechestvennoi voiny 1941–1945: Dokumenty i materialy* [Ministry of Foreign Affairs, Soviet-American Relations During the Great Patriotic War 1941–1945: Documents and Materials; hereafter *SAO*], vol. 2 (Moscow: Politizdat, 1984), pp. 347–48.

10. The complete record of the Hopkins-Stalin meeting has not been published. The Truman Library holds the complete minutes with accompanying cables, "Hopkins-Stalin Conference: Record of Conversations between Harry L. Hopkins and Marshal Stalin in Moscow," May 26–June 6, 1945, Papers of HST, Staff Member and Office File, Naval Aide to the President Files, 1945–1953, Subject File, Box 12, Hopkins-Stalin Conference in Moscow, Harry S. Truman Library. The record in *Foreign Relations of the United States: Conference: Diplomatic Papers: Conference of Berlin (The Potsdam Conference)* [hereafter *FRUS: Potsdam*] (Washington, DC: U.S. Government Printing Office, 1955) is not complete, lacking a portion of the fourth and the entire fifth conversation. For the Russian version, see Documents 258, 260, *SAO*, vol. 2, pp. 397–403, 404–11.

11. *Racing*, pp. 82–84; *Anto*, pp. 135–39.

12. Chaps. 2 and 3, *Racing* and *Anto*.

13. Doc. No. 57670, Toyoda Soemu Statement No. 57670, Office of the Chief of Military History, Historical Manuscript File, Statements of Japanese Officials on World War II; Toyoda Soemu chinjut-

susho, Boei kenkyujo senshishitsu (Toyoda Soemu's statement, Collection of Military History, Defense Institute).

14. As for Takagi's reports, I analyze them in more detail in *Anto*, pp. 50–51, 66–68.

15. Chaps. 2 and 3, *Racing* and *Anto*.

16. Chap. 3, *Racing* and *Anto*.

17. Chap. 4, *Racing* and *Anto*.

18. H.A. Craig's Memorandum for General Handy, July 13, 1945, Records of the Office of the Secretary of War, Stimson Safe File, RG 107, National Archive.

19. Although I add a new angle in the process in which the Potsdam Proclamation was revised, no one else except Richard Frank pays close attention to this issue. See *Racing*, pp. 110–15, 116–20, 145–48, 155–60; and *Anto*, pp. 181–89, 191–97, 247–52, 265–74. For Frank's comments, see www.h-net.org/~diplo/roundtables/#hasegawa (Mar. 2006).

20. Robert H. Ferrell, ed., *Off the Record: The Private Papers of Harry S. Truman* (New York: Harper & Row, 1980), p. 53; Harry S. Truman, *Memoirs* (Garden City, NY: Doubleday, 1955), vol. 1, p. 411; Robert H. Ferrell, ed., *Dear Bess: The Letters from Harry to Bess Truman, 1910–1959* (New York: Norton, 1983), p. 519; Richard Frank, *Downfall: The End of the Imperial Japanese Empire* (New York: Random House, 1999), p. 243.

21. Stimson Diary, July 17, 1945, Sterling Library, Yale University; also quoted in U.S. Department of State, *FRUS: Potsdam*, vol. 2, 1266.

22. "HF mtg w/Byrnes, 2-27-58," "Byrnes draft ms—HF notes," Herbert Feis Papers, Box 65, Library of Congress.

23. Walter Mills, ed., *Forrestal Diaries* (New York: Viking Press, 1951), p. 78.

24. Stimson Diary, July 23, 1945.

25. Ibid., July 24, 1945.

26. Chap. 4, *Racing* and *Anto*.

27. Whether Vasilievskii's telegram was prompted by Stalin or his recommendation was made on his own is an important issue over which David Holloway and I differ. See Holloway's review of my book in www.h-net.org/~diplo/roundtables/#hasegawa (Mar. 2006); as well as David Holloway, "Jockeying for Position in the Postwar World: Soviet Entry into the War with Japan in August 1945"; and Tsuyoshi Hasegawa, "The Soviet Factor in Ending the Pacific War: From the Neutrality Pact to Soviet Entry into the War in August 1945," in Hasegawa, *End of the Pacific War*.

28. Truman made a brief statement at the news conference announcing the Soviet entry into the war. Quoting the *New York Times* and *Washington Post* articles on this news conference, Michael Kort criticizes my account that Truman was disappointed. In fact, according to the *New York Times*, he "rocked with laughter." Kort, however, does not explain why Byrnes went out of his way to emphasize that the Soviet Union did not sign the Potsdam Proclamation, and in fact, as Truman indeed welcomed Soviet entry into the war, why Truman and Byrnes refused to accept Stalin's request that his signature be appended to the Potsdam Proclamation. See Michael Kort, "Racing the Enemy: A Critical Look," in *Hiroshima in History: The Myths of Revisionism*, ed. Robert James Maddox (Columbia: University of Missouri Press, 2007), pp. 194–95.

29. See chap. 5, *Racing* and *Anto*. In *Anto*, I examine in more detail the historiographical issues on the relationship between the atomic bombing on Hiroshima and Japan's decision to surrender. See also Tsuyoshi Hasegawa, "The Atomic Bombs and the Soviet Invasion: Which Was More Important in Japan's Decision to Surrender?" in Hasegawa, *End of the Pacific War*, pp. 113–44.

30. I presented an argument that the opposition of the Japanese specialists, especially by Joseph Balantine, played an important role in inducing Byrnes to reject Japan's conditional acceptance. Bernstein questions the reliability of Balantine's memoirs, while Richard Frank supports my contention.

31. See chap. 6, *Racing* and *Anto*.

32. See chap. 7, *Racing* and *Anto*.

33. See Hasegawa, "Atomic Bombs and the Soviet Invasion," pp. 113–44; see H-Diplo Roundtables.

34. Hasegawa, "Atomic Bombs and the Soviet Invasion," pp. 114–18. For the view that holds that Japan immediately decided to accept the Potsdam terms after the atomic bombing of Hiroshima, see Sadao Asada, "The Shock of the Atomic Bomb and Japan's Decision to Surrender—a Reconsideration," *Pacific Historical Review* 67, no. 4 (1998); and Richard Frank, *Downfall: The End of the Imperial Japanese Empire* (New York: Random House, 1999).

35. Frank, *Downfall*, pp. 119–20.

36. Sato Motohide and Kurosawa Bunki, eds., *GHQ rekishika chinjutsuroku: shusenshi shiryo* (Statements for the GHQ Division: Documents for the History of Japan's Surrender) (Tokyo: Hara Shobo, 2002), vol. 1, p. 73.

37. Chap. 5 of *Racing* and *Anto*; Hasegawa, "Atomic Bombs and the Soviet Invasion," pp. 120–22.

38. Originally, this view was presented by Lawrence Freedman and Saki Dockrill, "Hiroshima: A Strategy of Shock," in *From Pearl Harbor to Hiroshima: The Second World War in Asia and the Pacific, 1941–45*, ed. Saki Dockrill (New York: St. Martin's Press, 1994), pp. 201–9. Asada closely follows Dockrill's view in "Shock," p. 504. Frank also subscribes to the view that the Soviet role was merely secondary: Frank, *Downfall*, p. 348.

39. Hasegawa, "Atomic Bombs and the Soviet Invasion," pp. 123–31.

40. Hando Toshikazu, *Nihon no ichiban nagai hi* (Japan's Longest Day), ed. Oya Soichi (Tokyo: Bungenshunju, 1973), p. 36.

41. Michael S. Sherry, *The Rise of American Air Power: The Creation of Armageddon* (New Haven: Yale University Press, 1987), pp. 355–56.

42. Gordin, *Five Days*, pp. 10–11, 18.

43. Quoted in John W. Dower, *War Without Mercy: Race and Power in the Pacific War* (New York: Pantheon Books, 1986), pp. 38, 39.

44. Sherry, *Rise of American Air Power*, p. 117.

45. For graphic details of Japanese atrocities, see Dower, *War Without Mercy*, especially pp. 42–45.

46. Sherry, *Rise of American Air Power*, p. 171.

47. Quoted in ibid., p. 141.

48. Sherry, *Rise of American Air Power*, p. 141; Ronald Schaffer, *Wings of Judgment: American Bombing in World War II* (New York: Oxford University Press, 1985), p. 142.

49. Quoted in Dower, *War Without Mercy*, p. 55.

50. Sherry, *Rise of American Air Power*, pp. 245–46; Dower, *War Without Mercy*, pp. 55, 56.

51. Sherry, *Rise of American Air Power*, p. 321.

52. *Racing*, p. 66; *Anto*, pp. 110–11; Stimson Diary, Apr. 25, 1945; memorandum discussed with the president, Apr. 25, 1945, in Stimson Diary, pp. 70–72. Also see "The Atomic Bomb," Papers of Eben A. Ayers, Subject File, Box 5, Atomic Bomb [3 of 4], Harry S. Truman Library.

53. *Racing*, p. 77; *Anto*, p. 127; Stimson Diary, May 13, 1945, pp. 123–24; May 14, 1945, p. 126.

54. Robert S. Norris, *Racing for the Bomb: General Leslie R. Groves, the Manhattan Project's Indispensable Man* (South Royalton, VT: Steerforth Press, 2002), p. 381.

55. Stimson Diary, May 31, 1945; Martin J. Sherwin, *A World Destroyed: The Atomic Bomb and the Grand Alliance* (New York: Vintage Books, 1977), pp. 204–5.

56. Stimson Diary, July 18, 1945.

57. Ferrell, *Off the Record*, pp. 56–57; Dennis Merrill, ed., *Documentary History of the Truman Presidency* [hereafter *DHTP*], vol. 1, *The Decision to Drop the Atomic Bomb on Japan* (Bethesda, MD: University Publications of America, 1995), pp. 156, 157.

58. Winston S. Churchill, *The Second World War: Triumph and Tragedy* (Boston: Houghton Mifflin, 1953), pp. 638–39.

59. Quoted in Gar Alperovitz, *The Decision to Use the Atomic Bomb* (New York: Vintage Books, 1996), p. 345.

60. *DHTP*, pp. 9–11. Stimson's opposition to targeting Kyoto was motivated not only by his concerns for preserving cultural treasures, but also by his political concerns. He feared that bombing Kyoto would irretrievably make the Japanese anti-American in the coming postwar struggle with the Soviet Union. For Stimson's moral dilemma, see Sean L. Malloy, *Atomic Tragedy: Henry L. Stimson and the Decision to Use the Bomb Against Japan* (Ithaca: Cornell University Press, 2008).

61. "Notes of the Interim Committee Meeting," May 31, 1945, p. 11, Harrison-Bundy Files Relating to the Development of the Atomic Bomb, 1942–1946; Miscellaneous Historical Documents Collection, Item #661-79, Harry S. Truman Library; *DHPT*, pp. 46–47.

62. Norris, *Racing for the Bomb*, pp. 379–80. The quote is from p. 380.

63. *Racing*, pp. 90–91; *Anto*, p. 148; Stimson Diary, June 6, 1945; Memorandum of Conference with the President, June 6, 1945, Stimson Papers, Reel 118, Sterling Library, Yale University. On the same occasion, Stimson also told Truman that the Russians should not be told anything about the bomb until the first bomb was successfully dropped on Japan. The president said that he was thinking along the same line, especially with regard to the "settlement of the Polish, Rumanian, Yugoslavian, and *Manchurian* problems [italics added by the author]." Here is the direct evidence to show that Truman was interested in using the bomb as a political weapon against Soviet expansionism, not merely in Europe but also in Asia.

64. *Racing*, p. 159; *Anto*, pp. 273–74; *DHTP*, pp. 155, 156; Farrell, *Off the Record*, pp. 56–57. Here we face a difficult question of how to interpret Truman's diary. Did it accurately reflect his thinking at the time, or did Truman write the diary "for history," attempting to justify his actions for future historians? It should be pointed out that there is no truth to his statement that he instructed Stimson to target the atomic bombs only at the military objects and personnel, not "women and children."

65. H.H. Arnold, *Global Mission* (New York: Harper & Bros., 1949), p. 589.

66. Leslie R. Groves, *Now It Can Be Told: The Story of the Manhattan Project* (New York: Harper & Bros., 1962), p. 324.

67. For Stimson's conflicting views, see Schaffer, *Wings of Judgment*, pp. 166–70, 180.

68. Stimson Diary, from July 28 through Aug. 9, 1945; also see Hiroshima: The Henry Stimson Diary and Papers (Part 9), compiled by Doug Long, http://www.doug-long.com/stimson9.htm (accessed Sept. 11, 2007).

69. Henry L. Stimson and McGeorge Bundy, *On Active Service in Peace and War* (New York: Harper & Bros., 1948), p. 633.

70. Barton Bernstein's commentary on Racing the Enemy, www.h-net.org/~diplo/roundtables/#hasegawa (Mar. 2000); Gordin, *Five Days*, pp. 6–7.

71. Grew to Byrnes, Aug. 7, 1945, Letters of Joseph Grew, 1945, Grew Papers, Houghton Library, Harvard University.

72. Walter Brown Diary, July 18, 1945, and July 24, 1945, Folder 602, Folder 54 (1), James Byrnes Papers, Clemson University.

73. Mills, *Forrestal Diaries*, p. 78.

74. Stimson Diary, July 23, 1945.

75. Cyril Clemens, ed., *Truman Speaks* (New York: Columbia University Press, 1960), p. 69.

76. Telegram, Senator Richard Russell to Truman, Aug. 7, 1945, Truman to Russell, Papers of Harry S. Truman, Official File, Box 196 Misc (1946), Harry S. Truman Library; *DHTP*, pp. 210, 211–12.

77. John Morton Blum, ed., *The Price of Vision: The Diary of Henry A. Wallace, 1942–1946* (Boston: Houghton Mifflin, 1973), p. 374; Leahy Diary, Aug. 9, 1945, Library of Congress.

78. Truman to Eugene Meyer, Aug. 10, 1945, quoted in Barton Bernstein, "Truman and the A-Bomb: Targeting Noncombatants, Using the Bomb, and His Defending the 'Decision,'" *Journal of Military History* 62, no. 4 (1998): 557.

79. Truman to Thomas Murray, Jan. 19, 1953, quoted in Bernstein, "Truman and the A-Bomb," p. 562.

80. See Gordin, *Five Days*, chap. 7.

81. Stimson and Bundy, *On Active Service*, p. 617.

82. Sherwin, *World Destroyed*, pp. 200–202; Shaffer, *Wings of Judgment*, pp. 159–60; David Robertson, *Sly and Able: A Political Biography of James F. Byrnes* (New York: Simon & Schuster, 1992), pp. 400–406; Bernstein, "Truman and the A-Bomb," pp. 555–56.

83. Sherwin, *World Destroyed*, pp. 210–11; Shaffer, *Wings of Judgment*, p. 160.

84. Sherry, *Rise of American Air Power*, p. 326; Schaffer, *Wings of Judgment*, p. 161.

85. Sherry, *Rise of American Air Power*, p. 326.

86. "Ralph Bard's Dissent," in Sherwin, *World Destroyed*, pp. 307–8; Schaffer, *Wings of Judgment*, p. 165.

87. *Racing*, p. 299; *Anto*, pp. 511–12; *Asahi Shimbun*, Aug. 11, 1945. The full text is also in *FRUS* 1945, vol. 6, pp. 472–73.

88. Gordin, *Five Days*, p. 22; Sven Lindqvist, *A History of Bombing*, trans. Linda Haverty Rugg (New York: The New Press, 2000), p. 113; Geoffrey Best, *War and Law Since 1945* (Oxford: Clarendon Press, 1994), pp. 204–5; Norman Paech, "Nürnberg und die Nuclearfrage," in *Strafgerichte gegen Menshheitsverbrechen: Zum Völkerstrafrecht 50 Jahre nach den Nürnberger Prozessen*, ed. Gerd Hankel, Gernard Study (Hamburg: Hamburger Edition HIS Verlagsges, 1995), p. 481. For the London Agreement and the attached Convention, see Avalon Project at Yale Law School, www.yale.edu/lawweb/avalon/imt/pro/imtchart.htm (accessed Sept. 3, 2008).

89. Lindqvist, *History of Bombing*, p. 113.

90. For Pal's dissenting voice, see Elizabeth Borgwardt, "Ideology and International Law: The Dissent of the Indian Justice at the Tokyo War Crimes Trial," *War and Crimes Law*, vol. 2, in the series *International Library of Essays in Law and Legal Theory*, ed. Tom D. Campbell, Ashgate Publishing, July 2004,

pp. 373–44; and Hiro Saito, "Culpability and Responsibility in Hiroshima," *Journal of the International Institute* 11, no. 1 (2003).

91. Helen Fein, "Discriminating Genocide from War Crimes: Vietnam and Afghanistan Reexamined," *Denver Journal of International Law and Policy* 22, no. 1 (1993): 33, quoted in Markusen and Kopf, *Holocaust and Strategic Bombing*, p. 252.

92. Markusen and Kopf, *Holocaust and Strategic Bombing*, pp. 256–58.

93. Quoted by Sherry, *Rise of American Air Power*, p. 335.

94. Norman M. Naimark, *The Russians in Germany: A History of the Soviet Zone of Occupation, 1945–1949* (Cambridge, MA: Belknap Press of Harvard University Press, 1995), p. 112.

6. Strategic Bombing of Chongqing by Imperial Japanese Army and Naval Forces
by Tetsuo Maeda

1. P.M.S. Blackett, *The Military and Political Consequences of Atomic Energy* (London: Turnstile Press, 1949), passim.

2. Kaisen yomu rei koku-sen no bu, soan gunrei bu kimitu dai 209 go: Showa 15 nen 4 , 10 [Navy General Staff Confidential No. 209, Air Battle Section Draft, Sea Battle Operation, continued, April 10], collection of the War History Library, Japanese Ministry of Defense.

3. *Chugoku homen jaigiun sakusen 2* [Naval Operations in China vol. 2], in Boei-sho senshi shiryo sosho [War History Series, Japanese Ministry of Defense (hereafter WHS)], p. 77.

4. Liu Ching Shen, "Chongqing and the 8 Years of Resistance," in *Records of Resistance Movement at Chongqing*, ed. Chongqing City Committee, Sichuan, of the People's Republic of China (Chongqing Publishers, 1988).

5. *Shina jihen rikugun sakusen 2* (Army Operations of War with China, vol. 2), in WHS, p. 296.

6. Theodore H. White, *In Search of History: A Personal Adventure* (New York: Harper & Row, 1978).

7. *Kaigun koku-shi 4* [Navy Force Air Division History, vol. 4] in WHS, p. 475.

8. *Shina jihen rikugun sakusen 2* [Army Operations of War with China vol. 2] in WHS, p. 296.

9. *Chugoku homen kaigiun sakusen 2* [Naval Operations in China, vol. 2] in WHS, p. 49.

10. Nakayama Sadayoshi, *Ichi kaigun shikan no kaiso* [The Recollections of a Naval Officer] (Tokyo: Mainichi Press, 1981), p. 11.

11. *Chugoku homen rikugun koku sakusen* [Army Air Operations in China] in WHS, p. 130.

12. White, *In Search of History*, p. 81.

13. Han Suyin, *Birdless Summer* (London: Jonathan Cape, 1968) p. 125.

14. *Dai 3 kantai sento gaiho* [Third Fleet Outline Report], collection of the War History Library, Japanese Ministry of Defense.

15. Iwatani Fumio, *Chuko* [Attacking China] (Tokyo: Hara Shobo, 1976), p. 138.

16. *Shanghai tokumu kikan shusaeki bukan joho* [Shanghai Secret Military Agency, Chief Military Officer Information], collection of the War History Library, Japanese Ministry of Defense.

17. *101 go sakusen no gaiyo* [Brief Summary of No. 101 Operation] and abstract of same in *Chugoku homen kaigiun sakusen 2* [Naval Operations in China, vol. 2], in WHS. Both documents are stored in the War History Library, Japanese Ministry of Defense.

18. Liu Ching Shen, "Chongqing," p. 4.

19. White, *In Search of History*, p. 82.

20. Gaston Bouthoul and René Carrère, *Le défi de la guerre: Deux siècles de guerres et de revolution, 1740–1974* (Paris: Presses Universitaires de France, 1976), Japanese ed., p.156.

21. *Mainichi* newspaper, Dec. 14, 2001.

22. *Mainichi* newspaper, Mar. 28, 1997.

7. Bombing Civilians from the Twentieth to the Twenty-first Centuries
by Marilyn B. Young

1. Ronald Schaffer, *Wings of Judgment: American Bombing in World War II* (New York: Oxford University Press, 1985), p. 215.

2. The single best account is Bruce Cumings, *Origins of the Korean War* (Princeton, NJ: Princeton University Press, 1990), vol. 2; see also Conrad Crane, *American Airpower Strategy in Korea, 1950–1953* (Lawrence: University Press of Kansas, 1993), pp. 11–22.

3. Earl H. Tilford Jr., *Crosswinds: The Air Force's Setup in Vietnam* (College Station: Texas A&M University Press, 1993), p. 117.

4. Strategic bombing was directed at the "enemy's capability and will to resist"; tactical bombing was "designed to assist ground forces on the battlefield." Mark Clodfelter, *The Limits of Air Power: The American Bombing of North Vietnam* (New York: The Free Press, 1989), pp. 2, 3.

5. Col. Raymond Sleeper, "Air Power, the Cold War, and Peace," in *Airpower: The Decisive Force in Korea*, ed. James T. Stewart (Princeton, NJ: Van Nostrand, 1957); see also Schaffer, *Wings of Judgment*, p. 207.

6. H.R. McMaster, *Dereliction of Duty* (New York: HarperCollins, 1997), p. 62. The classic analysis of Johnson administration policy remains Wallace J. Thies, *When Governments Collide: Coercion and Diplomacy in the Vietnam Conflict, 1964–1968* (Berkeley: University of California Press, 1980).

7. It was not until quite late in the Vietnam War that Americans (and the rest of the world) saw television and still images of napalm victims. In 1974, Hans Blix, in an effort to ban the use of napalm, reminded his listeners of those images. His colleagues would, he knew, "coldly and rationally analyze the various factors which argue in favour of a ban on use of incendiaries and the factors which, on the contrary, militate against such a ban. But at the same time I confess that I hope and trust we shall be influenced by that picture." Quoted in Eric Prokosch, *Technology of Killing: A Military and Political History of Antipersonnel Weapons* (London: Zed, 1995), p. 170.

8. During the Korean War, the romance of flight was dimmed by the high toll Soviet MiGs took on U.S. jets. By 1952, the air force had identified "fear of flying" as a major problem in retention and recruitment. The air force took active measures to deal with the problem, and Hollywood helped out: in 1951, dozens of film stars joined in a celebration of the air force held in the Hollywood Bowl, and a number of films glorifying the past and present of the air force were produced, including *12 O'Clock High* and *Strategic Air Command*. See Crane, *American Airpower Strategy*, pp. 97–108.

9. Crane, *American Airpower Strategy*, pp. 132ff, discusses the development of these new bombs—the prototypes of today's "smart" bombs. Of the twenty-eight used in combat, only twelve had been controllable, of which only six hit their intended targets. On cluster bombs, see Prokosch, *Technology of Killing*, and Michael Krepon, "Weapons Potentially Inhumane: The Case of Cluster Bombs," *Foreign Affairs* 52, no. 3 (April 1974): 595–611.

10. The name of a popular children's song, which was number 2 on the charts in 1963. It was performed by Peter, Paul and Mary and used, with conscious irony, by troops in Vietnam to describe the
AC-47 gunship.

11. Raphael Littauer and Norman Uphoff, eds., *The Air War in Indochina*, rev. ed. (Boston: Beacon
Press, 1972), p. 209. The U.S. Air Force was responsible for the overwhelming majority of the bombing and
strafing, with the U.S. Navy and Marines Second and Third respectively. Non-U.S. air forces dropped
some 20,000 tons of the total.

12. Jeffrey Record, *The Wrong War* (Annapolis, MD: Naval Institute Press, 1998), p. 75.

13. Cecil Currey article in *VN Generation*. See also Paul Frederick Cecil, *Herbicidal Warfare* (New
York: Praeger, 1986); and J.B. Neilands et al., *Harvest of Death: Chemical Warfare in Vietnam and Cambodia*
(New York: The Free Press, 1972). For figures on cluster bombs, see Prokosch, *Technology of Killing*, and
Littauer and Uphoff, *Air War in Indochina*.

14. Micheal Clodfelter, *Vietnam in Military Statistics: A History of the Indochina Wars, 1772–1991* (Jefferson, NC: McFarland, 1995), p. 275; on Japan, see Littauer and Uphoff, *Air War in Indochina*, table B-2,
p. 204.

15. E.J. Kahn, *The Peculiar War: Impressions of a Reporter in Korea* (New York: Random House, 1952),
pp. 105, 132.

16. Reginald Thompson, *Cry Korea* (London: MacDonald, 1952), p. 94.

17. See Jonathan Schell, *The Real War: The Classic Reporting on the Vietnam War* (New York: Pantheon, 1987), pp. 302–3. At one point in the Korean War, a lack of targets had reduced medium-sized
bombers to twenty-five sorties a day. "Finding nothing better to bomb, one 92nd Group crew recorded that
it chased an enemy soldier on a motorcycle down the road, dropping bombs until one hit the hapless
fellow. . . ." Crane, *American Airpower Strategy*, pp. 122–23.

18. See Barton Bernstein, "New Light on the Korean War," in *MacArthur and the American Century*,
ed. William M. Leary (Lincoln: University of Nebraska Press, n.d.), p. 404. The head of the special weapons
project, General Kenneth D. Nichols, on the other hand, thought nuclear weapons should be used to "prevent our being pushed off the peninsula," irrespective of Chinese or Russian intervention.

19. Ibid., p. 405.

20. The flirtation with use of nuclear weapons ended only with the Korean War itself. For more details,
see Cumings, *Origins of the Korean War*. In 1951, this included a simulated atomic run by a single B-29 flying
from Okinawa to North Korea. For details on this flight, Operation Hudson Harbor, see Cumings.

21. Cumings, *Origins of the Korean War*, p. 755. John McNaughton, the assistant secretary of defense,
contemplated attacking North Vietnam's system of dikes and dams in 1966, though the suggestion was
never acted upon. If "handled right," he wrote in a memo, it "might offer promise. . . . Such destruction
does not kill or drown people. By shallow flooding the rice, it leads after a time to widespread starvation
(more than a million?) unless food is provided—which we could offer to do 'at the conference table.'" See
also Crane, *American Airpower Strategy*, pp. 159–61. General Mark Clark had expected some international
protest but "the dam attacks received very little notice in the world press. American newspapers were preoccupied with the exploits of the jet aces. . . ."

22. Freda Kirchwey, "Liberation by Death," *Nation*, March 10, 1951, p. 216.

23. Ibid.

24. Ibid., p. 215.

25. "The Bridges at Sinanju and Yongmidong," *Quarterly Review* Staff Study, in Stewart, *Airpower*, pp. 141ff.

26. William W. Stueck, *The Korean War: An International History* (Princeton, NJ: Princeton University Press, 1995), p. 342.

27. See ibid., pp. 326ff.

28. Stewart, *Airpower*, p. 290.

29. Crane, *American Airpower Strategy*, p. 178.

30. Michael Bechloss, LBJ Tapes book, 370.

31. McMaster, *Dereliction of Duty*, p. 62.

32. *The Pentagon Papers: The Defense Department History of U.S. Decisionmaking on Vietnam*, Senator Gravel ed. (Boston: Beacon Press, 1971–72), 3: 593, 599–600, 605; see also p. 225.

33. Ibid., p. 238. Any ongoing discussion of the possibility of using tactical nuclear weapons came to a head, for the Johnson administration, when four scientists associated with the Jason Division spent the summer of 1966 studying the feasibility of their use in Vietnam. The study was inspired by a remark one of the scientists associated with Jason overheard a high Pentagon official make, that it "might be a good idea to toss in a nuke from time to time, just to keep the other side guessing." The result was a fifty-five-page report unequivocally rejecting the notion; it was never raised again in the Johnson administration. See Peter Hayes and Nina Tannewald, "Nixing Nukes in Vietnam," *Bulletin of Atomic Scientists* 59, no. 1 (Jan.–Feb. 2003): 28–37, 72–73.

34. Clodfelter, *Limits of Air Power*, on Tuesday lunches and target selection, pp. 120–23; quote is on pp. 121–22.

35. Clodfelter, *Vietnam in Military Statistics*, p. 221.

36. *Pentagon Papers*, 3: 687–91.

37. Ibid., 4: 222–24. Several years later, in October 1972, the staff report to the Senate Foreign Relations Committee reached a similar conclusion: "There is no indication . . . that any of the major intelligence agencies believed that the bombing of the North could or would reduce the level of support for the war in the South. . . . Rather, the agencies placed their hopes in punishing North Vietnam and in possibly breaking her will."

38. Jeffrey Kimball, *Nixon's Vietnam War* (Lawrence: University Press of Kansas, 1998), pp. 83, 82.

39. William Burr and Jeffrey Kimball, "Nixon's Nuclear Ploy," *Bulletin of Atomic Scientists* 59, no. 1 (Jan.–Feb. 2003): 28–37, 72–73. Nixon called another full-scale alert during the October war in 1973 to demonstrate U.S. readiness to "to use threats of force to deter Soviet military intervention in regional conflicts (even if the Soviets had no plans to intervene)." The point, Kimball and Burr conclude, was to indicate Nixon and Kissinger's conviction "that a show of force was essential to salvage U.S. Vietnam policy and the credibility of American power."

40. Quoted in Seymour Hersh, *The Price of Power: Kissinger in the White House* (New York: Summit Books, 1983), pp. 125–27, p. 134 note.

41. Clodfelter, *Limits of Air Power*, p. 194.

42. Quoted in Nguyen Tien Hung and Jerrold L. Schecter, *The Palace File* (New York: Harper & Row, 1986), p. 146.

43. Kimball, *Nixon's Vietnam War*, pp. 209, 211, 363.

44. Schaffer, *Wings of Judgment*, p202.

45. Jim Lobe, "Pentagon Woos Vietnam," *Asia Times*, July 19, 2003. According to Rajan Menon, the

invitation is part of a "broader anti-China strategy in which Washington attempts to build up military ties with countries situated along China's periphery. . . ." Ian Bremer, "Talk, But Talk Tough," *New York Times*, July 19, 2003, p. A-27.

46. This would reverse the "traditional equation of air power." In World War II, Korea, and indeed in Vietnam, the issue was "how many planes were needed to take out one target; now it was a question of how many targets *one* plane with precision-guided weapons could take out." David Halberstam, *War in a Time of Peace: Bush, Clinton, and the Generals* (New York: Scribner's, 2001), p. 51. For a general discussion of the new tactics and those who opposed them, see chapter 5.

47. "Sir," Halberstam quotes General Charles Horner saying to General Schwarzkopf, "the last thing we want is a repeat of Vietnam where Washington picked the targets!" Ibid., p. 53. After the war, Warden projected what World War II would have been like had the United States possessed precision weapons then: it took 6,000 planes to shut down German military production at the rate of about 1,000 planes per target, with high military and civilian casualties. "The circle of error—that is, the circle into which you could realistically expect to put 50% of your bombs stood at 20 miles for night bombing at the start of the war and narrowing to 1000 meters towards the end. The new weapons allowed the circle of error to close to six feet or even smaller" [p. 55]. Warden quote, p. 52.

48. Paul Walker, "U.S. Bombing: The Myths of Surgical Bombing in the Gulf War," report to the New York Commission of Inquiry for the International War Crimes Tribunal, May 11, 1991, and the Boston hearing on June 8, 1991, http://deoxy.org/wc-myth.htm (accessed Feb. 20, 2006).

49. "Air Power in the Gulf War," anonymous, globalsecurity.org/military/library/report/1999/airpower (accessed June 30, 2008).

50. Edwin E. Moïse, "Limited War: the Stereotypes," www.clemson.edu/caah/history/FacultyPages/EdMoise/limit1.html (accessed June 30, 2008).

51. From official U.S. Air Force history, quoted in Fred Kaplan, "The Flaw in Shock and Awe," *Slate*, Mar. 26, 2003, http://www.slate.com/id/2080745 (accessed Feb. 21, 2006). The entire episode is reminiscent of Nixon's hunt for COSVN during the Vietnam War.

52. Quoted in Walker, "U.S. Bombing."

53. Quoted in Andrew J. Bacevich, *American Empire: The Realities and Consequences of U.S. Diplomacy* (Cambridge, MA: Harvard University Press, 2002), p. 48.

54. Quoted in ibid., p. 150. As Bacevich points out, p. 155, Clinton's bombing policy was Rolling Thunder redux.

55. Ibid., pp. 152, 154.

56. Oliver Burkeman, "Shock Tactics," *The Guardian*, Mar. 25, 2003, http://www.guardian.co.uk/world/2003/mar25/u.s.a.iraq/ (accessed Feb. 21, 2006).

57. Ullman makes the case for the nuclear bombs as it is usually made: the invasion would have cost a million American casualties and countless Japanese lives. He instructs Burkeman that the Japanese were "suicidal in the extreme. And they could comprehend 1,000 bombers, 100,000 dead Japanese, but they couldn't understand one plane, one bomb, one city gone." He goes further: "We could have de-peopled Japan: no more Japanese. We dropped two nuclear weapons, and they quit. So you focus on things that collapse their ability to resist."

58. Ira Chernus, "Shock & Awe: Is Baghdad the Next Hiroshima?" CommonDreams.org, Jan. 27, 2003, http://www.commondreams.org/views03/0127-08.htm (accessed Feb. 21, 2006).

59. Anthony Shadid, *Night Draws Near: Iraq's People in the Shadow of America's War* (New York: Henry Holt, 2005), pp. 90–91.

60. Ellen Knickmeyer, "U.S. Airstrikes Take Toll on Civilians," *Washington Post*, Dec. 24, 2005.

61. Drew Brown, "Air War May Intensify as Ground Forces Leave Iraq," *Detroit Times*, Jan. 11, 2006.

62. Dahr Jamail, "An Increasingly Aerial Occupation," Tomgram, Dec. 13, 2005, http://www .tomdispatch.com/post/163152.

63. Nick Turse, "America's Secret Air War in Iraq: Bombs Over Baghdad," TomDispatch.com, *Dahr* Feb. 7, 2007 (accessed Feb. 3, 2008). See also his report on the use of cluster bombs in Iraq, "Did the U.S. Lie About Cluster Bomb Use in Iraq?" TomDispatch.com, May 24, 2007 (accessed Feb. 3, 2008), and Tom Engelhardt, "Looking Up: Normalizing Air War from Guernica to Arab Jabour," TomDispatch.com, Jan. 29, 2008.

64. Associated Press, "Lynch: US 'Surge' Tipped Scales in Iraq," *New York Times*, Feb. 2, 2006.

65. Josh Meyer, "CIA Expands Use of Drones in Terror War," *Los Angeles Times*, Jan. 19, 2006.

66. See "Lawmakers Defend Pakistan Strike," CNN International.com, Jan. 16, 2006, http://edition .cnn.com/2006/US/01/15/alqaedastrike.us/index/htm.

67. Andrew J. Bacevich, "War in Error," *American Conservative*, Feb. 27, 2006.

8. The United States and Strategic Bombing: From Prophecy to Memory
by Michael Sherry

1. I examine that history through 1945 at length in Michael S. Sherry, *The Rise of American Air Power: The Creation of Armageddon* (New Haven: Yale University Press, 1987); Truman's words are quoted and analyzed on p. 349.

2. Ibid., p. 1.

3. Ibid., pp. 8–9, 44 (quotations). In addition to my book and other scholarship on interwar prophecy, see the excellent recent piece, Paul K. Saint-Amour, "Air War Prophecy and Interwar Modernism," *Comparative Literature Studies* 42, no. 2 (2005): 130–61.

4. Spencer R. Weart, *Nuclear Fear: A History of Images* (Cambridge, MA: Harvard University Press, 1988), p. 81.

5. These arguments are developed in my book *The Rise of American Air Power*. The Philco ad is reproduced in that book's photo essay.

6. Ibid., p. 289 (air force officer). For the bombing in Europe, see especially Ronald Schaffer's essay.

7. See especially Sharon Ghamari-Tabrizi, *The Worlds of Herman Kahn: The Intuitive Logic of Thermonuclear War* (Cambridge, MA: Harvard University Press, 2005).

8. Both quotations appear in many accounts. I analyze them in Michael S. Sherry, *In the Shadow of War: The United States Since the 1930s* (New Haven: Yale University Press, 1995), pp. 251, 312.

9. Paul Boyer, *When Time Shall Be No More: Prophecy Belief in Modern American Culture* (Cambridge, MA: Belknap Press of Harvard University Press, 1992), p. 127.

10. On the *Enola Gay* exhibition controversy, see Philip J. Nobile, ed., *Judgment at the Smithsonian* (New York: Marlowe & Co., 1995); Laura Hein and Mark Selden, eds., *Living with the Bomb: American and Japanese Cultural Conflicts in the Nuclear Age* (Armonk, NY: M.E. Sharpe, 1997); Edward T. Linenthal and Tom Engelhardt, eds., *History Wars: The* Enola Gay *and Other Battles for the American Past* (New York: Metropolitan Books, 1996).

11. W.G. Sebald, *On the Natural History of Destruction*, trans. Anthea Bell (New York: Random House, 2003), p. 69.

12. See Robert Moeller's essay in this volume.

13. Quotation from Sharon Ghamari-Tabrizi on her Web site, www.acdis.uiuc.edu/About/Staff/showstaff.php?id=33 (accessed Dec. 14, 2006). I also draw on informal communications with Ghamari-Tabrizi about her work in progress on this subject; on entries, each with extensive links, about "wargaming" and "military exercises" in Wikipedia (accessed Dec. 12, 2006); and the Air War College Web site, www.au.af.mil/au/awc/awcgate/awc-ndex.htm (accessed Dec. 10, 2006), also with extensive links.

14. Saint-Amour, "Air War Prophecy," p. 158, quoting E.B. White, *Here Is New York*, ed. Barbara Cohen and Judith Stonehill (New York: New York Review Books, 2000).

15. Ibid.

9. Bombing and the Morality of War *by C.A.J. Coady*

1. So, for instance, Hsun Tzu: "The king's army does not kill the enemy's old men and boys; it does not destroy crops . . . it does not punish the common people." *Hsun Tzu: Basic Writings*, trans. Burton Watson (New York: Columbia University Press, 1966), p. 67.

2. Virtually all noncombatants are civilians, although there is room to argue that military chaplains and medical personnel are military but not combatants.

3. McMahan's criticisms occur in several places. See especially, "The Ethics of Killing in War," *Ethics* 114, no. 4 (2004): 693–733.

4. Giulio Douhet, *The Command of the Air*, trans. Dino Ferrari (New York: Coward McCann, 1942); B.H. Liddell Hart, *Paris; or, the Future of War* (London: Kegan Paul, 1925).

5. B.H. Liddell Hart, *The Memoirs of Captain Liddell Hart*, vol. 1 (London: Cassell, 1965), p. 141.

6. Quoted in Brian Bond, *Liddell Hart: A Study of His Military Thought* (Aldershot, UK: Gregg Revivals in association with the Department of War Studies, King's College, London, 1991), p. 145.

7. See *The United States Strategic Bombing Survey: Summary Report*, Sept. 30, 1945, available online at http://www.anesi.com/ussbs02.htm#eaocar. Another good and fairly skeptical discussion of the effects of the bombing on the course of the war can be found in Barrie Paskins and Michael Dockrill, *The Ethics of War* (London: Duckworth, 1979), chap. 1, especially pp. 42–51.

8. The story of this opposition is told more fully in A.C. Grayling, *Among the Dead Cities* (London: Bloomsbury, 2006). See especially chap. 5, "Voices of Conscience," from which my information in this paragraph is drawn.

9. Grayling, *Among the Dead Cities*, pp. 201–5.

10. See Stephen A. Garrett, *Ethics and Airpower in World War II: The British Bombing of German Cities* (New York: St. Martin's Press, 1993), p. 192.

11. Quoted by Garrett in *Ethics and Airpower*, p. 193.

12. The exchange is quoted in Grayling, *Among the Dead Cities*, p. 88. He gets it from Christoph Kucklick, *Feuersturm: Der Bombenkrieg gegen Deutschland* (Hamburg: Ellert and Richter, 2003), p. 32. His translation slightly alters what was recorded by Casey. My quote is from Lord Casey, *Personal Experience: 1939–1946* (London: Constable, 1962), p. 166.

13. See the *United States Strategic Bombing Survey*.

14. Utilitarianism and its cousin consequentialism are both very flexible doctrines, and some have defended nonutilitarian morality as the best morality for ordinary mortals to have. Most utility is promoted if people don't act on utilitarian principles! Whether it is comfortable to embrace a theory that tells you that its truth requires that hardly anyone should believe it, I will leave for another occasion. (See my "Henry Sidgwick" in *Routledge History of Philosophy*, vol. 7, *The Nineteenth Century*, ed. C.L. Ten [New York: Routledge, 1994] chap. 5, pp. 122–47.) Consequentialists might even, I suppose, find some use in this connection for the Doctrine of Double Effect (discussed below), but typically they reject it.

15. These conditions are expressed differently by different authors. This list is my distillation of the sense of those treatments I have read.

16. I discuss this debate more fully in C.A.J. Coady, *Morality and Political Violence* (New York: Cambridge University Press, 2007), pp. 136–46.

17. Robert L. Holmes, *On War and Morality* (Princeton, NJ: Princeton University Press, 1989). See especially pp. 193–203.

18. The precondition is related in spirit to a direct qualification to the usual statements of the DDE that has been suggested by Michael Walzer. Walzer treats the precondition as part of the condition specifying that the apparent effect be not really a means to the intended goal. Walzer's version goes as follows: ". . . aware of the evil involved, he seeks to minimize it, accepting costs to himself." Beyond minimizing damage at cost to oneself once embarked on the attack, however, there is the issue of accepting cost in order to avoid making the attack and causing its collateral damage altogether. For Walzer's view, see Michael Walzer, *Just and Unjust Wars: A Moral Argument with Historical Illustrations*, 3rd ed. (New York: Basic Books, 2000), p. 155.

19. Francisco de Vitoria, *Political Writings*, ed. Anthony Pagden and Jeremy Lawrance (New York: Cambridge University Press, 1991), p. 316.

20. Article 54, paragraph 3, of Protocol 1 of the Additional Protocols to the Geneva Conventions.

21. There is an excellent discussion of the limits of dual purpose targeting and of the state of international law and military practice in Henry Shue and David Wippman, "Limiting Attacks on Dual-Use Facilities Performing Indispensable Civilian Functions," *Cornell International Law Journal* 35, no. 3 (2002): 559–80. This contains detailed proposals for new approaches to the problem.

22. *The Age* (Melbourne), Mar. 12, 2004

23. I have discussed this issue more fully in Coady, *Morality and Political Violence*, pp. 149–52.

10. Aerial Bombardment of Civilians: The Current International Legal Framework
by Timothy L.H. McCormack and Helen Dunham

The writers would like to gratefully acknowledge the research assistance provided by Paramdeep Mtharu.

1. Statute of the International Criminal Tribunal for the former Yugoslavia, annexed to SC Res 827, UN SCOR, 48th sess., 3,217th mtg., 29, UN Doc S/Res/827 (May 25, 1993).

2. Statute of the International Criminal Tribunal for Rwanda, annexed to Resolution 955, SC Res 955, UN SCOR, 49th sess., 3,453rd mtg., UN Doc S/RES/955 (1994).

3. Rome Statute of the International Criminal Court, opened for signature July 17, 1998, 2187 NTS 3, entered into force July 1, 2002 (Rome Statute).

4. The ICTY has passed judgment on the war crime of willful targeting of civilians during the siege

of Sarajevo in the Galić case. Although this case did not involve the aerial bombing of civilians but sniping and shelling from small arms and artillery, the key rules applied in the case are the same. See *Prosecutor v Stanislav Galić (Trial Chamber Judgment)*, Case no. IT-98-29-T (Dec. 5, 2003).

5. Geoffrey Best, *War and Law Since 1945* (New York: Oxford University Press, 1994), p. 14.

6. See Timothy L.H. McCormack, "From Sun Tzu to the Sixth Committee: The Evolution of International Criminal Law Regime," in *The Law of War Crimes: National and International Approaches*, ed. Timothy L.H. McCormack and Gerry Simpson (Boston: Kluwer Law International, 1997), p. 33.

7. For further discussion on the distinction between human rights law and IHL, see Louise Doswald-Beck and Sylvain Vité, "International Humanitarian Law and Human Rights Law," *International Review of the Red Cross*, no. 293 (1993): 94.

8. See Chris Jochnick and Roger Normand, "The Legitimation of Violence: A Critical History of the Laws of War," 35 *Harvard International Law Journal* 49 (1994).

9. *Geneva Convention for the Amelioration of the Condition of the Wounded and the Sick in Armed Forces in the Field*, opened for signature Aug. 12, 1949, 75 UNTS 31, entered into force Oct. 21, 1950 (Geneva Convention I); *Geneva Convention for the Amelioration of the Condition of the Wounded, Sick and Shipwrecked in Members of Armed Forces at Sea*, opened for signature Aug. 12, 1949, 75 UNTS 85, entered into force Oct. 21, 1950 (Geneva Convention II); *Geneva Convention Relative to the Treatment of Prisoners of War*, opened for signature Aug. 12, 1949, 75 UNTS 135, entered into force Oct. 21, 1950 (Geneva Convention III); *Geneva Convention Relative to the Protection of Civilian Persons in Times of War*, opened for signature Aug. 12, 1949, 75 UNTS 287, entered into force Oct. 21, 1950 (Geneva Convention IV); (collectively, "Geneva Conventions"). As of March 2007, there are 194 state parties.

10. *Protocol Additional to the Geneva Conventions of 12 August 1949, and Relating to the Protection of Victims of International Armed Conflicts*, opened for signature June 8, 1977, 1125 UNTS 3, entered into force Dec. 7, 1978) (Additional Protocol I); *Protocol Additional to the Geneva Conventions of 12 Aug. 1949, and Relating to the Protection of Victims of Non-International Armed Conflicts*, opened for signature June 8, 1977, 1125 UNTS 609, entered into force Dec. 7, 1978 (Additional Protocol II).

11. For a more detailed discussion on IHL, see Frits Kalshoven and Liesbeth Zegveld, *Constraints on the Waging of War: An Introduction to International Humanitarian Law*, 3rd ed. (Geneva: International Committee of the Red Cross, 2001).

12. *Convention for the Protection of Cultural Property in the Event of Armed Conflict*, opened for signature May 14, 1954, 249 UNTS 240, entered into force Aug. 7, 1956.

13. See Robert J. Mathews and Timothy L.H. McCormack, "The Relationship Between International Humanitarian Law and Arms Control," in *The Changing Face of Conflict and the Efficacy of International Humanitarian Law*, ed. Helen Durham and Timothy L.H. McCormack (Boston: Kluwers Law International, 1999), p. 65.

14. *Convention on the Prohibition of the Use, Stockpiling, Production and Transfer of Anti-Personnel Mines and on Their Destruction*, opened for signature Sept. 18, 1997, 2056 UNTS 241, entered into force Mar. 1, 1999 (Ottawa Treaty).

15. Ibid.

16. *Convention on the Prohibition of the Development, Production and Stockpiling of Bateriological (Biological) and Toxin Weapons and on Their Destruction*, opened for signature April 10, 1972; 11 ILM 3320; (BWC) (entered into force March 26, 1975). *Convention on the Prohibition of the Development, Production,*

Stockpiling and Use of Chemical Weapons and on their Destruction, opened for signature January 13, 1993; 32 ILM 800 (entered into force April 29, 1997) (CWC).

17. William Hays Parks, "The Protection of Civilians from Air Warfare," *Israeli Yearbook of Human Rights* 27 (1998): 72.

18. Ian Henderson, "Targeting in Armed Conflict: A Legal Analysis" (doctoral thesis, University of Melbourne, 2007). Note that it is not the official policy of the ADF but a proposal by a Royal Australian Air Force legal officer.

19. Trial Judgment in the Blaškić case, para. 512. As in sec. III.2.3 supra, the ICTY's case law has considered indiscriminate attacks as attacks directed against civilian population.

20. See, e.g., ibid., p. 16.

21. See, e.g., Alexandra Boivin, "The Legal Regime Applicable to Targeting Military Objectives in the Context of Contemporary Warfare," University of Geneva Centre for International Humanitarian Law Research Paper, Series no. 2, Feb. 2006, available at http://www.ucihl.org/research/military_objec tives_ research.pdf.

22. Article 51(7) states: "The presence or movements of the civilian population or individual civilians shall not be used to render certain points or areas immune from military operations, in particular in attempts to shield military objectives from attacks or to shield, favour, or impede military operations. The parties to the conflict shall not direct the movement of the civilian population or individual civilians in order to attempt to shield military objectives from attacks or to shield military operations."

23. Boivin, "Legal Regime," p. 17.

24. See Rule 14 in Jean-Marie Henckaerts and Louise Doswald-Beck, *Customary International Humanitarian Law (2005)*, vol. 1, *Rules*, p. 46.

25. Additional Protocol I, art. 57(2)(b). This is a rule of customary international law and is therefore binding on states not party to Additional Protocol I.

26. Algeria, Australia, Austria, Belgium, Canada, Egypt, Germany, Ireland, Italy, the Netherlands, New Zealand, Spain, and the United Kingdom have all made declarations to this effect.

27. Judge Advocate General's School, U.S. Army, Charlottesville, *Operational Law Handbook* (2001), p. 9.

28. *Legality of the Threat or Use of Nuclear Weapons (Advisory Opinion)* [1996], ICJ Rep.

29. "Refusing to Learn to Love the Bomb: Nations Take Their Case to Court," *New York Times*, Jan. 14, 1996.

30. Timothy L.H. McCormack, "A Non Liquet on Nuclear Weapons—the ICJ Avoids the Application of General Principles of International Humanitarian Law," *International Review of the Red Cross*, no. 316 (1997): 76–91.

31. Frits Kalshoven, *Belligerent Reprisals* (Leyden: Martin Nijhoff, 1971), p. 162.

32. R.J. Overy, *The Air War, 1939–1945* (London: Europa Publications, 1980), p. 26.

33. Ibid., p. 35.

34. *Hague Convention IX Concerning Bombardment by Naval Forces in Time of War*, Oct. 18, 1907, CTS 345, art. 1 and 2, entered into force Jan. 26, 1910.

35. See Additional Protocol I, art. 20: "Reprisals against persons and objects protected by this Part are prohibited."

36. Kalshoven, *Belligerent Reprisals*, p. 176.

37. Michael Bothe, "The Protection of the Civilian Population and NATO Bombing on Yugoslavia: Comments on a Report to the Prosecutor of the ICTY," *European Journal of International Law* 12, no. 3 (2001): 532.

38. Paolo Benvenuti, "The ICTY Prosecutor and the Review of the NATO Bombing Campaign Against the Federal Republic of Yugoslavia," *European Journal of International Law* 12, no. 3 (2001): 506.

39. W.J. Fenwick, "Targeting and Proportionality during the NATO Bombing Campaign Against Yugoslavia," *European Journal of International Law* 12, no. 3 (2001): 502.

40. Final Report to the Prosecutor by the Committee Established to Review the NATO Bombing Campaign Against the Federal Republic of Yugoslavia (June 2000), p. 59, available at http://www.un.org/icty/pressreal/nato061300.htm.

41. U.S. Deputy Defense Secretary John Hamre cited in ibid., p. 59.

42. Amnesty International claims that sixteen civilians were killed and a further sixteen were wounded as a result of the attack. See Amnesty International, "NATO/Federal Republic of Yugoslavia: "'Collateral Damage' or Unlawful Killings? Violations of the Laws of War by NATO During Operation Allied Force," June 6, 2000.

43. NATO press conferences, Apr. 28 and 30, 1999, quoted in the Final Report to the Prosecutor, p. 22, para. 76.

44. Amnesty International, "NATO/Federal Republic of Yugoslavia," p. 39.

45. The Amnesty International report reinforces this opinion with a quote from the German Military Manual, which states that "if weakening the enemy population's resolve to fight were considered a legitimate objective of armed forces, there would be no limit to war," and another from the British Defence Doctrine, which states "the morale of an enemy's civilian population is not a legitimate target." See ibid., p. 40.

46. Ibid., p. 41.

47. There were estimated to be at least 120 civilians working in the RTS building at the time of the attack. See ibid., p. 38, quoting Inter Press Service (IPS), "NATO and Serbian TV Accused of Rights Crimes," Oct. 19–26, 1999.

48. The Amnesty International report quotes SACEUR General Wesley Clark stating: "We knew when we struck that there would be alternate means of getting Serb Television. There's no single switch to turn off everything but we thought it was a good move to strike it and the political leadership agreed with us." See Amnesty International, "NATO/Federal Republic of Yugoslavia," p. 41 (citing "Moral Combat— NATO at War," broadcast on BBC2, Mar. 12, 2000).

49. Final Report to the Prosecutor, p. 22, para. 77.

50. This particular wording is taken from the Italian Statement of Interpretation to its Ratification of Additional Protocol I & II, Feb. 27, 1986, printed in Adam Roberts and Richard Guelff, eds., *Documents on the Laws of War* (New York: Oxford University Press, 2000), pp. 506–7.

51. Attacks were also aimed at electricity grids, radio, and TV relay sites at Novi Pazar, Krosovaka, and Krusevac. See Final Report to the Prosecutor, p. 23, para. 78.

52. Ibid., p. 23, para. 77.

53. This is a view shared by Prime Minister Tony Blair, who is quoted in the Final Report to the Prosecutor as saying, "They could have moved those people out of the building. They knew it was a target and they didn't . . . it was probably for . . . very clear propaganda reasons." See Final Report to the Prosecutor, p. 23, para. 77.

54. Michael Schmitt, "Precision Attack and International Humanitarian Law," *International Review of the Red Cross*, no. 859 (2005): 445–66, 461.

55. Marco Sassoli, Transnational Armed Groups and International Humanitarian Law (Program on Humanitarian Policy and Conflict Research, Occasional Paper Series, no. 6, 2006), p. 7.

56. Michael Schmitt, "Fault Lines in the Law of Attack," *Testing the Boundaries of International Humanitarian Law*, ed. Susan Breau and Agnieszka Jachec-Neale (London: British Institute of International and Comparative Law, 2006), pp. 277–307.

57. See Daniel Muñoz-Rojas and Jean-Jacques Frésard, "The Roots of Behaviour in War: Understanding and Preventing IHL Violations," *International Review of the Red Cross*, no. 853 (2004): 189–206.

58. See Richard Price, "Reversing the Gun Sights: Transnational Civil Society Targets Landmines," *International Organizations* 52 (1998): 613.

59. Bothe, "Protection of the Civilian Population," p. 535.

ABOUT THE CONTRIBUTORS

C.A.J. (Tony) Coady is a professorial fellow in the Centre for Applied Philosophy and Public Ethics at the University of Melbourne. He has published widely on ethical issues to do with war and terrorism. In 2008, he published *Morality and Political Violence* and *Messy Morality: The Challenge of Politics*.

Helen Durham is the program director for research and development for the Asia Pacific Centre for Military Law and a senior research fellow at Melbourne Law School. She teaches and researches in the area of international humanitarian law and previously worked as a legal adviser for the International Committee of the Red Cross

Tsuyoshi Hasegawa is a professor of history at the University of California at Santa Barbara. His major publications include *The February Revolution: Petrograd, 1917*; *The Northern Territories Dispute and Russo-Japanese Relations*; *Racing the Enemy: Stalin, Truman, and the Surrender of Japan*; and *The Deadly Struggles: Stalin, Truman, and Japan's Surrender*. He also edited *The End of the Pacific War: Reappraisals* and *East Asia's Haunted Present: Historical Memories and the Resurgence of Nationalism*.

Tetsuo Maeda is a former professor of international studies at Tokyo International University. He retired from teaching in 2007 and currently works as a freelance researcher. He has published many books and essays in Japanese, most of which are critical analyses of the conduct of Japanese Imperial Forces as well as contemporary Japanese Self-Defense Forces. For many years he has been conducting research on the Japanese bombing of Chongqing during the Asia Pacific War.

Tim McCormack was appointed the Foundation Australian Red Cross Professor of International Humanitarian Law at Melbourne Law School in 1996 and is the foundation director of the Asia Pacific Centre for Military Law, a collaborative initiative established in 2001 between the University of Melbourne Law School and the Australian Defence Force Legal Service.

Robert G. Moeller teaches European history at the University of California, Irvine. He has published widely on the social and political history of Germany in the twentieth century, and he is the author of *War Stories: The Search for a Usable Past in the Federal Republic of Germany*.

Ronald Schaffer is professor emeritus at California State University, Northridge. A graduate of Columbia College and Princeton University, he has written a series of books and articles on military history, notably *Wings of Judgment: American Bombing in World War II* and *America in the Great War: The Rise of the War Welfare State*. He has also written about the history of American counterinsurgency warfare and contributed to such television series as *The Great War and the Shaping of the Twentieth Century* and *Woodrow Wilson*, both PBS productions.

Mark Selden is research associate in the East Asia Program at Cornell University and a coordinator of the Asia-Pacific e-journal *Japan Focus*. His recent books include *War and State Terrorism: The United States, Japan, and the Asia-Pacific in the Long Twentieth Century* and *Revolution, Resistance and Reform in Village China*.

Michael S. Sherry is the Richard W. Leopold Professor of History at Northwestern University, where he has taught since 1976, and received his PhD from Yale University in 1975. Among his books are *The Rise of American Air Power: The Creation of Armageddon*, which won the Bancroft Prize in History, and *In the Shadow of War: The United States since the 1930s*.

Yuki Tanaka is research professor at Hiroshima Peace Institute of Hiroshima City University. He lived and taught at several universities in Australia for about twenty years until 2000. Since the mid-1980s he has been concentrating his research on war crimes, and his publications include *Japan's Comfort Women: Sexual Slavery and Prostitution During World War II* *and the US Occupation* and *Hidden Horrors: Japanese War Crimes in World War II*.

Marilyn B. Young is a professor of history at New York University. She has been a Guggenheim Fellow and is the author of numerous books, including *The Vietnam Wars, 1945–1990*. With Lloyd C. Gardner, she co-edited *Iraq and the Lessons of Vietnam* (The New Press). She lives in New York City.

INDEX